The

PAULO FREIRE
READER

The
PAULO FREIRE
READER

EDITED BY

Ana Maria Araújo Freire

and Donaldo Macedo

CONTINUUM · NEW YORK

1998

The Continuum Publishing Company
370 Lexington Avenue
New York, NY 10017

Printed in the United States of America

Library of Congress Cataloging-in-Publication Data

Freire, Paulo, 1921–
    [Selections. English. 1998]
    The Paulo Freire reader / edited by Ana Maria Araújo Freire
and Donaldo Macedo.
        p.   cm.
    Includes bibliographical references and index.
    ISBN 0-8264-1088-X (hardbound : alk. paper)
    1. Education—Philosophy. 2. Popular education. 3. Critical
pedagogy. I. Freire, Ana Maria Araújo, 1933– . II. Macedo,
Donaldo P. (Donaldo Pereira), 1950– . III. Title.
LB880.F73S4513   1998
370.11'5—dc21   98-17039
                                                    CIP

CONTENTS

INTRODUCTION

The Reagan era educational legacy can be best characterized by an unrelenting assault on schools and public schoolteachers. Reactionary educators and political pundits all jumped on the bandwagon to blame public schools and public schoolteachers for the unacceptably high dropout rates, particularly in urban schools, for producing graduates who are semiliterates, and for the general failure that has made public schools moribund and teachers who are not able to pass state mandate standard tests. For example, in Massachusetts, "59 percent of 1,800 education students taking first-ever certification exams in April have failed."[1] While there has been a cacophony of assaults on public schools and public schoolteachers, reactionary educators and politicians have conspicuously failed to recognize a fundamental issue.

Although there has been a barrage of teacher bashing in the media and political circles, very few people are asking the simple, yet crucial question: who trained these teachers? In fact, when Chairman of the Massachusetts State Board of Education James F. Carlin demanded "almost immediate feedback from college presidents on how education schools can better prepare graduates [with the threat that] he will not tolerate defensiveness or oblique educational rhetoric,"[2] the chairman of the board got precisely what he would not tolerate: defensiveness and oblique educational rhetoric.

Unfortunately the chairman of the board is betrayed by his own rhetoric to the extent that he is part and parcel of a social order that supports a form of education designed to de-skill and domesticate teachers and only later to blame them for the skills they do not have and the general failure of public schools. This "politics of deception"[3] is very much linked to a pedagogy of entrapment when the system requires of students, including teachers, what it does not give them. That is, schools of education, by and large, are informed by an ideology characteristic of the Trilateral Commission, whose members, among them former President Jimmy Carter, referred to schools as "institutions responsible for the indoctrination of the young."[4] Noam Chomsky stated simply: the Trilateral Commission argued that schools should be institutions for indoctrination, "for imposing obedience, for blocking the possibility of independent thought, and they play an institutional role in a system of control and coercion."[5] This approach to education invariably has given rise to an instrumentalist and domesticating education that sets the stage for the anesthetization of the mind, as poet John Ashbery eloquently captured in "What Is Poetry":

> *In school*
> *All the thoughts get combed out:*
>
> *What was left was like a field.*[6]

The educational "comb" for those teachers who have blindly accepted the dominant ideological perspective on education is reflected in an instrumentalist literacy for the poor characterized by mindless, meaningless skills and exercises given "in preparation for multiple choice exams and writing gobbledygook in imitation of the psychobabble that surrounds them."[7]

As reactionary educators and politicians fail to critically understand the root cause for the present educational malaise, a young teacher who successfully passed the exam had no difficulties understanding what teachers need most and, in our view, schools of education, in general, fail to teach them:

> I am a recent graduate of Tufts University, and I took the exam for the first time on July 11. Although it was long and grueling, it is a fair judge of one of the many aspects of teaching.
>
> Creativity, enthusiasm, compassion, and positive disciplining skills are essential characteristics of a good teacher. But the bottom line is that teachers must be able to read, write, and think analytically. How will our students learn to formulate an opinion and back it up with a logical argument if the teachers cannot do this? Many test-takers complain that the exam does not test what they learned in education class. But the goal is not for examiners to regurgitate their class lecture notes. The purpose is to assess candidates' abilities to think critically.[8]

This young teacher, Carolyn S. Cohen, amply understands what college presidents, deans of schools of education, and political pundits have failed to understand. That is, how can schools of education prepare teachers to become critical thinkers when they, by and large, blindly embrace a domesticating instrumentalist approach to education designed, along the lines of the Trilateral Commission, to produce readers who meet the basic requirements of our contemporary society and "learned ignoramuses" trained at the highest level of literacy: specialism and hyperspecialization?

The instrumentalist approach to literacy, even at the highest level of specialism, functions to domesticate the consciousness via a constant disarticulation between the narrow reductionist reading of one's field of specialization and the reading of the universe within which one's specialism is situated. This inability to link the reading of the word and the world is part of a literacy for stupidification that, at best, produces semiliterates. Thus, we should not at all be surprised by the fact that 59 percent of teachers who took the first state-mandated certification exam failed in Massachusetts. In fact this so-called teacher failure serves as a prime example of the highest level of literacy for stupidification. In other words, at the lowest level of instrumental literacy, a semiliterate reads the word but is unable to read the world. At the highest level of instrumental literacy achieved via specialization, the semiliterate is able to read the text of his or her specialization but is ignorant of all the other bodies of knowledge that constitute the world of knowledge. This semiliterate specialist was characterized by Ortega y Gasset as a "learned ignoramus." That is to say, "he is not learned, for he is formally ignorant of all that does not enter into his specialty: but neither is he ignorant, because he is a 'scientist' and 'knows' very well his own tiny portion of the universe."[9]

Instead of bashing teachers we should put the blame squarely on institutions and schools of education that trained them in an approach that abstracts methodological issues from their ideological contexts and consequently ignores the interrelationships between sociopolitical structures of a society and the act of learning and knowing. In part, the exclusion of social, cultural, and political dimensions from learning and teaching practices gives rise to an ideology of cultural reproduction that produces teachers who are de-skilled and acritical without much independent thought.

In general, most schools of education, under the rubric of science, specialism, and specialization, rupture with philosophies and cultural relations that are indispensable for the development of the critical thinking skills that the young teacher, Carolyn S. Cohen, called for. In addition, specialization also hides behind an ideology that creates and sustains false dichotomies rigidly delineated by disciplinary boundaries. This ideology also informs the view that "hard science," "objectivity," and "scientific rigor" must be divorced from the messy data of "soft science" and from the social and political practices that generate those categories in the first place.

We are not at all surprised that reactionary educators and politicians could not put the blame squarely where it belongs: in schools of education whose culture, with a few exceptions, demonstrates an aversion toward critical theory and the development of independent critical thought. This is abundantly clear, for example, in a Harvard Graduate School of Education professor's written comment on his graduate student Pepi Leistyna's research paper:

> The assumption that ideological sophistication is a sign of cultural progress ignores the fact that many people just don't give a damn about this kind of complex verbalization. They may be temperamentally bent toward building, or singing, or hoeing corn. So the problem for me is to prevent the overinterpretative egghead from claiming a special corner on sacred (significant) knowledge—but still get his or her due. It always makes me a little wary about the extent to which the critical theorists (Freire, Giroux, etc.) appreciate the great range of talents of people who are not so much deluded by all this professional garbage complex elaboration of language.[10] So they often cannot protect themselves, either from specialized professors of literacy or specialized professors of critical literacy.[11]

How else can one explain a culture that pontificates about intellectual rigor and yet allows a graduate course titled The Politics of Literacy to be taught without any reference to Freire? The syllabus for this course further revealed its hidden politics: The professor even allotted one week to covering the politics of literacy in Latin America without any reference to Freire. This is tantamount to offering an introduction to a linguistics course without mentioning Noam Chomsky or an introduction to a British literature course without mentioning Shakespeare. Not only is this evidence of the fear that many professors feel toward Freire's critical theories, but it also points to an extreme level of academic dishonesty and the ahistorical nature of the course. One may not agree with Freire's theories, but one cannot arrogantly ignore the best-known literacy educator in the world. Failure to expose students of literacy to Freire is not only a form of extreme antiintellectualism but also a de facto censorship. Here is where the HGSE faculty mantra of objectivity and scientific rigor is subverted by a more insidious force: ideology. But what can one expect from a culture in which another professor responded to Freire's death in the following manner: "Freire's coming to Harvard would have made twenty students very happy while making the rest of the students extremely unhappy. Now he is dead and we are all unhappy."

This comment regarding Freire's death not only epitomizes the level of dehumanization and insensitivity that exists at the highest level of education,[12] but it also points to the arrogance (which borders on stupidification) ascribed to many professors by the sheer power, resources, and authority of institutions such as Harvard. Many of these professors' identities are tied solely to Harvard's prestige, which gives many of them the illusion that they can dismiss any body of knowledge, views, or perspectives that do not conform to their preestablished ways of seeing the world. In fact, if one applies rigorous standards of the academy, one soon realizes (1) that most of the professors at the HGSE are not among the most-cited educators in the United States, much less in the world; (2) that their work has done little to advance the present theoretical debate in the field; and (3) that they have contributed few earthshaking ideas that might help to raise schools—particularly urban schools, with their outrageously high dropout rate and high numbers of students who graduate as semiliterates—out of their moribund condition. On the contrary, most of these schools are very much informed by the positivistic and management models that character-ize the very culture of ideologies and practices to which Freire was in opposition all his life. It is no wonder that in a lecture at Harvard that analyzed Paulo Freire's theories given by professor Ramón Flecha from the University of Barcelona, Spain, a Harvard Graduate School of Education doctoral student approached Donaldo Macedo and asked the following: "I don't want to sound naive, but who is this Paulo Freire that professor Flecha is citing a lot?" Then again, how can one expect this doctoral student to know the work of the most significant educator in the world during the last half of the century[13] when the Harvard Graduate School of Education sanctions a graduate course entitled the Literacy Politics and Policy without requiring students to read, critique, and analyze the work of Freire.

It is this form of academic selective selection of bodies of knowledge that borders on censorship of critical educators that is partly to blame for the lack of knowledge of Paulo Freire significant contributions to the field of education. Even many liberals who have embraced his ideas and educational practices, often reduce his theoretical work to a mechanical methodology. According to Stanley Aronowitz,

> In fact, in concert with many liberal and radical educators some teachers have interpreted liberatory education to chiefly mean instilling humanis-tic values in a non-repressive way. The school seems to be a massive values clarification exercise. . . . Many read Freire's dialogic pedagogy as a tool for student motivation and cannot recognize that for him dialogue is a content whose goal is social as much as individual change. In

Freire's educational philosophy the first principle is that the conventional distinction between teachers as expert and learner as an empty bio-physiological shell is questioned. Education takes place when there are two learners who occupy somewhat different spaces in an ongoing dialogue. But both participants bring knowledge to the relationship and one of the objects of the pedagogic process is to explore what each knows and what they can teach each other. A second object is to foster reflection on the self as actor in the world in consequence of knowing.[14]

Paulo Freire Is Not a Method

In contrast to the market notion of school reform in the United States, many liberal and neoliberal educators have rediscovered Freire as an alternative to the conservative domestication education that equates free-market ideology with democracy. Part of the problem with some of these pseudocritical educators is that, in the name of liberation pedagogy, they reduce Freire's leading ideas to a method. Stanley Aronowitz correctly suggested that the North American fetish for method has allowed Freire's philosophical ideas to be "assimilated to the prevailing obsession of North American education, following a tendency in all human and social sciences, with methods—of verifying knowledge and, in schools, of teaching, that is, transmitting knowledge to otherwise unprepared students."[15]

This fetish for method works insidiously against adhering to Freire's own pronouncement against the importation and exportation of methodology. In a long conversation Paulo had with Donaldo about this issue he said: "Donaldo, I don't want to be imported or exported. It is impossible to export pedagogical practices without reinventing them. Please tell your fellow American educators not to import me. Ask them to re-create and rewrite my ideas."

Before problematizing the reductionism of Freire's leading philosophical ideas into a mechanistic world, it is necessary to comment on the "Paulo Freire Method," since it still is widely used today, with some adaptations, all over the world. Another reason is that, often when one speaks of Freire and literacy, they become reduced to a mere set of techniques associated with the learning of reading and writing. It is necessary to clarify, especially for the sake of those who are being initiated in Freire.

Freire's "invitation" to adult literacy learners is, initially, that they look at themselves as a man or a woman living and producing in a given society. He invites learners to come out of the apathy and the conformism akin to being "dismissed from life," as they often find themselves. Freire challenges them to understand that they are themselves the makers of culture, leading them to learning the anthropological meaning of culture. The popular classes' status of "being less" is worked on so as not to be understood as divine determination or fate, but rather as determined by the economic-political-ideological context of the society they live in.

When men and women realize themselves as the makers of culture, they have conquered, or nearly conquered, the first step toward feeling the importance, the necessity, and the possibility of owning reading and writing. They become literate, politically speaking.

As they discuss the object to be known and the representation of reality to be decodified, the members of a "circle of culture" respond to questions generated by the group coordinator, gradually deepening their readings of the world. The ensuing debate makes possible a rereading of reality from which may well result the literacy learner's engagement in political practices aiming at social transformation.

What? Why? How? To what end? For whom? Against whom? By whom? In favor of whom? In favor of what? These are questions that provoke literacy learners to focus on the substantiveness of things, their reasons for being, their purpose, the way they are done, etc.

Literacy activities require research on what Freire calls a "minimum vocabulary universe" among literacy learners. It is through work on this universe that words become chosen to integrate the program. These words, more or less seventeen of them, called "generative words," should be phonemically rich words and necessarily ordered in increasing progression of phonetic difficulty. They should be read within the widest possible context of the literary learners' life and of the local language, thus becoming national as well.

Decodifying the written word, which follows the decodifying of a codified existential situation, implies certain steps that must be strictly followed.

Let us take the word *tijolo* (brick), used as the first word in Brasilia, in the sixties. This word was chosen because Brasilia was a city under construction at the time, in order to facilitate the reader's understanding.

- The generative word *tijolo* is presented, inserted in the representation of a concrete situation: men at work at a construction site.

- The word is simply written: *tijolo*.
- The same word is written with its syllables separated: *ti-jo-lo*.
- The "phonemic family" of the first syllable is presented: *ta-te-ti-to-tu*.
- The "phonemic family" of the second syllable is presented: *ja-je-ji-jo-ju*.
- The "phonemic family" of the third syllable is presented: *la-le-li-lo-lu*.
- The "phonemic families" of the word being decodified are presented:
  ta-te-ti-to-tu
  ja-je-ji-jo-ju
  la-le-li-lo-lu

This set of "phonemic families" of the generative word has been termed "discovery form," for it allows the literacy learner to put together "pieces," that is, come up with new phonemic combinations that necessarily will result in words of the Portuguese language.

- Vowels are presented: *a-e-i-o-u*.

In sum, the moment the literacy learner is able to articulate syllables to form words, he or she is literate. The process evidently requires deepening; that is, a postliteracy component.

The effectiveness and validity of the "method" lie in having the learner's reality as a starting point—in starting from what they already know, from the pragmatic value of the things and the facts of their daily life; that is, their existential situations. By respecting and starting from common sense, Freire proposes overcoming it.

The "method" follows methodological and linguistic rules, but also goes beyond them, for it challenges men and women who are becoming literate to take ownership of the written code and to politicize themselves, acquiring a totality view of language and the world.

The "method" rejects mere narrow-minded and mind-narrowing repetition of phrases, words, and syllables, as it proposes that the learners "read the world" and "read the word," which, as Paulo Freire emphasizes, are inseparable actions. Thus, he has positioned himself against *"cartilhas,"* or literacy workbooks.

In short, Paulo Freire's work is more than a method for literacy education; it is a broad and deep understanding of education that has its political nature at the core of its concerns.

We would conclude these comments on the "Paulo Freire method" by saying that the literacy education of the Brazilian people—since when

Freire created the "method" he never expected that it would spread around the world—was, then, in the good sense of the word, an educational tactic designed to achieve a necessary strategy: politicizing the Brazilian people. In this sense, it is revolutionary, for it can remove those who do not yet know the written word from a condition of submission, of immersion and passivity. The revolutionary thought by Freire does not presuppose an inversion of the oppressed-oppressor poles; rather, it intends to reinvent, in communion, a society where exploitation and the verticalization of power do not exist, where the disenfranchised segments of society are not excluded or interdicted from reading the world.

Paulo Freire was in exile for almost sixteen years, precisely because he understood education this way, and because he fought to give a large number of Brazilians access to this asset traditionally denied them: the act of reading the world by reading the word.

As it becomes abundantly clear, Freire's method to teach peasants how to read was not designed to be a method as an end in itself but as part of a larger goal of politicizing the Brazilian peasants so they can also read the world and be able to connect the world with the word. For this reason, Freire's leading ideas concerning the act of knowing transcend the methods for which he is known. In fact, according to Linda Bimbi, "the originality of Freire's work does not reside in the efficacy of his literacy methods, but, above all, in the originality of its content designed to develop our consciousness"[16] as part of a humanizing pedagogy. According to Freire, "a humanizing education is the path through which men and women can become conscious about their presence in the world. The way they act and think when they develop all of their capacities, taking into consideration their needs, but also the needs and aspirations of others."[17]

Freire's efficacy to develop students' capacities to be aware of their presence in the world was achieved through the dialogical model for which he is also known. Unfortunately, many educators who embrace his notion of dialogue mechanistically reduce the epistemological relationship of dialogue to a vacuous, feel-good comfort zone. In this sense, the dialogical model loses clarity with respect to the object of knowledge under study while reducing dialogue as a mere conversation about individuals' lived experiences.

With that said, we can begin to understand why some educators, in their attempt to cut the chains of oppressive educational practices, blindly advocate for the dialogical model, creating, in turn, a new form of methodological rigidity laced with benevolent oppression—all done under the guise of democracy with the sole purpose that it is for your own good. Many of us have witnessed pedagogical contexts in which you are implicitly or explicitly required to speak, or to talk about your experience as an act of liberation. We all have been at conferences where the speaker is chastised because he or she failed to locate himself or herself in history. In other words, he or she failed to give primacy to his or her experiences in addressing issues of critical democracy. It does not matter that the speaker had important and insightful things to say. This is tantamount to dismissing Marx because he did not entrance us with his personal lived experiences.

The appropriation of the dialogical method as a process of sharing experiences is often reduced to a form of group therapy that focuses on the psychology of the individual. Although some educators may claim that this process creates a pedagogical comfort zone, in my view it does little beyond make the oppressed feel good about his or her own sense of victimization. In other words, the sharing of experiences should not be addressed in psychological terms only. It invariably requires a political and ideological analysis as well. That is, the sharing of experiences must always be understood within a social praxis that entails both reflection and political action. In short, it must always involve a political project with the objective of dismantling oppressive structures and mechanisms.

This overdose of experiential celebration that characterizes some strands of critical pedagogy offers a reductionist view of identity and experience within, rather than outside, the problematics of power, agency, and history. By overindulging in the legacy and importance of their respective voices and experiences, these educators often fail to move beyond a notion or difference structured in polarizing *binarisms* and uncritical appeal to the discourse of experience.[18] For this reason, they invoke a romantic pedagogical mode that exoticizes lived experiences as a process of coming to voice. By refusing to link experiences to the politics of culture and critical democracy, these educators reduce their pedagogy to a form of middle-class narcissism. On the one hand, the dialogical method provides the participants with a group therapy space for stating their grievances and, on the other hand, it offers the educator or facilitator a safe pedagogical zone to deal with his or her class guilt.

By refusing to deal with the issue of class privilege, the pseudocritical educator dogmatically pronounces the need to empower students, to give them voices. These educators are even betrayed by their own language. Instead of creating pedagogical structures that would enable oppressed students to empower themselves, they paternalistically proclaim, "We need to empower students." This position often leads to the creation of what we could call literacy and poverty pimps to the extent that, while proclaiming the need to empower students, they are in fact strengthening their own privileged position.

The following example will clarify my point: a progressive teacher of mine who had been working in a community-based literacy project betrayed her liberal discourse to empower the community when one of the agencies we work with solicited a colleague's help to write a math literacy proposal for them. The colleague agreed and welcomed the opportunity. One of his goals is to develop structures so that community members and agencies can take their own initiative and chart their own course, thus eliminating the need for our continued presence and expertise. In other words, our success in creating structures so that community members empower themselves rests on the degree to which our presence and expertise in the community are no longer necessary because community members have acquired their own expertise, thus preventing a type of neocolonialism.

When the progressive teacher heard about the math literacy proposal she was reticent but did not show outward opposition. However, weeks later, when she learned that the community-based math literacy grant written by community members competed with the progressive teacher's own university-based proposal, which was designed to provide literacy training to community members, she reacted almost irrationally. She argued that the community agency that had written the math literacy grant did not follow a democratic process in that it had not involved her in the development of the grant. A democratic and participatory process in her view referred to the condition that community action needed to include her, this despite the fact that she is not a member of the particular community the math literacy grant was designed to serve. Apparently, in her mind, one can be empowered so long as the empowerment does not encroach on the "expert's" privileged, powerful position. This is position of power designed to paternalistically empower others.

When it was pointed out the obvious ideological contradictions in her behavior, her response was quick, aggressive, and almost automatic: "I'll be very mad if they get their proposal and we don't get ours." It became very clear to me that the progressive teacher's real political commitment to the community hinged on the extent to which her "expert" position remained unthreatened. That is, the literacy "expert," do-gooder, antiestablishment persona makes sure that his or her privileged position within the establishment as an antiestablishment "expert" is never absorbed by empowered community members.

It is this colonizer, paternalistic attitude that led this same progressive teacher to pronounce publicly, at a major conference, that community people don't need to go to college because, since they know so much more than do members of the university community, there is little that the university can teach them. While making such public statements, she was busily moving from the inner city to an affluent suburb, making sure that her children would attend better schools.

A similar attitude emerged in a recent meeting to develop a community-university relationship grant proposal. During the meeting a liberal white professor rightly protested the absence of community members in the committee. However, in attempting to valorize the community knowledge base, she rapidly fell into a romantic paternalism by stating that the community people knew much more than the university professors and that they should be invited to come to teach us rather than the reverse. This position not only discourages community members from having access to the cultural capital from which these professors have benefitted greatly but it also disfigures the reality context that makes the university cultural capital indispensable for any type of real empowerment. It also smacks of a false generosity of paternalism that Freire aggressively opposes:

> The pedagogy of the oppressed animated by authentic humanism (and not humanitarianism) generously presents itself as a pedagogy of man. Pedagogy which begins with the egoistic interests of the oppressors (an egoism cloaked in the false generosity of paternalism) and makes of the oppressed the objects of its humanitarianism, itself maintains and embodies oppression. It is an instrument of dehumanization.[19]

Childhood, Adolescence, and First Professional Experiences

Paulo Reglus Neves Freire became known in Brazil and abroad simply as Paulo Freire. He was born at 724 Enchantment Road, in Recife, PE, on September 19, 1921, the son of Joaquim Temístocles Freire and Edeltrudes

Neves Freire. He died in the city of São Paulo on May 2, 1997, of a massive heart attack.

Paulo always spoke of his first childhood as of a very happy moment. He admired and valued his parents' patience, tolerance, and ability to love. He understood that those were the reasons why they were able to create a harmonious family atmosphere for their four children, one where it was possible to experience emotions naturally, think out argumentations, and live a life of religious faith. His mother was an extremely important person in Paulo's emotional and intellectual development, for she always believed in him. She sensed that the shy, strong-willed, and jealous boy would be the man he was. His father would not only put him to sleep by singing, but also read him children's storybooks. Paulo understood and respected him from a very early age. The reverse was also true.

He was initiated in the reading of the word by his parents. He started by writing words and sentences from his life experiences with twigs from the mango trees, in their shade, down on the ground, in the backyard of the house where he was born, in the Yellow House District, as he liked so much to remember and to say.

At the age of ten he moved to the outskirts of the Pernambucan capital, to Jaboatão, a small town about eleven miles from Recife that, to Paulo, had a flavor of pain and pleasure, suffering and love, anguish and growth. There he experienced the pain of losing his father, at the age of thirteen; he learned the pleasure of hanging out with friends and acquaintances who were in solidarity with him during those difficult times; he learned suffering when he saw his mother, widowed so soon, fight to support herself and four children; he was strengthened from the love that grew among them due to the difficulties they faced together; he suffered the anguish of things lost and material trials, he was startled with the growth of his body, but not allowing the boy to abandon him definitively, he did gradually allow the adult to gain space in his existence. As he saw his body grow, he also felt his passion for knowledge increasing.

In one of the notes Nita Freire (Paulo's second wife) wrote to Paulo's *Pedagogy of Hope*, she said something about his relationship with Jaboatão that would be interesting to quote here:

> But it was also in Jaboatão that he felt, learned, and lived the fun of playing soccer and swimming in the Jaboatão river, while watching the women hunched over rocks washing and scrubbing their own families' laundry and that of better off families as well. It was there where he

learned how to sing and how to whistle, which to this day he still likes very much to do to relieve the fatigue from thinking and the stresses of daily life. He also learned how to dialogue within "circles of friends," and he learned to value women sexually, to date them, and to love them. Finally, it was there where he learned to take up for himself, with passion, the studies of the Portuguese language, its popular and erudite syntaxes.

Thus, Jaboatão was a space-time for learning, a time of difficulties and happiness which, lived intensely, taught him how to harmonize and balance between having and not having, being and not being, being able and not being able, wanting and not wanting. That is how the discipline of hope was forged in Freire.[20]

In Jaboatão, Paulo also concluded his elementary education, after having attended, still in Recife, Eunice Vasconcelos's elementary school.

Following that, he went through his first year of secondary schooling at the July 14 School, which while operating in the São José district, was in reality an extension of the Francês Chateaubriand School, located at 150 Harmony Street, Yellow House district, where final exams were held. After this first year of secondary schooling, under the tutelage of mathematics professor Luiz Soares, he entered the then called Oswaldo Cruz School, also in Recife. At this institute, he completed the seven years of secondary school—the fundamentals and the prelaw programs—being accepted at the age of twenty-two into the secular School of Law of Recife, where he studied from 1943 to 1947.

He made his choice, for it was the one that presented itself in the humanities; at the time there were no higher education programs in Pernambuco for the training of educators. For this reason, he never really practiced law even though he did open a small office and try to get started into litigation. He gave it up on his first attempt: a creditor wanted to confiscate the instruments from a dentist and family head.

In 1944, before graduating from college, he married the elementary school teacher Elza Maria Costa Oliveira, with whom he had five children: Maria Madalena, Maria Cristina, Maria de Fátima, Joaquim, and Lutgardes.

Nita Freire met Paulo in the hallways of the "Oswaldo Cruz," owned by her father, Aluízio Pessoa de Araújo, in that distant Recife of 1937, when she was almost four years old and he, almost at the age of seventeen, was belatedly starting the second year of secondary school. In 1942, he became a teacher of Portuguese at the same institute. In 1985, he spoke about the opportunity of receiving his secondary education at a school well known in the Brazilian northeast for its high-quality standards and, consequently, of having the level of schooling that helped his intellectual development:

> In my first year of junior high school, I attended one of these private schools in Recife; in Jaboatão there were only elementary schools. But my mother was not able to continue paying tuition; then, it was a real struggle to find a school which would accept me as a scholarship student. She finally found the Oswaldo Cruz School and its owner. Aluízio Araújo, who had been a seminary student and was married to an extraordinary woman, whom I like immensely, decided to grant my mother's request. I remember she came home glowing and said, "You know, the only thing he demanded is that you be studious." Wow, I loved studying, so I went to the Oswaldo Cruz School, where later on I became a teacher. Aluízio Araújo has already passed, but Elza and I had the great pleasure to host him and his wife for fifteen days at our house in Geneva, in 1977. And in 1979, after sixteen years in exile, when we came to visit Brazil, both Aluízio and Genove were at the airport in Recife waiting for us. He was already looking quite old; we had dinner together after. Upon our return to Geneva, he passed away. And I can say here in this interview, with no doubt, that had it not been for them, this interview would never have taken place. They were the ones who created the necessary conditions for my development. . . . It is obvious that they could not have made me, but the dimensions of my individual experience have a great deal to do with them.[21]

It is interesting to recall that it was due to this job as a Portuguese teacher and his scrawny build that the army doctor spared him from having to fight with the Brazilian Expeditionary Force (F.E.B.) in the battlefields of Italy during World War II.

After having gained teaching experience in some other educational institutes, he took the position of director at the Division of Education and Culture within SESI, an agency recently created by the National Confederation of Industry through an agreement with the Vargas government. There he came in contact with adult education and realized how badly adults and the nation needed to face the issue of education and, in particular, of literacy.

He began work at SESI—Pernambuco on August 1, 1947, as Assistant in the Division of Public Relations, Education, and Culture (Ordinance number 20, of July 17, 1947). In that same year he earned his legal degree and was promoted to Director of the Division of Education and Culture. On December 1, 1954, he was appointed to the post of Superintendent, which he held until October 23, 1956, when through Ordinance number

2627, he requested to be divested of the position. In 1957, Lídio Lunardi, Director of SESI-National requested from the Pernambuco Regional that Paulo be released to the national agency justifying his choice "with the experience and knowledge the appointee will lend to the Division of Research and Planning, where we are encouraging studies and the recruitment of individuals able to provide us with the effective means to formulate viable solutions pertaining to the pressing social issues in the current state of the nation." The request was granted through Ordinance number 216, of October 18, 1957. Thus, from this time until April 14, 1961, Paulo traveled through some Brazilian states as a consultant. On May 14, 1964, Célio Augusto de Melo sends a memo (G.D.S. 58/64), unsigned, requesting Paulo's return to work within eight days, at a time when he had already been released and was fulfilling different duties. On May 20, 1964 he requested, irrevocably so, revision of his employment contract, renouncing all his labor rights. This request was only filed on August 17, 1966, under number 1429. On September 30, 1966 he was legally dismissed, having by then long been in exile.

Along with other educators and individuals interested in formal education, under the leadership of Raquel Castro, he founded the Capibaribe Institute in the fifties. A private educational institution, to this day it is well known in Recife for its high-level scientific, ethical, and moral education toward democratic conscience.

On August 9, 1956, the progressive Mayor Pelópidas Silveira, exercising the authority given him by Decree number 1.555, of 08/0956, appointed Paulo Freire member of Recife's Educational Consulting Board. A few years later he was also made Director of the Division of Culture and Recreation of the City of Recife's Department of Archives and Culture, as per instrument signed by Germano Coelho, on July 14, 1961.

He had his first teaching experience in higher education as professor of History and Philosophy of Education at the School of Fine Arts of Recife—Social Service School.

At the end of 1959, through a process of exams and credentials review, he was tenured as Professor of History and Philosophy of Education of the School of Fine Arts, earning a doctoral degree.

This credential ensured his appointment, through Ordinance number 30, of November 30, 1960, signed by University President João da Costa Lima, as tenured Professor (level 17) of Philosophy and History of Education of the University of Recife's Faculty of Philosophy, Sciences, and

Letters. He taught from January 2, 1961, until he was retired by the military coup.

Through Ordinance number 37, of August 14, 1961, signed by the same University President, he was also granted the certificate of "Livre-Docente"° in History and Philosophy of Education at the Fine Arts School, where he used to teach before taking the exam. Freire was awarded the diploma for this degree on April 23, 1962, before a school congregation, according to an invitation from the school's secretary dated April 18, 1962.

Paulo Freire was also one of the "Pioneer Council Members" of Pernambuco's State Council on Education. "Pioneer Council Members," as indicated in the archive records, was the phrase the original members of the council used to name themselves. These first fifteen council members were chosen by Governor Miguel Arraes, according to the law, from among "individuals of noted knowledge and experience in matters of education and culture" in the state of Pernambuco. They took seat in the council on November 29, 1963, and according to the state law cited in article number 10 of the National Education Guidelines and Bases Law, number 4,024/61, they authored the Council's first set of bylaws, which were approved by the same governor who appointed them, through Decree number 928, of March 3, 1964, published in the Official Gazette on March 6.

On March 31, 1964, when the encircling coup was full-blown, thirteen of them collectively renounced their terms. Paulo Freire, who was in Brasilia actively involved in the National Literacy Program project and was, therefore, unable to sign the collective notice of resignation, was dismissed from his position as council member by Decree number 942, of April 20, 1964, signed by Vice-Governor Paulo Guerra, for Governor Miguel Arraes had already been arrested by the new power-seizing forces.

It was as Chief Writer and creator of the ideas in Theme Three of Pernambuco's Regional Commission, "Education of Adults and Marginal Populations: The Mocambos Problem," presented in the Second National Conference on Adult Education in July 1958, in Rio de Janeiro, that Paulo Freire established himself as a progressive educator. With a very particular language and an educational philosophy marked by absolute renewal, he proposed that adult education in the Mocambo zones in the state of Pernambuco had to have its foundation in consciousness of the day-to-day conduct

---

°Livre-Docente: a higher academic credential obtained through examination that qualifies faculty members to teach certain types of courses and/or to serve as examiners of candidates to higher education teaching.

lived by the learners so that it could never be reduced to a mere knowing of letters, words, and sentences. He also stated that educational work toward democracy would only be achieved if the literacy process was not *about* or *for* man, but with man (in the fifties, and until just after the publication of *Pedagogy of the Oppressed* in the United States, Freire did not employ nonsexist language; he mistakenly believed that he included women when he used the word man), with the learners, and with their reality. He proposed an adult education that encouraged cooperation, decision making, participation, social and political responsibility. Freire, focused on that category of knowledge that is learned existentially, through the living knowledge of his own problems and those of his local community, already made explicit his respect for popular knowledge, common knowledge.

He spoke of social education, of the need for learners to discover themselves, as well as to know the social problems that afflicted them. He did not see education simply as a means toward mastering academic standards of schooling or toward professionalization. He spoke about the need to encourage the people to participate in their process of immersion into public life by becoming engaged in society as a whole.

He added that it would be up to the learners themselves, in part, to plan the content of their studies and that pedagogical work in the Mocambos should be encouraged to lead to women's overcoming their state of destitution by changing the nature of their own domestic practices.

The Second National Conference on Education took place between July 6 and July 16, 1958, the year when Juscelino Kubitscheck was becoming established as the force in power and beginning to show concern for our people's misery. He wanted and needed to find solutions to social problems, education among them. He tried to solve them within the bounds of populism, the favored ideology of the day. Freire's ideas, his discourse and practice, however, already treaded a legitimately popular path.

The aspirations of political society in the fifties converged with those of part of civil society, making for an atmosphere conducive to mobilization, to reflection, and to action for social and political change. Hence, Freire translated the needs of his time and engaged himself with them.

This more progressive segment of Brazilian society Freire belonged to—made up of industry workers, countrymen, students, university professors, intellectuals, and the Catholic clergy—was inclined not to settle for, but rather to break away from the archaic, authoritarian, discriminatory, elitist, and interdictive traditions that for centuries were in effect in Brazil.

While many representatives of the day's hegemonic political society thought hard to try and formulate solutions toward economic development, some within civil society were revolted by the poverty, the social injustice, and the illiteracy widespread among our people. Freire was among those, and that is how he gradually became, since that period, the educator of indignation.

His pedagogy contained a clear perception of the discriminatory nature of daily existence in our predominantly patriarchal and elitist society. Toward overcoming the conditions in effect, he pointed to solutions that were advanced for the times and to an ampler and more progressive conception: that of education as a political art. All this was new in Brazil, which continued to reproduce, inhumanely so and for centuries, the interdiction of the bodies of the socially unvalued, who were thus left to live in prohibition, from being, from knowing, from having, and from being able.

Such political nature of education, even before its pedagogical specificity, had been at the core of Freirean concerns, both in his theoretical reflection and in his educational practice.

Freire forged himself out of his lived praxis as educator of the oppressed—even before having written *Pedagogy of the Oppressed*—because he started from popular knowledge, from popular language, popular needs, from respect for the concreteness of the people and their daily lives of limitations, and from the ability to listen to the people. Beyond the starting point, he proposed overcoming such a world of submission, of silence, and of destitution, pointing to a world of possibilities.

With all these innovations, Freire's report presented at the Second Conference on Adult Education doubtlessly became a milestone in pedagogical thought at the time, a definitive boundary between "neutral," mind-numbing, universalizing education, and one essentially rooted in the adult learner's daily political existence without being reduced to it. This report, thus, irreversibly inserted Freire into the history of Brazilian education. His understanding of adult education was absolutely revolutionary.

The Popular Educator, Exile, and Return

Going beyond academia and institutional life, Paulo Freire also engaged in the movements for popular education of the early sixties. He was one of the founders of the Movement for Popular Culture (MCP) in Recife, where he worked, alongside other intellectuals and the people, in order to contribute to a more participatory presence of the masses in Brazilian society, through attributing a higher value to popular culture.

This first Movement for Popular Culture in Brazil deeply marked the Pernambucan educator's professional, political, and emotional development.

Through his identification with popular progressive education, he influenced the "bare feet can also learn how to read" campaign, successfully carried out by the then popular administration of Mayor Djalma Maranhão, in Natal, Rio Grande do Norte.

As he organized and directed the literacy campaign in Angicos, also in Rio Grande do Norte, Freire became better known nationally as the educator dedicated to the issues of the people. Soon after that, he went to Brasilia at the invitation of the recently inaugurated Minister of Education Paulo de Tarso Santos, of the Goulart administration, in order to implement a national literacy campaign.

Under his coordination was then born the National Literacy Program, which, through the Paulo Freire method, intended to make literate, while politicizing them, five million adults. As per the law of the time, those adults could, in a near future, become part of the still restricted Brazilian electoral college of the early sixties. Only a few more than 11,600,000 voters had participated in the recent presidential election, where victory went to Mr. Jânio da Silva Quadros and João Belchior Goulart.

In the process of becoming literate, those new voters, coming from the popular classes, would be challenged to realize the injustice that oppressed them and the need to fight for change. The dominant classes identified the threat and, obviously, positioned themselves against the program, which, made official on January 21, 1964, by decree number 53,465, was eliminated by the military government on April 14 of the same year, through decree number 53,886.

Arrested twice in Recife, Paulo Freire was forced to come to Rio de Janeiro to testify in a military-police inquiry. Feeling threatened, he sought exile at the Bolivian embassy and departed to that country in September 1964. He was only forty-three years old, and he carried with him the "sin" of having loved his people too much and having worked hard to politicize them so they would suffer less and participate more in the country's decisions. He wanted to contribute to the building of consciousness on the part of the oppressed and to overcoming their centuries-old interdiction from society. He never spoke, nor was he ever an advocate, of violence or of the taking of power through the force of arms. He was always, from a young age, reflecting on education and engaging in political action mediated by an educational practice that can be transformative. He fought and had been fighting for a more just and less perverse society, a truly democratic one, one where there are no repressors against the oppressed, where all can have a voice and a chance.

Having left São Paulo, under the protection of the Bolivian Ambassador himself, to go to that neighboring country, which generously welcomed him, Freire found his health was affected by the high altitude of La Paz, which lies at the top the Andes. It was, however, the military coup that took place in Bolivia shortly after his arrival that drove him out to Chile. In Santiago, with his family beside him, he started, like so many other Brazilians who were granted political asylum in Chile, a new phase of his life and work. He lived in that country from November 1964 to April 1969, working as an aide to the Instituto de Desarollo Agropecuario and to Chile's Ministry of Education, and as a consultant to UNESCO with Chile's Instituto de Capacitación en Reforma Agraria. At that time, he was also invited to teach in the United States and to work in the World Council of Churches. He accepted both invitations.

From April 1969 to February 1970, he lived in Cambridge, Massachusetts, and taught a course on his own ideas at Harvard University as a guest lecturer. After that, he moved to Geneva to serve as a special consultant in the department of education of the World Council of Churches.

At the council's service, he "trod a path," as he likes to say, throughout Africa, Asia, Australia, and America, except for Brazil—for his sadness. In particular, he helped those countries that had conquered their political independence to systematize their plans in education. In Cape Verde, Angola, and Guinea-Bissau, he became known for that work, when those countries struggled in the sixties to free themselves from the claws of colonialism, to rid themselves of the remaining traces of the oppressor who had turned many of the black African bodies into white Portuguese heads overseas. Those peoples wanted and needed to free themselves from their "oppression-hosting conscience" to become citizens of their countries and of the world.

Paulo Freire also lectured at the University of Geneva, in Switzerland, bringing his ideas and reflections to the students at the College of Education.

He has his first Brazilian passport issued in June 1979 and in August of the same year, within the atmosphere of political amnesty, arrives in Brazil through the Viracopos Airport in São Paulo, where he was warmly welcomed by relatives, friends, and admirers; he comes, as he states to the Brazilian press at that moment, "to relearn my country."

He was able to visit his country thanks to the efforts of Monsignor Paulo Evaristo Arns, Archbishop of São Paulo, who asked the then Minister of Justice to guarantee protection for the educator and his family during their stay. Months before, the Brazilian government had released the name of eight Brazilians—Paulo among them—who would continue to be denied the Brazilian passport they were entitled to as Brazilian citizens.

He was in Brazil for one month, visiting São Paulo, Rio de Janeiro, and Recife. He accepted an invitation to teach at the Catholic University in São Paulo (PUC-SP). Then, he returned to Europe to organize his definitive return to Brazil. This university, which had been an enclave of resistance against the dictatorship, promised that there would be room for a professor like Paulo Freire.

He returned to Europe and planned his permanent return to Brazil. He declined the rights granted by the Swiss government to reside in that country and travel around the world with credentials that provided personal guarantees.

Indeed, in June 1980 he returned to integrate and immerse himself definitively in his country and his people. However, a still-difficult political context kept him from returning, as he had dreamed in exile, to his beloved and praised Recife. He came to São Paulo, which opened its doors to him as if he were its own son coming back home, thanks to the opportunity opened by the Amnesty Law and to the democratic spirit of PUC's leadership, I repeat, not only that of its president. He was a professor at this university—having only had two periods of leave: when his first wife Elza passed away; and when he became Secretary of Education for the City of São Paulo—from that time until the day of his death, May 2, 1997.

In 1980, Paulo Freire had to start all over again, from the beginning, for the Amnesty Law required that the ex-exiled request the study of his case by the government. Considering such demand offensive, he refused to accept it. He did not request reinstatement in his professorship or management appointment at the Federal University of Pernambuco, which is how the former University of Recife had been renamed.

Thinking and acting this way, he started everything once again, from the beginning since April 1, 1964, had brought his summary dismissal from the position of Director of the Cultural Extension Service (SEC) at the University of Recife. He, who had been one of its founders and who had enthusiastically and coherently directed it, was not spared by right-wing forces. At the University of Recife's SEC, he had the opportunity to systematize the "Paulo Freire method" and, along with his team, enjoy the initial and motivating experience of adult literacy. There he was also able to serve the local population through the University's Educational Radio Station, also conceived by him.

In September 1980, pressured by the students and some professors, the University of Campinas (UNICAMP) made him professor, and he taught there until the end of school year 1990.

The UNICAMP president's office requested a "report on Paulo Freire" from its Board of Directors, in the person of full professor Rubem Alves. The request seemed absurd and reminiscent of the persecution Freire suffered when in exile. Then, there were denied passports, now it was reports. Then, "things of dictatorship," it was the repudiation from the MOBRAL° president and his entourage at a 1975 event in Iran, when in obedience to the military government's orders from Brasilia, the delegation left so as not to be present at the presentation of a UNESCO international prize to the Brazilian educator; now, "things of authoritarianism," it was a "legitimacy" requirement before he could be granted full professorship.

The words by Rubem Alves, one of the most renowned and respected intellectuals in the country, speak for themselves:

> The purpose of a report, as the very word might suggest, is to tell someone who supposedly has heard nothing, and thus knows nothing, about what seems to be in the eyes of the one who speaks or writes. One who reports lends his eyes and judgment to another who has not seen and cannot meditate on the issue in question. That is necessary because problems are too many, and our eyes are only two. . . .
>
> There are, however, certain issues on which producing such a report is almost an offense. Producing such a report on Nietzsche or Beethoven or Cecília Meireles? In order for that to happen, it would be necessary for the report's signatory to be greater than they are, and his name would have to be better known and worthier of trust than are those of the ones he writes about. . . .
>
> A report on Paulo Reglus Neves Freire.
>
> His name is known in universities across the whole world. Would it not be also here, at UNICAMP? Would that be the reason why I should add my signature (a well known domestic name) as a co-signer?

°Brazilian Literacy Movement: a nationwide government literacy program whose conception is largely credited to Paulo Freire and his ideas.

His books are translated into more languages than I can recall. I would imagine (and I could be wrong about that) that none other among our faculty has published so much, in so many languages. The dissertations which have been written about his thought form a bibliography of many pages. And the articles written about his ideas and his educational practice could be compiled into many books.

His name, in its own right, without domestic reports to recommend it, transits in universities in North America and Europe. And anyone wishing to add to this name his own "letter of recommendation" would certainly be playing a ridiculous role.

No. I cannot presuppose that this name is not known at UNICAMP. That would be an offense to those who make up its leadership.

For this reason, my report is a refusal to provide a report. And in this refusal is included, in implicit and explicit fashion, my absolute surprise at having to add my name to Paulo Freire's. As if, without mine, his could not stand.

But he stands alone.

Paulo Freire has reached the highest peak an educator can reach.

The question is whether we want to have him with us.

The question is whether he wishes to work by our side.

It is good to say to friends, "Paulo Freire is my colleague. We have offices along the same hallway at UNICAMP's College of Education. . . .

This is all I had to say.

This report, dated May 25, 1985, written by Rubem Alves, full professor II, is filed under number 4,838/80 in the administrative records of the State University of Campinas.

From 1964 to the day he died, Freire maintained the status of retired professor from the Federal University of Pernambuco, a position that, in light of conditions imposed, represents to him a greater moment than that of his longing for the time when he could communicate his accumulated knowledge, his knowledge in creation, and all his loving in relating to his students. He held the affiliation as one of his highest honors.

As for his appointment as Education Specialist within the Cultural Extension Service, a position he held with so much enthusiasm at the Federal University of Pernambuco, only much later did he have his rights recognized by the Ministry of Education. Thus, he was reinstated in the position, but he was immediately retired on partial time in March 1991, obviously without receiving anything for the twenty-seven years lost.

At the time, he wrote the minister thanking the government in his own name and in his family's for the recognition of "an act of sane injustice committed such a long time ago."

For this reason, he resigned from the position of professor at UNICAMP, since the Brazilian constitution of 1988 forbids the accumulation of more than two public service posts or retirements. In his resignation letter to the university's president, he expressed his regret at leaving UNICAMP at the beginning of school year 1991, due to both the support students and teachers had lent to his appointment and the university's environment, conducive to high-quality work since its creation by Professor Zeferino Vaz.

The blow suffered with his first wife's death took Freire down, until he opted for life and was married again, on March 27, 1988, in Recife, this time to the author of this biography. Having been childhood friends, after he had been my teacher at the Oswaldo Cruz School, we met again in the master's program at the Catholic University. I was his student/advisee and he, my teacher/advisor. Both widowed. Our relationship gained new meaning; it changed its nature, he was fond of saying. We felt that to the warmth of friends passion and love were added. We were married.

With his second wife, Nita (the endearing name he always called her), he was able to start a new phase of his life, even accepting fresh challenges in public. On January 1, 1989, he took office as Secretary of Education for the city of São Paulo, precisely, as a result of the Worker Party's victory with the election of Luiza Erundina de Sousa for mayor of São Paulo.

In Freire's highly democratic administration, he proved that more team-work methods and mutual understanding lead to collective responsibility and to reinventing the act of education, making it more effective and adequate.

His political decisions, born from his own theory and from his educational practice throughout the world—without exaggeration—and from the educational practice of all the members of the team of specialists who assisted him and who translated the wishes and needs of communities, have indelibly marked education in the city of São Paulo's public-school system.

His work was most fruitful, indeed "changing the face of schools," as he used to say. He rebuilt the schools, returning them to local communities in perfect conditions for the exercise of pedagogical activities. He also reformed the curriculum, adapting it to the needs of children from the popular classes as well, and he sought to improve the level of teaching through providing permanent professional development opportunities. He did not forget also to include the support staff of schools, providing them with development as well, in order that they too could perform their task adequately. Security guards, cooks, janitors, and secretaries, side by side with principals, teachers, students, and parents made the act of educating into an act of knowledge discovery, developed in cooperation and on the basis of socially felt needs.

He left the position of São Paulo's Secretary of Education, but he remained a member of the team until the end of 1992. He then left public service in São Paulo "to be returned to the world," as Maria Erundina put it at the grand farewell party he was given at São Paulo's Municipal Theater.

Thus, since May 27, 1991, he had been dedicating himself to other activities previously interrupted so he could fully commit to "changing the face of schools," to organize a quality public school that was also popular and democratic.

He went back to writing, with great passion. And with no less pleasure he also went back to teaching, at PUC—SP, in the then Supervision and Curriculum Program within their graduate program. The program innovated redefining the teaching-learning act and brought many of its teachers to the classroom at the same time, so that together with the students, they could engage in dialogue about the theses and dissertations the latter were writing or on certain objects of knowledge the educators may still need for their professional development. Paulo Freire was one of those teachers.

From 1987 to 1995 Freire was also a member of the UNESCO International Jury, which convenes every year in Paris in the summer in order to choose the best literacy projects and experiences from five continents. The prizes are awarded every September 8, International Literacy Day.

In the second semester of 1991, Paulo worked as invited professor at USP, the oldest and one of the most famous universities in the country, and there he engaged in broad activities, delivering lectures in the different colleges, recording videos, and discussing new and pioneering projects within the university. In 1987, also as Invited Professor, he had taught a regular course at the same university's College of Communications.

The Impact of Paulo Freire's Work

Paulo Freire's work has been published almost all over the world. His body of work comprises numerous books, some exclusively his, others "spoken" in partnership with other educators, essays and articles in specialized magazines, interviews to people who wrote about him, to radio stations, TV networks, various newspapers and magazines, thesis orientation, seminars and debates in universities all over the world, and prefaces in books by other authors.

Pedagogy of the Oppressed, which is with no doubt his most important work, has been translated and sold in more than twenty languages. That proves the currency of his thought at the end of this century, for the liberation of the oppressed is a problem that continues, especially with the current burst of neoliberalism, to constitute the greatest challenge for men and women who build their own time and historical space.

His theory, which constitutes a reflection upon his practice, has served as the foundation for academic work and inspired practices in different parts of the world, from the *mocambos* of Recife to the *barakumin* communities of Japan, through the most renowned educational institutions in Brazil and abroad.

This influence encompasses the most varied areas of knowledge: pedagogy, philosophy, anthropology, social service, ecology, medicine, psychotherapy, psychology, museology, history, journalism, the arts, theater, music, physical education, sociology, participatory research (Paulo was in fact the creator of participatory research), educational methodology in arts and sciences, political science, school curriculum, policy on the education of street boys and girls. His unmatched impact has been on adult education.

Unfortunately, today it would be impossible to list all citation to his work spread all around the world; that is why he received invitations from the most varied countries to speak, coordinate seminars, sit in juries, to orient or review dissertations and theses, to write prefaces and articles, to give interviews, to support educational or political movements, or simply to receive honors.

The following institutions had adopted Paulo Freire's name even before his death.

- Schools: Niteroi and Itaguai, RJ, Recife and Olinda, PE, São Paulo (2), Guarulhos, Jundiai, and Pindamonhangaba, SP, Pimenta Bueno, RO, Angicos, RN, Brasilia, DF, Macapa, and Amapa in Brazil; Arequipa in Peru, Mexico City, Cochabamba in Bolivia, Mendoza in Argentina, Malaga and Granada in Spain.
- Unions and Student Organizations in Schools of Education: at the University of São Paul, USP; at the Federal University of Ceará, in Fortaleza; at the University of Mogi das Cruzes; in Mogi das Cruzes; at the University of Ijuá in Campos de Santa Rosa, in Rio Grande

do Sul; at the Federal University of Goiás, in Goiânia; at the State University of Maringá, in Goiorerê, and at the Santa Fé College of Sciences and Letters, in Santa Fé do Sul (SP).

- Libraries: a popular one in Campinas, São Paulo; and another at SESI's Adult Education (GDE) Center, in Recife, Pernambuco.
- Academia: The Highlander Center in Tennessee, USA; and the Paulo Freire Institute in São Paulo, Brazil.
- Graduate Research Scholarship: the University of Glasgow, in Scotland.
- An organization in Holland, founded in the 1980s to orient and benefit country people in Nicaragua, also took Paulo Freire's name, for it has Freirian thought as its principle.

After his death, at the request of Monsignor Mauro Morelli, I authorized the Diocese of Duque de Caxias, in Baixada Fluminense, to open the "Paulo Freire Association" and the Rio de Janeiro Department of Social Service to create the "Professor Paulo Freire Opportunity Center."

Three days after Paulo's death the Ministry of Education and Culture of Argentina created, in his name, the award "Maestro Ejemplar." In July 1997 in Hamburg, Germany, during the V International Conference on Adult Education (V CONFITEA), organized by UNESCO, its General Director, Federico Mayor, announced the decision to create the "Paulo Freire Award" in recognition of innovative theoretical projects and experiments about the educator. The State Board of Education in Pernambuco instituted a medal with his name in order to recognize outstanding figures in Brazilian education, in December 1997.

Paulo Freire was awarded **Honorary Doctoral Degrees** by the following institutions: Alberta University in Landon, England, on June 23, 1973; The Catholic University of Louvain, Belgium, in February, 1975; University of Michigan, Ann Arbor, USA, on April 29, 1978; University of Geneva, Switzerland, on June 6, 1979; New Hampshire College, USA, on July 29, 1986; San Simon University in Cochabamba, Bolivia, on March 29, 1987; on March 29, 1987; University of Barcelona, Spain, on February 2, 1988; State University of Campinas, Brazil, on April 27, 1988; Federal University of Goiás, Brazil, on November 11, 1988; Pontifical Catholic University of São Paulo, Brazil, on November 23, 1988; University of Bologna, Italy, January 23, 1989; Claremont University, USA, on May 13, 1989; Piaget Institute, Portugal, on November 11, 1989; University of Massachusetts Amherst, USA, on May 26, 1990; Federal University of Pará, Brazil, on November 15, 1991; Complutense University of Madrid, Spain, on December 16, 1991; University of Mons-Hainaut, Belgium, March 20, 1992;

Wheelock College, Boston, USA, on May 15, 1992; University of El Salvador, El Salvador, on July 3, 1992; Fielding Institute, Santa Barbara, USA, on February, 6, 1993; Federal University of Rio de Janeiro, Brazil, on April 30, 1993; University of Illinois, Chicago, USA, on May 9, 1993; Federal University of Rio Grande do Sul, Brazil, on October 20, 1994; Rural Federal University of Rio de Janeiro, on December 6, 1994; Stockholm University, Sweden, on September 29, 1995 (presented at PUC—SP, in São Paulo, on October 17, 1995); Federal University of Alagoas, Brazil, on January 25, 1996; University of Nebraska, Omaha, USA, on March 19, 1996; National University of San Luis, Argentina, on August 16, 1996; Fluminense Federal University, Niterói, Brazil, on August 27, 1996; Federal University of Juiz de Fora, Brazil, on November 21, 1996; University of Lisbon, on January 10, 1996 (presented at PUC—SP, São Paulo, on November 27, 1996). I was invited to receive, in his memory, titles from the University of Oldenburgh, Germany, on July 7, 1997, and National University of Rio Cuarto, Argentina, on November 20, 1997.

He received the title *Professor Emeritus* from the Federal University of Pernambuco, Brazil, on December 13, 1984, and from Uniplac Foundation, Lajes, Brazil, on July 10, 1995, and that of Distinguished Educator for Northeastern University, Boston, USA, on March 14, 1994.

He was also given the title *Investigator Emeritus* by the Joaquim Nabuco Foundation for the Social Sciences, on December 17, 1996, in Recife.

Freire holds honorary citizenship of the following cities in Brazil: Rio de Janeiro, since October 6, 1983; São Paulo, since April 30, 1986; São Bernardo do Campo, since April 13, 1987; Campinas, since April 28, 1987; Belo Horizonte, since October 27, 1989; Itabuna, since April 13, 1992; Porto Alegre, since May 26, 1992; Angicos, since August 28, 1993; and Uberaba since November 17, 1995; Juiz de Fora, since November 22, 1996; Porto Velho, since March 13, 1997; and Brasília (posthumously), since November 8, 1997. He has also been citizen of the state of Ceará since April 10, 1996.

He was honored with "Fraternal Recognition" by the cities of Los Angeles, USA, on March 13, 1986, and Cochabamba, Bolivia, on May 29, 1987.

A street takes his name in Itabuna, Bahia, law #1400, signed by Mayor Ubaldo Dantas on December 23, 1987, which says among other things:

Article 19—Henceforth the street is now named Paulo Freire, which goes from Posto Timbaúba, on Ibicaraí Ave, to the street known as "A" block.

He also received public recognition for his educational practice through the following *honors*, among others: Merit Decoration from Marim dos Caetés, Olinda, in August 1979; William Rainey Harper Prize by the Religious Education Association of the US and Canada, California, USA, on November 20, 1985 (jointly awarded to Elza Freire); "Estácio de Sá" Award, from the Government of the State of Rio de Janeiro, in February, 1985; the title of "Comendador" for the National Educational Merit Award, by the Ministry of Education and Culture of Brazil, on June 13, 1987; the "Master of Peace" Award by the Associación de Investigación y Especialización sobre Temas Iberoamericanos, AIETI, in Spain, in January 1988; "Frei Tito de Alencar" Award, by the city of Fortaleza, on March 25, 1988; Merit Medal—Gold Class—by the city of Recife, March 28, 1988; the "Manchete" Educational Award, in 1989 and 1990; Diploma of International Merit—specifically for the book *The Importance of the Act of Reading*, by the International Reading Association, Stockholm, Sweden, in July, 1990; recognition from the World University Service, on October 22, 1990, in São Paulo; the Educator of the Year title given by the City Council in Mogi das Cruzes, SP, on October 26, 1990; the Liberator of Humanity Medal awarded on April 27, 1993, by the Bahia State House of Representatives; a medal awarded during the International Conference in Education for the Future, in São Paulo, on October 4, 1993; title of "Grand-Master" from the "National Order of Educational Merit" from the Ministry of Education and Culture of Brazil, on November 11, 1993; the "Chico Mendes Title of Resistance," from the Never Again Torture Group, in Rio de Janeiro, on March 30, 1994; the Jam Amos Comenius Medal, from the government of the Czech Republic and UNESCO, in Geneva, Switzerland, on October 4, 1994; the "Pedro Ernesto" Medal, from the Rio de Janeiro Legislature, Rio de Janeiro, on November 6, 1995; the "Alberto Maranhão Medal," from the Government of Rio Grande do Norte, Brazil, on April 18, 1996; the "Diploma of Educational Merit of the City of Campinas," Campinas, on October 30, 1996; "Outstanding Achievement in Education Medal," from SESI–Pernambuco, in December 1996. I was invited to accept in his memory the "Decoration of Education et Labor," from Senai-Firjan, Rio de Janeiro, on July 7, 1997.

On November 9, 1994, Paulo Freire received the "Paulo Freire Award," from the International Consortium for Experimental Learning in Washington, DC. He also received, during the First Conference on Education and Cooperation among Lusophone Countries, in September 1995, in Faro,

Portugal, the medal "Paulo Freire—peace education, freedom, literacy and conscientization."

He was also recognized for his work in the field of education with the following *awards:* "Mohammad Reza Pahlevi," from Iran, by UNESCO, in Iran, 1975; "Balduine King Award for Development," from Belgium, for 1980, on November 15, 1980, in Brussels; "UNESCO Award for Peace Education," from UNESCO, for 1986, in Paris, in September 1986; "Andres Bello Award," from the Organization of American States—OAE, as the Educator of the Continent of 1992, on November 17, 1992, in Washington, DC, USA; and the "Santista Mill Award," from the Santista Mill Foundation, in São Paulo, Brazil, on September 29, 1995.

We could list here, among others, institutions that created centers for documentation, information dissemination, and studies by and about Paulo Freire. In fairness, we should begin with CEDIF—The Center for Studies, Documentation, and Information Paulo Freire—through the effort of Professor Admardo Serafim de Oliveira, passed away a few years ago, with the Federal University of Pernambuco, both in Brazil. We should add, A.G.SPAK, Munich, Germany; CAAP—Centro di Animazioni per L'Autofestione Popolare, Alia, Italy; CEDI—Ecumenical Center for Documentation and Information—based in Espírito Santo, Brazil; Center for Study and Development at Social Change, Cambridge, Massachusetts, USA; Center for Popular Education, Sedes Sapientae Institute, São Paulo, Brazil; VEREDA—Center for Education Studies, São Paulo, Brazil; CEP—Pastoral Vergueiro Center, São Paul, Brazil; CIDOC—Intercultural Center for Documentation, Cuernavaca, Mexico; Latin America Adult Education Council—CEAAL, Chile; INODEP—Institute Oecuménique au Service du Dévelopment des Peuples, Paris, France; Institute of Adult Education at the University of Dar-Es-Salam, Tanzania; LARU—Latin America Research Unit, Toronto, Canada; MABIC—Mouvement d'Animation de Base International Outmoetings, Hasselt, Belgium; Birgit Wingerrath (private collection), Drie-Benst, Germany, Research Library, Washington, DC, US; SPE—Scuola Professional Emigranti, Zurich, Switzerland; Syracuse University, Syracuse, NY, USA; The Ontario Institute for Studies in Education—OISE, Toronto, Canada; UNIMEP—Vale dos Sinos University, São Leopoldo, Rio Grande do Sul, Brazil; University of Michigan, Ann Arbor, Michigan, USA; and the Paulo Freire Institute, based in São Paulo, Brazil (source: Committee for Readings on Paulo Freire, Moacir Gadotti).

Freire is also honorary president of some institutions: CEAAL, CECIP (Center for the Creation of Popular Image, Rio de Janeiro), INODEP

(Institute Oecuménique au Service du Dévelopment des Peuples, Paris), VEREDA (Center for Education Studies, São Paulo), INCA (Cajamar Institute, São Paulo), ICAE (International Council for Adult Education, Toronto), CECUP (Center for Education and Popular Culture, Salvador, Bahia) among others throughout the world.

His published **books** are: *Education as the Exercise of Freedom; Pedagogy of the Oppressed; Extension or Communication?, Cultural Action for Freedom; Pedagogy in Process; Letters to Guinea-Bissau; Conscientization: Theory and Practice of Liberation; The Importance of the Reading Act; Politics and Education Pedagogy of the City; Pedagogy of Hope—A Rereading of Pedagogy of the Oppressed; Teachers as Cultural Workers: Letters to Cristina°; Pedagogy of the Heart; Pedagogy of Freedom.* He left unfinished "Pedagogical Letters."

Published dialogues with other educators are: *Paulo Freire Live*, with faculty and students of the College of Sciences and Letters of Sorocaba; *For a Pedagogy of Questioning*, with Antonio Faundez; *This School Called Life*, with Frei Betto; *Fear and Daring: The Teacher's Day-to-day*, with Ira Shor; *Pedagogy: Dialogue and Conflict*, with Moacir Gadotti and Sérgio Guimarães; *Learning with History Itself*, Vol. I, with Sérgio Guimarães (he left incomplete volume 2), *Theory and Practice in Popular Education*, with Andriano Nogueira; *Literacy: Reading of the World, Reading of the Word*, with Donaldo Macedo; and *We Make the Road Walking*, with Myles Horton. Also with Donaldo Macedo he cowrote *Ideology Matters*.

All of Paulo Freire's books, except for the one written in partnership with Myles Horton, are published in Brazil, in Portuguese, obviously. Almost all are also published in English, French, and Spanish, and most of them are also published in Italian and German.

Pedagogy of the Oppressed was translated into the languages mentioned above and at least two dozen others, from Japanese, Hindu, and other Asian languages to Yiddish, Hebrew, Swedish, Dutch, and other European languages. *Education as the Exercise of Freedom* was also translated into the Basque language, and *Pedagogy of Hope* was translated among others into Danish.

Brazilian songwriter Chico César paid Paulo homage in his song called Bérodêro with the verse, "And the illiterate Gypsy read Paulo Freire's hand."

°Nita Freire wrote explanatory notes for these last three books. In some cases, she expanded and deepened them after conducting research on issues and problems raised by Freire.

In honor of those who fought against oppression, the Swedish artist Pye Engstron sculpted him, in 1972, in stone, next to Pablo Neruda, Angela Davis, Mao Tse-Tung, Sara Lidman, Elise Ottosson-Jense, and Georg Borgström. Sculpted into the shape of a bench, in a small square in the Västertorp district of Stockholm, covered by the Northern cold, Freire remains open to anyone wanting to take a seat, very much as he was to so many friends, intellectuals, and family members, who always had in his warm, welcoming, generous, and ever-open-to-the-other body a cozy space of understanding and solidarity.

Paulo Freire was invited to visit about one hundred cities throughout the world, including those in Brazil and in other continents. He was, thus, able to know and appreciate the ways of thinking, feeling, and acting of the peoples in the following places: in North America: USA, Canada, Mexico; Central America: Nicaragua, Costa Rica, El Salvador, Panama, Cuba, Haiti, Dominican Republic, Barbados, and Granada; in South America: Colombia, Venezuela, Ecuador, Peru, Bolivia, Chile, Argentina, Paraguay, and Uruguay; in Europe: Portugal, Spain, France, England, Scotland, Ireland, Belgium, Holland, Germany, Switzerland, Italy, Austria, Greece, Poland, Denmark, Sweden, and Norway; in Africa: Senegal, Guinea-Bissau, Cape Verde, Gabon, Angola, Botswana, Zambia, Tanzania, and Kenya; in Asia: Iran, India, and Japan; and in Australia: Papua New-Guinea, New Zealand, Fiji, and Australia.

Paulo Freire the Writer

It is very important to call attention to the manner in which Paulo Freire wrote his texts. His writing process, as he would confess himself, was not merely that of transcribing his conceived ideas, with a pencil or, as was more habitual to him, with a fountain or ballpoint pen, on a sheet of paper. Rather, it was one of producing an appealing text that could accurately express his philosophical-political reasoning as an educator of the world. Freire was never in a hurry to produce articles or books in order to count them up at the end of each year—this was never his goal, as it should not be for any intellectual in the world. He developed his ideas mentally; then he would note them down on pieces of paper or index cards, or he would store them away "in a little corner of his head" when they came up on the street, in his conversations, or during his own speaking in a conference or interview.

He would, thus, accumulate these ideas, and after he had epistemologically and politically filtered, organized, and systematized them, he would sit in the rotating chair in his office and, while reflecting, with tranquility, as if "clean copying," making sure he had completed and matured what he wanted to say, he would write. Every time he returned to the writing act, he would reread what was already written and then begin a new cycle of ideas and to put them on paper. Facing his desk, and leaning over a leather support, with unruled paper and in his own handwriting, almost always with no erasures or corrections, he would write out his text, encircling his topic, going deeper into it until he had fully exploited it; it was as if he was "drawing" on the white paper, in blue ink, often emphasizing segments in green or red, the image created in his intelligence, the language created in his "conscious body," in his whole body, for his writing came from his passion for the act of discovering, of reading-writing, and from his personal experience as a sensitive man of his time.

Thus, when he sat down to write he did not scribble, "searching for inspiration." No. He would sit, reflect once again, and then write. He almost never changed his paragraphs or his words (when he did substitute one or a few words already written down, he would delicately cut up little strips of paper with small scissors, measure them before gluing them in order to be sure that they would be just the necessary size; he would wait for the glue to dry, and only then would he carefully write the new), his syntax, or the division of chapters in his books. He would stop to think or to look words up in the dictionary. He was disciplined, attentive, patient in the act of writing. He never finished a text hurriedly, or feeling vexed, because he had a deadline for concluding the work. He respected his own time limits, his writing rhythm.

Paulo never placed himself before a computer desk to oversee the word processing of any of his writing. Whenever he would turn copy over to the secretary who assisted us, he did it because he had the conviction that he had said all he needed to say—not that this meant he had exhausted all the possibilities of a topic—and in the form he wanted to speak about the topic exploited.

He wrote the first three chapters of *Pedagogy of the Oppressed* in just fifteen days, for he had been thinking them through and "writing them in his head" for over a year. He, then, spent months writing the forth and last chapter, because he wrote it at the same time he was conceiving and organizing his ideas.

Pedagogy of Hope came in a pace of maturity; thus, he wrote the whole book in the same rhythm. The substance of content, accompanied by greater homogeneity in his style, grows and deepens with each paragraph. His enthusiasm with his involvement in the work and in the world is present from the first to the last line, and his passion and hope for people and the world permeate each of his words.

Once finished with *Pedagogy of Hope*, Freire wrote *Teachers as Cultural Workers*. Even though the letters change topics, the richness and maturity of his language as political educator remains in all of them. It is a passionate and critical language that respects the teacher-reader as it exposes the subliminal ideologies embodied in an apparent paternalistic benevolence the educational professional has to be aware of in order to radicalize his/her professional competence.

Letters to Cristina (promised to his niece Cristina when he lived in Switzerland, but only completed more than ten years later), even having been interrupted various times, carries also Freire's characteristic coherence and continuity. There is coherence among the letters themselves and between those and his work as a whole. In these letters he exploited themes ranging from the difficulties faced by his impoverished family in the thirties and his important work at SESI–PE to the ethics of the advising professor's role and his/her emotional-epistemological-ideological relationship to the adult advisee.

Convinced that social injustice does not exist because it has to exist, he responded to the challenges of our times by writing *Pedagogy of the Heart*, where he sought to demystify the theses of neoliberalism.

The format used by Freire in these last two books mentioned differs from that employed in other works. In these books, he addresses the issues and problems discussed in the form of letters, for he deems them more communicative than traditional essay narrative. In *Pedagogy of Hope*, however, he opted for a format that does not appear to be the closest and most direct manner to address the reader, but that, in reality, since it deals with people's positive and negative reactions to *Pedagogy of the Oppressed*, came very close to the reader, provoking him/her just as much as the "letters," even though it is a book without chapters. He wrote *Pedagogy of the Heart* in the same format, for he understood the reader will rewrite it at other times, without dividing it into chapters, items, and sub items.

Politics and Education is made up of small essays and conferences on various topics. *Pedagogy of the City* compiles some interviews about his term as Secretary of Education for the City of São Paulo.

Pedagogy of Freedom, launched on April 10, 1997, deals with the knowledge necessary for educational practice. With much simplicity, he compiles and goes deeper into the qualities, according to his view, required of the revolutionizingly progressive educator. The text weaves and reweaves his ideas step by step, like threads of hope for the liberating educational practice. Freire put forth his already weak body through the clarifying power of his unprecedented mind. As we read, we can, more so than in other books hear his voice passionately speaking of his convictions.

Pedagogical Letters was left unfinished. In the twenty-nine pages completed, Freire approached distortions akin to the a-ethicalness of humanity: neoliberalism, globalization, and the manner in which landless and Indian workers have been treated (the death of Pataxó Indian Galdino) within our elitist and discriminatory society, leading to the question of ethical limits and the necessary act of educating will.

All these books by Paulo Freire have, above all, one point in common—the mature and convincing manner in which he dealt with the theory and practice of education. He did it with conscience, lucidity, and transparency. His clear political option for the oppressed and his life ethic came through in his aesthetically beautiful language, the language of someone who knew what he wanted and knew how to say it. He translated the aspirations of all men and women who want the necessary liberation of all men and women, not only their own.

One thing was with him always, from his earliest writings in the fifties—his own style of writing and relating to his readers, coming closer to them, inviting them to reflect with him, to become involved in his plot.

Finally, his texts have a lot of power because they are able to transcribe into paper, with beauty and truth, his reflections and options generated in his daily practice.

It is fundamental to emphasize that in Paulo Freire there was not a time to write and a time to read. Rather, there was a time to read-write or time to write-read. It is just that these acts, almost always taken and accepted as separate, two distinct moments of the act of knowing, were understood by Paulo as one single moment, not disassociable from knowing. He never tired of denouncing such dichotomy that destroys real knowledge.

When Freire wrote, he would be "reading" other authors and himself along the way, the same way he would write and rewrite himself and others as he read them.

It is important to conclude this analysis of Paulo's writing act by saying that his manuscripts insert themselves on the paper with such harmony that they more resemble a drawing that can be observed and admired even before one reads the meaning of his words and sentences or of the reading of the world written in.

The determination he had devoted in recent years to the act of writing is due to his dream of a democratic utopia. He was forever convinced that we should do everything possible today to build a democratic society for tomorrow. As a political educator, he realized most clearly that we—educators—are in part responsible for this task of transforming our society. While writing as a political educator he felt himself and knew himself to be fulfilling a challenge and duty that imposed itself on him.

Thus, he had been surrendering to the task, writing, disputing, arguing, seeking to interfere more directly in the educational process, in order dialectically to transform societies, above all Brazilian society, so that it can become less authoritarian, less discriminatory, in sum, more just, as he always liked to say.

Therefore, Freire did not write just for the sake of writing, and he did not become an educator just to be the educator of the people, but rather to be an educator-writer who wanted to provide men and women with epistemological instruments so that they could, while transforming and reinventing their societies, assert themselves as the subjects of their own histories, conscious, engaged, and happy.

The act of writing in Paulo was not simply the act of communicating or engaging in dialogue with readers on the ethics, politics, and pedagogy of knowledge, or of prodding them to think and engage. It also consisted of aesthetic moments of rare beauty, perceptible to those who read his work, but also aesthetic due to the extremely beautiful manner in which he manipulated the books and simple objects needed for the scribing of his texts. His writing was also aesthetic in the way that he rested his whole body, not only his hand, before those objects that he knew symbolized a special moment in his existence.

His efforts for and his dedication to the pressing necessity that is education motivated educators, unions, unionists, leaders, and members of various organizations of diverse natures from around the world, convinced that peace begins with better days and equal rights for all peoples, to present his name, in 1993, to the committee that awards the Nobel Peace Prize each year in Norway.

Fighting for peace through education presupposes a new understanding of peace that is enlisting more and more supporters each day. Freire, who participated and, above all, decisively contributed to this understanding of peace, who had been dedicating himself to education as love and tenacity, has his name in the roster of those who could one day have received such recognition. This new understanding of peace does not simply yearn for the putting down of arms, of all arms, but also for social, religious, and political peace.

✿   ✿   ✿

Recommendation for the Nobel Peace Prize

Motion

SBPC (The Brazilian Society for the Progress of Science), an entity bringing together Brazilians from all areas of knowledge, during its 45th Annual Meeting, held in Recife, at the Federal University of Pernambuco, from July 11 to July 17, 1993, wishes to express its support for the nomination of Professor Paulo Freire as recipient of the Nobel Peace Prize. We believe the initiative to award the Prize to the Brazilian and Recifean educator to constitute official recognition of his pedagogical project, which has spread throughout the world in the second half of the twentieth century.

Paulo Freire's work is oriented towards the emancipation of human beings, towards the freedom of all peoples, towards justice among men, towards legitimate democracy as popular sovereignty, and towards peace among citizens, in an atmosphere of humanization and conscientization.

Awarding Paulo Freire the Nobel Peace Prize represents more than the recognition of the work of a lifetime, but also the recognition of many people who fight for the nearly impossible: giving marginalized individuals the opportunity to live a dignified existence, awakening them from apathy and honoring their rights.

SBPC, Recife, 07.17.93

Paulo Freire's personal experience, his activism, and his reflections were enriched by the influence received from different people: his parents, especially his mother, this extraordinary woman who not only gestated and educated him, but also believed in him as a generous beloved son, and as a man who had much to give of himself to many more people than herself and his family.

Elza, he always used to say, gave him his taste for literacy—she had been a literacy educator of children—for making others able to write the word and for sharing the excitement of those who learn how to read. His own elementary schoolteacher, Eunice Vasconcelos, introduced him to the enjoyment of the Portuguese language.

Aluísio Araújo gave him the sense of duty and pleasure in the struggle for education. He influenced Freire from adolescence, not only for his democratic spirit, for his character of extreme respect for others, but also for his authentic Christian humanism. Aluísio, my father, had as principle, as a dream, the right to schooling for all men and women. Hence, he made his school into a space open to whoever wanted to study, even those who could not pay or belonged to a religion, race, or social class different from his own. He represented an example of life, of seriousness, and human understanding for Paulo.

Also very important to Freire, as he so clearly reveals in his work, especially in *Pedagogy of Hope*, the influences from a great number of people with whom he lived, discussed knowledge, or worked throughout the world. He gives testimony to people who touched him for their sensibility, purity, and the wisdom in their actions and narratives, and to those who instigated him towards elaborate and lucid reason of scientific knowledge.

The influence in Paulo's own way of thinking—because he reinvented and surpassed in part or in the whole many of his masters—of Marxism cannot be denied, as well as that of existentialism, personalism, or phenomenology. These are present in his reading of the reading of the world: Marx, Lukács, Sartre, and Mounier, as well as Albert Memmi, Erich Fromm, Franz Fanon, Merleau-Ponty, Antonio Gramsci, Karel Kosik, H. Marcuse, Agnes Heller, Simone Weill, and Amilcar Cabral.

Freire never denied these influences, for he knew himself as living, working, and doing in given situations—which he did not create—and, therefore, suffering like every man and every woman—historical beings—the influences of his time's culture, and those before, even while knowing himself as a critic and creator.

That is why in his work, in his reflection, he brought along his sweated personal experiences, as he liked to say, the influences of this world, which was his and not his at the same time. And from his relationship with the world he knew that he should include the other.

Freire, while reinventing and surpassing, in part or in the whole, many of his masters, was—and will doubtlessly continue to be a political-philosopher-educator—a humanist educator, who built a theory of knowledge plentiful in ethics and of knowing at the service of liberation.

Paulo Freire the Human Being

Proud and happy, modest and conscious of his position in the world, Paulo Freire lived his life with faith, with humility and with contained happiness. With curiosity, serenity, and a desire for transformation, he lived, learning with the oppressed and fighting to overcome relationships of oppression. Living through the tensions and the conflicts of the world, but hopeful in its necessary changes, he lived. Impatiently patient, he fought his whole life for a more democratic world.

He was afraid of flying, and he enjoyed "going for a car ride," to see people, sights and buildings, for he liked urban life. He used to sing Brazilian popular music, and to the end of his life, he continued to whistle. Villa Lobos knows it!

Patiently, quietly he waited almost sixty years, precisely until Christmas 1995, when Nita Freire found out that one of his most secluded wishes was to "get the gift" of a leather soccer ball. He was happy with the guessed gift, which he had kept secret from the time when his poor boyhood did not allow for anything more than balls made with old and rotten socks to play soccer in the fields of Recife and Jaboatão. Riding bicycles and driving cars forever remained a boy's dream not realized.

He felt comfortable talking to people from the popular classes. He valued their ideas, their talk, customs, and beliefs. Such things had caused in him a feeling of solidarity and cooperation and had enabled him to understand more dialectically, with them and starting from them, the philosophy, the politics, and the science of life itself.

It was from this uncommon ability to listen to the people, that is, to hear, embrace, elaborate the ideas, reasons, needs, aspirations, the pains, and the happiness of common men and women, that Paulo created so concrete, engaged, revolutionary, and rigorously scientific a theory of knowledge. He loved São Paulo, Santiago, Cambridge, Geneva—cities that embraced him generously—but he loved Recife as if it were a person, his mother-soil, the warm land of a fresh afternoon breezes. He loved people regardless of their religion, age, or ideological choices. He had many friends and received the affection and love from men and women wherever he went, conversed, spoke, or did other work.

He liked dogs, but above all, he loved birds.

He was tolerant and calm, but aggressive enough to defend his personal and professional spaces. He never offended, but he could not stand for being offended either.

Northeasterly, he liked the warmth of the waters and walking on the beach. After the exile he suffered with the cold that brings with it the dark of eternal night, and he rejoiced in the heat that the strong, bright sun imposes on the Brazilian Northeast.

The typical food from the Northeast, whose flavor was' kept in his memory, was almost exclusively present in his menu. He wouldn't trade for anything the *"canidela"* chicken served with beans or the "fish in coconut milk," served with beans seasoned with cilantro and coconut milk. Ice-cream? Only those in "tropical fruit" flavors: *pitanga, cajá,* starfruit, *graviola,* and *mangaba.* Desserts? *Jaca* preserve and Guava paste, above all. Fruits? Mango, *sapoti, araçá, jaca,* banana, pineapple, papaya, starfruit, *pinha,* and cashew fruit.

He was an avid smoker, and only when he sensed the harm tobacco was causing to his health did he quit, angrily, as he liked to emphasize, the smoke and the drags. Certainly, it was too late, for he had been suffering the consequences that his anger at smoking could not erase from his body. The heart attack that took him from our lives, in the early morning of May 2, 1997, was caused by the mercilessness with which tobacco attacks its lovers. He was the victim of this sad, tragic contradiction.

Freire was, no doubt, a sensitive, strong man and one of passionate feelings: his rejection of anything outside his ideological-political-ethical principles; the manner in which he spoke and wrote metaphorically through histories; his dietary habits; his way of respecting the honor and good faith of men and women; and above all, his creative, revolutionary intelligence of a man unable to accept the injustice that historically has been imposed on a large part of the world's population.

He considered himself privileged for having been able to witness so many important historic events: the 1930 Revolution; the emergence of the masses and the popular education movements; man's journey to the moon; women's struggle for liberation and the battles won; the "magnificent deeds" of computers and fax machines; the return of the people to the streets of Brazil demanding "direct elections now," or more recently, repudiating corruption and demanding both ethics in politics and the impeachment of the corrupt president—elected by our people's "democratic inexperience." Thus he was touched to see the enthusiastic and decided participation of the young "painted faces" that turned out in the millions to the streets and squares of the entire country in the nineties.

A few days before his death he cried when, also by the hands of young people, our Indian-father Pataxó Galdino was burned alive. He had been happy with the peaceful, conscious march and the struggle of all MTS members, who rallied different groups to march equally peacefully for their rights: the schooless, the homeless, the shelterless, the hungry, and others.

Calm semblance, long gray hair and beard, medium height, slender body, eyes the color of honey, and his constant disposition for exchanging experiences, to dialogue, especially when he was explaining his ideas about education or discussing those of others, were some of his most marked characteristics. Equally significant were his strong, compassionate, profound, communicating gaze and his always expressive gestures, his hands so often touching those with whom he spoke. His gaze and hand gestures revealed the desires and the hope of his being forever in love with life. Anyone who knew Paulo will hardly forget these traits that translated his personality, secure, tender, communicative, and forever concerned about others.

One could not forget his generosity, coherence, humility, tolerance, ability to understand, to respect, and to value others. Also his intelligence and outrage at injustices, his political engagement while an educator, and the coherence of his ethical conduct will not be forgotten. In sun, his ability to be human and to live passionately will be remembered. This is how he wished to die, loving and working passionately, and he did.

He wished he could have been a famous singer and renowned grammarian of the Portuguese language, but he himself reserved the right and the privilege of being, recognizably so, one of the greatest educators of this century.

Ana Maria Araújo Freire
and
Donaldo Macedo

Bibliography

Ashbery, J. (1977). *Houseboat Days, Poems.* New York: Penguin Books.

Chomsky, N. and C. P. N. Otero (1988). *Language and Politics.* Montreal; New York: Black Rose Books.

Courts, P. L. (1991). *Literacy and Empowerment: The Meaning Makers.* New York: Bergin & Garvey.

Freire, P., Betto, et al. (1985). *Essa Escola Chamada Vida: Depoimentos ao Reporter Ricardo Kotscho.* São Paulo: Editora Atica.

Freire, P. (1993). *Pedagogy of the Oppressed: New Revised 20th-Anniversary Edition* New York: Continuum.

Freire, P. and A. M. A. Freire. (1994). *Pedagogy of Hope: Reliving "Pedagogy of the Oppressed."* New York: Continuum.

Freire, P. (1998). *Pedagogy of Freedom: Ethics, Democracy, and Civic Courage.* Lanham, Md.: Rowman & Littlefield Publishers.

Gadotti, M. (1989). *Convite à Leitura de Paulo Freire.* São Paulo: Editora Scipione.

Leistyna, P. (1998). *Presence of Mind: Education and the Politics of Deception.* Boulder, Colo.: Westview Press.

McLaren, P. and P. Leonard. (1993). *Paulo Freire: A Critical Encounter.* London, New York: Routledge.

Ortega y Gasset, J. (1993). *The Revolt of the Masses.* New York: W. W. Norton.

Notes

1. Stephen Ebbert, "Carlin Demands Teacher Strategy from Colleges," *The Boston Globe,* July 3, 1998, p. B1.

2. Ibid, p. B1

3. See Pepi Leistyna, *Presence of Mind: Education and the Politics of Deception* (Boulder, Colorado: Westview Press) In press.

4. Noam Chomsky, *Language and Politics,* ed. C. P. Otero (New York: Black Rose Books, 1988), p. 681.

5. Ibid., p. 671.

6. John Ashbery, "What Is Poetry," in *Houseboat Days: Poems by John Ashbery* (New York: Penguin Books, 1977), p. 47.

7. Patrick L. Counts, *Literacy and Empowerment: The Meaning Makers* (South Hadley, Mass.: Bergin & Garvey Publishers, 1991), p. 4.

8. Carolyn S. Cohen, "Exam Measures Candidates' Ability to Think Critically," *The Boston Globe,* July 27, 1998, p. A9.

9. José Ortega y Gasset, *The Revolt of the Masses* (1930; reprint, New York: W. W. Norton, 1964), p. 111.

10. Pepi Leistyna. "The Fortunes of My Miseducation at Harvard Graduate School of Education," in Donaldo Macedo (ed.) Tongue-Tying Multiculturalism: The Politics of Race and Culture in the Ivy League. Forthcoming.

11. Ibid.

12. Herbert Kohl, "Paulo Freire: Liberation Pedagogy" in *The Nation,* May 26, 1997. p.7.

13. Ibid.

14. Stanley Aronowitz, Introduction. In Paulo Freire, *Pedagogy of Freedom.*

15. Stanley Aronowitz, "Paulo Freire's Radical Democratic Humanism," in Peter McLaren and Peter Leonard, eds., *Paulo Freire: A Critical Encounter* (London: Routledge, 1993), p. 8.

16. Linda Bimbi, cited in Moacir Gadotti, *Convite a Leitura de Paulo Freire* (São Paulo: Editora Scipione, 1989), p. 32.

17. Paulo Freire and Frei Betto, *Essa Escola Chamada Vida* (Sao Paulo: Attica, 1985), pp. 1–15.

18. Henry Giroux, "The Politics of Difference and Multiculturalism in the Era of the Los Angeles Uprising," *Journal of the Midwest Modern Language Association.* In press.

19. Paulo Freire, *Pedagogy of the Oppressed* (New York: Continuum, 1993), p. 39.

20. Paulo Freire, *Pedagogy of Hope: "Reliving Pedagogy of the Oppressed"* (New York: Continuum, 1994).

21. Paulo Freire: In: *Ensaio* Magazine, number 14, 1985, p. 5.

· 1 ·

PEDAGOGY OF
THE OPPRESSED

Chapter 1: The Fear of Freedom

While the problem of humanization has always, from an axiological point of view, been humankind's central problem, it now takes on the character of an inescapable concern.[1] Concern for humanization leads at once to the recognition of dehumanization, not only as an ontological possibility but as an historical reality. And as an individual perceives the extent of dehumanization, he or she may ask if humanization is a viable possibility. Within history, in concrete, objective contexts, both humanization and dehumanization are possibilities for a person as an uncompleted being conscious of their incompletion.

But while both humanization and dehumanization are real alternatives, only the first is the people's vocation. This vocation is constantly negated, yet it is affirmed by that very negation. It is thwarted by injustice, exploitation, oppression, and the violence of the oppressors; it is affirmed by the yearning of the oppressed for freedom and justice, and by their struggle to recover their lost humanity.

Dehumanization, which marks not only those whose humanity has been stolen, but also (though in a different way) those who have stolen it, is a *distortion* of the vocation of becoming more fully human. This distortion

---

1. The current movements of rebellion, especially those of youth, while they necessarily reflect the peculiarities of their respective settings, manifest in their essence this preoccupation with people as beings in the world and with the world—preoccupation with *what* and *how* they are "being." As they place consumer civilization in judgment, denounce bureaucracies of all types, demand the transformation of the universities (changing the rigid nature of the teacher-student relationship and placing that relationship within the context of reality), propose the transformation of reality itself so that universities can be renewed, attack old orders and established institutions in the attempt to affirm human beings as the Subjects of decision, all these movements reflect the style of our age, which is more anthropological than anthropocentric.

occurs within history; but it is not an historical vocation. Indeed, to admit of dehumanization as an historical vocation would lead either to cynicism or total despair. The struggle for humanization, for the emancipation of labor, for the overcoming of alienation, for the affirmation of men and women as persons would be meaningless. This struggle is possible only because dehumanization, although a concrete historical fact, is *not* a given destiny but the result of an unjust order that engenders violence in the oppressors, which in turn dehumanizes the oppressed.

Because it is a distortion of being more fully human, sooner or later being less human leads the oppressed to struggle against those who made them so. In order for this struggle to have meaning, the oppressed must not, in seeking to regain their humanity (which is a way to create it), become in turn oppressors of the oppressors, but rather restorers of the humanity of both.

This, then, is the great humanistic and historical task of the oppressed: to liberate themselves and their oppressors as well. The oppressors, who oppress, exploit, and rape by virtue of their power, cannot find in this power the strength to liberate either the oppressed or themselves. Only power that springs from the weakness of the oppressed will be sufficiently strong to free both. Any attempt to "soften" the power of the oppressor in deference to the weakness of the oppressed almost always manifests itself in the form of false generosity; indeed, the attempt never goes beyond this. In order to have the continued opportunity to express their "generosity," the oppressors must perpetuate injustice as well. An unjust social order is the permanent fount of this "generosity," which is nourished by death, despair, and poverty. That is why the dispensers of false generosity become desperate at the slightest threat to its source.

True generosity consists precisely in fighting to destroy the causes which nourish false charity. False charity constrains the fearful and subdued, the "rejects of life," to extend their trembling hands. True generosity lies in striving so that these hands—whether of individuals or entire peoples—need be extended less and less in supplication, so that more and more they become human hands which work and, working, transform the world.

This lesson and this apprenticeship must come, however, from the oppressed themselves and from those who are truly solidary with them. As individuals or as peoples, by fighting for the restoration of their humanity they will be attempting the restoration of true generosity. Who are better prepared than the oppressed to understand the terrible significance of an oppressive society? Who suffer the effects of oppression more than the oppressed? Who can better understand the necessity of liberation? They will not gain this liberation by chance but through the praxis of their quest for it, through their recognition of the necessity to fight for it. And this fight, because of the purpose given it by the oppressed, will actually constitute an act of love opposing the lovelessness which lies at the heart of the oppressors' violence, lovelessness even when clothed in false generosity.

But almost always, during the initial stage of the struggle, the oppressed, instead of striving for liberation, tend themselves to become oppressors, or "sub-oppressors." The very structure of their thought has been conditioned by the contradictions of the concrete, existential situation by which they were shaped. Their ideal is to be men; but for them, to be men is to be oppressors. This is their model of humanity. This phenomenon derives from the fact that the oppressed, at a certain moment of their existential experience, adopt an attitude of "adhesion" to the oppressor. Under these circumstances they cannot "consider" him sufficiently clearly to objectivize him—to discover him "outside" themselves. This does not necessarily mean that the oppressed are unaware that they are downtrodden. But their perception of themselves as oppressed is impaired by their submersion in the reality of oppression. At this level, their perception of themselves as opposites of the oppressor does not yet signify engagement in a struggle to overcome the contradiction;[2] the one pole aspires not to liberation, but to identification with its opposite pole.

In this situation the oppressed do not see the "new man" as the person to be born from the resolution of this contradiction, as oppression gives way to liberation. For them, the new man and woman themselves become oppressors. Their vision of the new man or woman is individualistic; because of their identification with the oppressor, they have no consciousness of themselves as persons or as members of an oppressed class. It is not to become free that they want agrarian reform, but in order to acquire land and thus become landowners—or, more precisely, bosses over other workers. It is a rare peasant who, once "promoted" to overseer, does not become more of a tyrant towards his former comrades than the owner himself. This is because the context of the peasant's situation, that is, oppression, remains unchanged. In this example, the overseer, in order to make sure of his job, must be as tough as the owner—and more so. Thus is illustrated our previous

---

2. As used throughout this book, the term "contradiction" denotes the dialectical conflict between opposing social forces.—Translator's note.

assertion that during the initial stage of their struggle the oppressed find in the oppressor their model of "manhood."

Even revolution, which transforms a concrete situation of oppression by establishing the process of liberation, must confront this phenomenon. Many of the oppressed who directly or indirectly participate in revolution intend—conditioned by the myths of the old order—to make it their private revolution. The shadow of their former oppressor is still cast over them.

The "fear of freedom" which afflicts the oppressed,[3] a fear which may equally well lead them to desire the role of oppressor or bind them to the role of oppressed, should be examined. One of the basic elements of the relationship between oppressor and oppressed is *prescription*. Every prescription represents the imposition of one individual's choice upon another, transforming the consciousness of the person prescribed to into one that conforms with the prescriber's consciousness. Thus, the behavior of the oppressed is a prescribed behavior, following as it does the guidelines of the oppressor.

The oppressed, having internalized the image of the oppressor and adopted his guidelines, are fearful of freedom. Freedom would require them to eject this image and replace it with autonomy and responsibility. Freedom is acquired by conquest, not by gift. It must be pursued constantly and responsibly. Freedom is not an ideal located outside of man; nor is it an idea which becomes myth. It is rather the indispensable condition for the quest for human completion.

To surmount the situation of oppression, people must first critically recognize its causes, so that through transforming action they can create a new situation, one which makes possible the pursuit of a fuller humanity. But the struggle to be more fully human has already begun in the authentic struggle to transform the situation. Although the situation of oppression is a dehumanized and dehumanizing totality affecting both the oppressors and those whom they oppress, it is the latter who must, from their stifled humanity, wage for both the struggle for a fuller humanity; the oppressor, who is himself dehumanized because he dehumanizes others, is unable to lead this struggle.

However, the oppressed, who have adapted to the structure of domination in which they are immersed, and have become resigned to it, are inhibited from waging the struggle for freedom so long as they feel incapable

---

3. This fear of freedom is also to be found in the oppressors, though, obviously, in a different form. The oppressed are afraid to embrace freedom; the oppressors are afraid of losing the "freedom" to oppress.

of running the risks it requires. Moreover, their struggle for freedom threatens not only the oppressor, but also their own oppressed comrades who are fearful of still greater repression. When they discover within themselves the yearning to be free, they perceive that this yearning can be transformed into reality only when the same yearning is aroused in their comrades. But while dominated by the fear of freedom they refuse to appeal to others, or to listen to the appeals of others, or even to the appeals of their own conscience. They prefer gregariousness to authentic comradeship; they prefer the security of conformity with their state of unfreedom to the creative communion produced by freedom and even the very pursuit of freedom.

The oppressed suffer from the duality which has established itself in their innermost being. They discover that without freedom they cannot exist authentically. Yet, although they desire authentic existence, they fear it. They are at one and the same time themselves and the oppressor whose consciousness they have internalized. The conflict lies in the choice between being wholly themselves or being divided, between ejecting the oppressor within or not ejecting them; between human solidarity or alienation; between following prescriptions or having choices; between being spectators or actors; between acting or having the illusion of acting through the action of the oppressors; between speaking out or being silent, castrated in their power to create and re-create, in their power to transform the world. This is the tragic dilemma of the oppressed which their education must take into account.

This book will present some aspects of what the writer has termed the pedagogy of the oppressed, a pedagogy which must be forged *with*, not *for*, the oppressed (whether individuals or peoples) in the incessant struggle to regain their humanity. This pedagogy makes oppression and its causes objects of reflection by the oppressed, and from that reflection will come their necessary engagement in the struggle for their liberation. And in the struggle this pedagogy will be made and remade.

The central problem is this: How can the oppressed, as divided, unauthentic beings, participate in developing the pedagogy of their liberation? Only as they discover themselves to be "hosts" of the oppressor can they contribute to the midwifery of their liberating pedagogy. As long as they live in the duality in which *to be* is *to be like*, and *to be like* is *to be like the oppressor*, this contribution is impossible. The pedagogy of the oppressed is an instrument for their critical discovery that both they and their oppressors are manifestations of dehumanization.

Liberation is thus a childbirth, and a painful one. The man or woman who emerges is a new person, viable only as the oppressor-oppressed contradiction is superseded by the humanization of all people. Or to put it another way, the solution of this contradiction is born in the labor which brings into the world this new being: no longer oppressor nor longer oppressed, but human in the process of achieving freedom.

This solution cannot be achieved in idealistic terms. In order for the oppressed to be able to wage the struggle for their liberation, they must perceive the reality of oppression not as a closed world from which there is no exit, but as a limiting situation which they can transform. This perception is a necessary but not a sufficient condition for liberation; it must become the motivating force for liberating action. Nor does the discovery by the oppressed that they exist in dialectical relationship to the oppressor, as his antithesis—that without them the oppressor could not exist[4]—in itself constitute liberation. The oppressed can overcome the contradiction in which they are caught only when this perception enlists them in the struggle to free themselves.

The same is true with respect to the individual oppressor as a person. Discovering himself to be an oppressor may cause considerable anguish, but it does not necessarily lead to solidarity with the oppressed. Rationalizing his guilt through paternalistic treatment of the oppressed, all the while holding them fast in a position of dependence, will not do. Solidarity requires that one enter into the situation of whose with whom one is solidary; it is a radical posture. If what characterizes the oppressed is their subordination to the consciousness of the master, as Hegel affirms,[5] true solidarity with the oppressed means fighting at their side to transform the objective reality which has made them these "beings for another." The oppressor is solidary with the oppressed only when he stops regarding the oppressed as an abstract category and sees them as persons who have been unjustly dealt with, deprived of their voice, cheated in the sale of their labor—when he stops making pious, sentimental, and individualistic gestures and risks an act of love. True solidarity is found only in the plenitude of this act of love, in its existentiality, in its praxis. To affirm that men and women are persons

---

4. See Hegel, pp. 236–37.

5. Analyzing the dialectical relationship between the consciousness of the master and the consciousness of the oppressed, Hegel states: "The one is independent, and its essential nature is to be for itself; the other is dependent, and its essence is life or existence for another. The former is the Master, or Lord, the latter the Bondsman." *Ibid.* p. 234.

and as persons should be free, and yet to do nothing tangible to make this affirmation a reality, is a farce.

Since it is a concrete situation that the oppressor-oppressed contradiction is established, the resolution of this contradiction must be *objectively* verifiable. Hence, the radical requirement—both for the individual who discovers himself or herself to be an oppressor and for the oppressed—that the concrete situation which begets oppression must be transformed.

To present this radical demand for the objective transformation of reality, to combat subjectivist immobility which would divert the recognition of oppression into patient waiting for oppression to disappear by itself, is not to dismiss the role of subjectivity in the struggle to change structures. On the contrary, one cannot conceive of objectivity without subjectivity. Neither can exist without the other, nor can they be dichotomized. The separation of objectivity from subjectivity, the denial of the latter when analyzing reality or acting upon it, is objectivism. On the other hand, the denial of objectivity in analysis or action, resulting in a subjectivism which leads to solipsistic positions, denies action itself by denying objective reality. Neither objectivism nor subjectivism, nor yet psychologism is propounded here, but rather subjectivity and objectivity in constant dialectical relationship.

To deny the importance of subjectivity in the process of transforming the world and history is naïve and simplistic. It is to admit the impossible: a world without people. This objectivistic position is as ingenuous as that of subjectivism, which postulates people without a world. World and human beings do not exist apart from each other, they exist in constant interaction. Marx does not espouse such a dichotomy, nor does any other critical, realistic thinker. What Marx criticized and scientifically destroyed was not subjectivity, but subjectivism and psychologism. Just as objective social reality exists not by chance, but as the product of human action, so it is not transformed by chance. If humankind produce social reality (which in the "inversion of the praxis" turns back upon them and conditions them), then transforming that reality is an historical task, a task for humanity.

Reality which becomes oppressive results in the contradistinction of men as oppressors and oppressed. The latter, whose task it is to struggle for their liberation together with those who show true solidarity, must acquire a critical awareness of oppression through the praxis of this struggle. One of the gravest obstacles to the achievement of liberation is that oppressive reality absorbs those within it and thereby acts to submerge human beings' consciousness.[6] Functionally, oppression is domesticating. To no

---

6. "Liberating action necessarily involves a moment of perception and volition. This action both precedes and follows that moment, to which it first acts as a prologue and which it subsequently

longer be prey to its force, one must emerge from it and turn upon it. This can be done only by means of the praxis: reflection and action upon the world in order to transform it.

Hay que hacer al opresión real todavía mas opresiva añadiendo a aquella la *conciéncia* de la opresión haciendo la infamia todavía mas infamante, al pregonarla.[7]

Making "real oppression more oppressive still by adding to it the realization of oppression" corresponds to the dialectical relation between the subjective and the objective. Only in this interdependence is an authentic praxis possible, without which it is impossible to resolve the oppressor-oppressed contradiction. To achieve this goal, the oppressed must confront reality critically, simultaneously objectifying and acting upon that reality. A mere perception of reality not followed by this critical intervention will not lead to a transformation of objective reality—precisely because it is not a true perception. This is the case of a purely subjectivist perception by someone who forsakes objective reality and creates a false substitute.

A different type of false perception occurs when a change in objective reality would threaten the individual or class interests of the perceiver. In the first instance, there is no critical intervention in reality because that reality is fictitious; there is none in the second instance because intervention would contradict the class interests of the perceiver. In the latter case the tendency of the perceiver is to behave "neurotically." The fact exists; but both the fact and what may result from it may be prejudicial to the person. Thus it becomes necessary, not precisely to deny the fact, but to "see it differently." This rationalization as a defense mechanism coincides in the end with subjectivism. A fact which is not denied but whose truths are rationalized loses its objective base. It ceases to be concrete and becomes a myth created in defense of the class of the perceiver.

Herein lies one of the reasons for the prohibitions and the difficulties designed to dissuade the people from critical intervention in reality. The oppressor knows full well that this intervention would not be to his interest. What *is* to his interest is for the people to continue in a state of submersion,

---

serves to effect and continue within history. The action of domination, however, does not necessarily imply this dimension; for the structure of domination is maintained by its own mechanical and unconscious functionality." From an unpublished work by José Luiz Fiori, who has kindly granted permission to quote him.

7. Karl Marx and Friedrich Engels, *La Sagrada Familia y otros Escritos* (Mexico, 1962), p. 6. Emphasis added.

impotent in the face of oppressive reality. Of relevance here is Lukács's warning to the revolutionary party:

> . . . il doit, pour employer les mots de Marx, expliquer aux masses leur propre action non seulement afin d'assurer la continuité des expériences révolutionnaires du prolétariat, mais aussi d'activer consciemment le développement ultérieur de ces expériences.[8]

In affirming this necessity, Lukács is unquestionably posing the problem of critical intervention. "To explain to the masses their own action" is to clarify and illuminate that action, both regarding in relationship to the objective facts by which it was prompted, and regarding its purposes. The more the people unveil this challenging reality which is to be the object of their transforming action, the more critically they enter that reality. In this way they are "consciously activating the subsequent development of their experiences." There would be no human action if there were no objective reality, no world to be the "not I" of the person and to challenge them; just as there would be no human action if humankind were not a "project," if he or she were not able to transcend himself or herself, if one were not able to perceive reality and understand it in order to transform it.

In dialectical thought, world and action are intimately interdependent. But action is human only when it is not merely an occupation but also a preoccupation, that is, when it is not dichotomized from reflection. Reflection, which is essential to action, is implicit in Lukács's requirement of "explaining to the masses their own actions" just as it is implicit in the purpose he attributes to this explanation that of "consciously activating the subsequent development of experience."

For us, however, the requirement is seen not in terms of explaining to, but rather dialoguing with the people about their actions. In any event, no reality transforms itself,[9] and the duty which Lukács's ascribes to the revolutionary party of "explaining to the masses their own action" coincides with our affirmation of the need for the critical intervention of the people in reality through the praxis. The pedagogy of the oppressed, which is the pedagogy of people engaged in the fight for their own liberation, has its roots here. And those who recognize, or begin to recognize, themselves as

---

8. Georg Lukács, *Lénine* (Paris, 1965), p. 62.

9. "The materialist doctrine that men are products of circumstances and upbringing, and that, therefore, changed men are products of other circumstances and changed upbringing, forgets that it is men that change circumstances and that the educator himself needs educating." Karl Marx and Friedrich Engels, *Selected Works* (New York, 1968), p. 28.

oppressed must be among the developers of this pedagogy. No pedagogy which is truly liberating can remain distant from the oppressed by treating them as unfortunates and by presenting for their emulation models from among the oppressors. The oppressed must be their own example in the struggle for their redemption.

The pedagogy of the oppressed, animated by authentic, humanist (not humanitarian) generosity, presents itself as a pedagogy of humankind. Pedagogy which begins with the egoistic interests of the oppressors (an egoism cloaked in the false generosity of paternalism) and makes of the oppressed the objects of its humanitarianism, itself maintains and embodies oppression. It is an instrument of dehumanization. This is why, as we affirmed earlier, the pedagogy of the oppressed cannot be developed or practiced by the oppressors. It would be a contradiction in terms if the oppressors not only defended but actually implemented a liberating education.

But if the implementation of a liberating education requires political power and the oppressed have none, how then is it possible to carry out the pedagogy of the oppressed prior to the revolution? This is a question of the greatest importance. One aspect of the reply is to be found in the distinction between *systematic education*, which can only be changed by political power, and *educational projects*, which should be carried out *with* the oppressed in the process of organizing them.

The pedagogy of the oppressed, as a humanist and libertarian pedagogy, has two distinct stages. In the first, the oppressed unveil the world of oppression and through the praxis commit themselves to its transformation. In the second stage, in which the reality of oppression has already been transformed, this pedagogy ceases to belong to the oppressed and becomes a pedagogy of all people in the process of permanent liberation. In both stages, it is always through action in depth that the culture of domination is culturally confronted.[10] In the first stage this confrontation occurs through the change in the way the oppressed perceive the world of oppression; in the second stage, through the expulsion of the myths created and developed in the old order, which like specters haunt the new structure emerging from the revolutionary transformation.

The pedagogy of the first stage must deal with the problem of the oppressed consciousness and the oppressor consciousness, the problem of men and women who oppress and men and women who suffer oppression. It must take into account their behavior, their view of the world, and their

---

10. This appears to be the fundamental aspect of Mao's Cultural Revolution.

ethics. A particular problem is the duality of the oppressed: they are contradictory, divided beings, shaped by and existing in a concrete situation of oppression and violence.

Any situation in which "A" objectively exploits "B" or hinders his and her pursuit of self-affirmation as a responsible person is one of oppression. Such a situation in itself constitutes violence, even when sweetened by false generosity, because it interferes with the individual's ontological and historical vocation to be more fully human. With the establishment of a relationship of oppression, violence has *already* begun. Never in history has violence been initiated by the oppressed. How could they be the initiators, if they themselves are the result of violence? How could they be the sponsors of something whose objective inauguration called forth their existence as oppressed? There would be no oppressed had there been no prior situation of violence to establish their subjugation.

Violence is initiated by those who oppress, who exploit, who fail to recognize others as persons—not by those who are oppressed, exploited, and unrecognized. It is not the unloved who initiate disaffection, but those who cannot love because they love only themselves. It is not the helpless, subject to terror, who initiate terror, but the violent, who with their power create the concrete situation which begets the "rejects of life." It is not the tyrannized who initiate despotism, but the tyrants. It is not the despised who initiate hatred, but those who despise. It is not those whose humanity is denied them who negate humankind, but those who denied that humanity (thus negating their own as well). Force is used not by those who have become weak under the preponderance of the strong, but by the strong who have emasculated them.

For the oppressors, however, it is always the oppressed (whom they obviously never call "the oppressed" but—depending on whether they are fellow countrymen or not—"those people" or "the blind and envious masses" or "savages" or "natives" or "subversives") who are disaffected, who are "violent," "barbaric," "wicked," or "ferocious" when they react to the violence of the oppressors.

Yet it is—paradoxical though it may seem—precisely in the response of the oppressed to the violence of their oppressors that a gesture of love may be found. Consciously or unconsciously, the act or rebellion by the oppressed (an act which is always, or nearly always, as violent as the initial violence of the oppressors) can initiate love. Whereas the violence of the oppressors prevents the oppressed from being fully human, the response of the latter to this violence is grounded in the desire to pursue the right to be human. As the oppressors dehumanize others and violate their rights, they themselves also become dehumanized. As the oppressed, fighting to be human, take away the oppressors' power to dominate and suppress, they restore to the oppressors the humanity they had lost in the exercise of oppression.

It is only the oppressed who, by freeing themselves, can free their oppressors. The latter, as an oppressive class, can free neither others nor themselves. It is therefore essential that the oppressed wage the struggle to resolve the contradiction in which they are caught; and the contradiction will be resolved by the appearance of the new man: neither oppressor nor oppressed, but man in the process of liberation. If the goal of the oppressed is to become fully human, they will not achieve their goal by merely reversing the terms of the contradiction, by simply changing poles.

This may seem simplistic; it is not. Resolution of the oppressor-oppressed contradiction indeed implies the disappearance of the oppressors as a dominant class. However, the restraints imposed by the former oppressed on their oppressors, so that the latter cannot reassume their former position, do not constitute *oppression*. An act is oppressive only when it prevents people from being more fully human. Accordingly, these necessary restraints do not *in themselves* signify that yesterday's oppressed have become today's oppressors. Acts which prevent the restoration of the oppressive regime cannot be compared with those which create and maintain it, cannot be compared with those by which a few men and women deny the majority their right to be human.

However, the moment the new regime hardens into a dominating "bureaucracy"[11] the humanist dimension of the struggle is lost and it is no longer possible to speak of liberation. Hence our insistence that the authentic solution of the oppressor-oppressed contradiction does not lie in a mere reversal of position, in moving from one pole to the other. Nor does it lie in the replacement of the former oppressors with new ones who continue to subjugate the oppressed—all in the name of their liberation.

But even when the contradiction is resolved authentically by a new situation established by the liberated laborers, the former oppressors do not feel liberated. On the contrary, they genuinely consider themselves to be oppressed. Conditioned by the experience of oppressing others, any

---

11. This rigidity should not be identified with the restraints that must be imposed on the former oppressors so they cannot restore the oppressive order. Rather, it refers to the revolution which becomes stagnant and turns against the people, using the old repressive, bureaucratic State apparatus (which should have been drastically suppressed, as Marx so often emphasized).

situation other than their former seems to them like oppression. Formerly, they could eat, dress, wear shoes, be educated, travel, and hear Beethoven; while millions did not eat, had no clothes or shoes, neither studied nor traveled, much less listened to Beethoven. Any restriction on this way of life, in the name of the rights of the community, appears to the former oppressors as a profound violation of their individual rights—although they had no respect for the millions who suffered and died of hunger, pain, sorrow, and despair. For the oppressors, "human beings" refers only to themselves; other people are "things." For the oppressors, there exists only one right: their right to live in peace, over against the right, not always even recognized, but simply conceded, of the oppressed to survival. And they make this concession only because the existence of the oppressed is necessary to their own existence.

This behavior, this way of understanding the world and people (which necessarily makes the oppressors resist the installation of a new regime) is explained by their experience as a dominant class. Once a situation of violence and oppression has been established, it engenders an entire way of life and behavior for those caught up in it—oppressors and oppressed alike. Both are submerged in this situation, and both bear the marks of oppression. Analysis of existential situations of oppression reveals that their inception lay in an act of violence—initiated by those with power. This violence, as a process, is perpetuated from generation to generation of oppressors, who become its heirs and are shaped in its climate. This climate creates in the oppressor a strongly possessive consciousness—possessive of the world and of men and women. Apart from direct, concrete, material possession of the world and of people, the oppressor consciousness could not understand itself—could not even exist. Fromm said of this consciousness that, without such possession, "it would lose contact with the world." The oppressor consciousness tends to transform everything surrounding it into an object of its domination. The earth, property, production, the creations of people, people themselves, time—everything is reduced to the status of objects at its disposal.

In their unrestrained eagerness to possess, the oppressors develop the conviction that it is possible for them to transform everything into objects of their purchasing power; hence their strictly materialistic concept of existence. Money is the measure of all things, and profit the primary goal. For the oppressors, what is worthwhile is to have more—always more—even at the cost of the oppressed having less or having nothing. For them, *to be is to have* and to be the class of the "haves."

As beneficiaries of a situation of oppression, the oppressors cannot perceive that if *having* is a condition of *being*, it is a necessary condition for all women and men. This is why their generosity is false. Humanity is a "thing," and they possess it as an exclusive right, as inherited property. To the oppressor consciousness, the humanization of the "others," of the people, appears not as the pursuit of full humanity, but as subversion.

The oppressors do not perceive their monopoly on *having more* as a privilege which dehumanizes others and themselves. They cannot see that, in the egoistic pursuit of *having* as a possessing class, they suffocate in their own possessions and no longer *are;* they merely *have.* For them, *having more* is an inalienable right, a right they acquired through their own "effort," with their "courage to take risks." If others do not have more, it is because they are incompetent and lazy, and worst of all is their unjustifiable ingratitude towards the "generous gestures" of the dominant class. Precisely because they are "ungrateful" and "envious," the oppressed are regarded as potential enemies who must be watched.

It could not be otherwise. If the humanization of the oppressed signifies subversion, so also does their freedom; hence the necessity for constant control. And the more the oppressors control the oppressed, the more they change them into apparently inanimate "things." This tendency of the oppressor consciousness to "in-animate" everything and everyone it encounters, in its eagerness to possess, unquestionably corresponds with a tendency to sadism.

> The pleasure in complete domination over another person (or other animate creature) is the very essence of the sadistic drive. Another way of formulating the same thought is to say that the aim of sadism is to transform a man into a thing, something animate into something inanimate, since by complete and absolute control the living loses one essential quality of life—freedom.[12]

Sadistic love is a perverted love—a love of death, not of life. One of the characteristics of the oppressor consciousness and its necrophilic view of the world is thus sadism. As the oppressor consciousness, in order to dominate, tries to deter the drive to search, the restlessness, and the creative power which characterize life, it kills life. More and more, the oppressors are using science and technology as unquestionably powerful instruments for their purpose; the maintenance of the oppressive order through manipu-

---

12. Eric Fromm, *The Heart of Man* (New York, 1966), p. 32.

lation and repression.[13] The oppressed, as objects, as "things," have no purposes except those their oppressors prescribe for them.

Given the preceding context, another issue of indubitable importance arises: the fact that certain members of the oppressor class join the oppressed in their struggle for liberation, thus moving from one pole of the contradiction to the other. Theirs is a fundamental role, and has been so throughout the history of this struggle. It happens, however, that as they cease to be exploiters or indifferent spectators or simply the heirs of exploitation and move to the side of the exploited, they almost always bring with them the marks of their origin: their prejudices and their deformations, which include a lack of confidence in the people's ability to think, to want, and to know. Accordingly, these adherents to the people's cause constantly run the risk of falling into a type of generosity as malefic as that of the oppressors. The generosity of the oppressors is nourished by an unjust order, which must be maintained in order to justify that generosity. Our converts, on the other hand, truly desire to transform the unjust order; but because of their background they believe that they must be the executors of the transformation. They talk about the people, but they do not trust them; and trusting the people is the indispensable precondition for revolutionary change. A real humanist can be identified more by his trust in the people, which engages him in their struggle, than by a thousand actions in their favor without that trust.

Those who authentically commit themselves to the people must reexamine themselves constantly. This conversion is so radical as not to allow of ambiguous behavior. To affirm this commitment but to consider oneself the proprietor of revolutionary wisdom—which must then be given to (or imposed on) the people—is to retain the old ways. The man or woman who proclaims devotion to the cause of liberation yet is unable to enter into *communion* with the people, whom he or she continues to regard as totally ignorant, is grievously self-deceived. The convert who approaches the people but feels alarm at each step they take, each doubt they express, and each suggestion they offer, and attempts to impose his "status," remains nostalgic toward his origins.

Conversion to the people requires a profound rebirth. Those who undergo it must take on a new form of existence; they can no longer remain as they were. Only through comradeship with the oppressed can

---

13. Regarding the "dominant forms of social control," see Herbert Marcuse, *One-Dimensional Man* (Boston, 1964) and *Eros and Civilization* (Boston, 1955).

the converts understand their characteristic ways of living and behaving, which in diverse moments reflect the structure of domination. One of these characteristics is the previously mentioned existential duality of the oppressed, who are at the same time themselves and the oppressor whose image they have internalized. Accordingly, until they concretely "discover" their oppressor and in turn their own consciousness, they nearly always express fatalistic attitudes towards their situation.

> The peasant begins to get courage to overcome his dependence when he realizes that he is dependent. Until then, he goes along with the boss and says "What can I do? I'm only a peasant."[14]

When superficially analyzed, this fatalism is sometimes interpreted as a docility that is a trait of national character. Fatalism in the guise of docility is the fruit of an historical and sociological situation, not an essential characteristic of a people's behavior. It almost always is related to the power of destiny or fate or fortune—inevitable forces—or to a distorted view of God. Under the sway of magic and myth, the oppressed (especially the peasants, who are almost submerged in nature)[15] see their suffering, the fruit of exploitation, as the will of God—as if God were the creator of this "organized disorder."

Submerged in reality, the oppressed cannot perceive clearly the "order" which serves the interests of the oppressors whose image they have internalized. Chafing under the restrictions of this order, they often manifest a type of horizontal violence, striking out at their own comrades for the pettiest reasons.

> The colonized man will first manifest this aggressiveness which has been deposited in his bones against his own people. This is the period when the "niggers" beat each other up, and the police and magistrates do not know which way to turn when faced with the astonishing waves of crime in North Africa.... While the settler or the policeman has the right the livelong day to strike the native, to insult him and to make him crawl to them, you will see the native reaching for his knife at the slightest hostile or aggressive glance cast on him by another native; for the last resort of the native is to defend his personality vis-à-vis his brother.[16]

---

14. Words of a peasant during an interview with the author.
15. See Candido Mendes, *Memento dos vivos—A Esquerda católica no Brasil* (Rio, 1966).
16. Frantz Fanon, *The Wretched of the Earth* (New York, 1968), p. 52.

It is possible that in this behavior they are once more manifesting their duality. Because the oppressor exists within their oppressed comrades, when they attack those comrades they are indirectly attacking the oppressor as well.

On the other hand, at a certain point in their existential experience the oppressed feel an irresistible attraction towards the oppressors and their way of life. Sharing this way of life becomes an overpowering aspiration. In their alienation, the oppressed want at any cost to resemble the oppressors, to imitate them, to follow them. This phenomenon is especially prevalent in the middle-class oppressed, who yearn to be equal to the "eminent" men and women of the upper class. Albert Memmi, in an exceptional analysis of the "colonized mentality," refers to the contempt he felt toward the colonizer, mixed with "passionate" attraction towards him.

> How could the colonizer look after his workers while periodically gunning down a crowd of colonized? How could the colonized deny himself so cruelly yet make such excessive demands? How could he hate the colonizers and yet admire them so passionately? (I too felt this admiration in spite of myself.)[17]

Self-depreciation is another characteristic of the oppressed, which derives from their internalization of the opinion the oppressors hold of them. So often do they hear that they are good for nothing, know nothing and are incapable of learning anything—that they are sick, lazy, and unproductive—that in the end they become convinced of their own unfitness.

> The peasant feels inferior to the boss because the boss seems to be the only one who knows things and is able to run things.[18]

They call themselves ignorant and say the "professor" is the one who has knowledge and to whom they should listen. The criteria of knowledge imposed upon them are the conventional ones. "Why don't you," said a peasant participating in a culture circle,[19] "explain the pictures first? That way it'll take less time and won't give us a headache."

Almost never do they realize that they, too, "know things" they have learned in their relations with the world and with other women and men.

---

17. *The Colonizer and the Colonized* (Boston, 1967), p. x.
18. Words of a peasant during an interview with the author.
19. See chapter 3, p. 113 ff.—Translator's note.

Given the circumstances which have produced their duality, it is only natural that they distrust themselves.

Not infrequently, peasants in educational projects begin to discuss a generative theme in a lively manner, then stop suddenly and say to the educator: "Excuse us, we ought to keep quiet and let you talk. You are the one who knows, we don't know anything." They often insist that there is no difference between them and the animals; when they do admit a difference, it favors the animals. "They are freer than we are."

It is striking, however, to observe how this self-depreciation changes with the first changes in the situation of oppression. I heard a peasant leader say in an *asentamiento*[20] meeting, "They used to say we were unproductive because we were lazy and drunkards. All lies. Now that we are respected as men, we're going to show everyone that we were never drunkards or lazy. We were exploited!"

As long as their ambiguity persists, the oppressed are reluctant to resist, and totally lack confidence in themselves. They have a diffuse, magical belief in the invulnerability and power of the oppressor.[21] The magical force of the landowner's power holds particular sway in the rural areas. A sociologist friend of mine tells of a group of armed peasants in a Latin American country who recently took over a latifundium. For tactical reasons, they planned to hold the landowner as a hostage. But not one peasant had the courage to guard him; his very presence was terrifying. It is also possible that the act of opposing the boss provoked guilt feelings. In truth, the boss was "inside" them.

The oppressed must see examples of the vulnerability of the oppressor so that a contrary conviction can begin to grow within them. Until this occurs, they will continue disheartened, fearful, and beaten.[22] As long as the oppressed remain unaware of the causes of their condition, they fatalistically "accept" their exploitation. Further, they are apt to react in a passive and alienated manner when confronted with the necessity to struggle for their freedom and self-affirmation. Little by little, however, they tend to try out forms of rebellious action. In working towards liberation, one must neither lose sight of this passivity nor overlook the moment of awakening.

---

20. *Asentamiento* refers to a production unit of the Chilean agrarian reform experiment.—Translator's note.

21. "The peasant has an almost instinctive fear of the boss." Interview with a peasant.

22. See Regis Debray, *Revolution in the Revolution?* (New York, 1967).

Within their unauthentic view of the world and of themselves, the oppressed feel like "things" owned by the oppressor. For the latter, *to be* is *to have*, almost always at the expense of those who have nothing. For the oppressed, at a certain point in their existential experience, *to be* is not to resemble the oppressor, but *to be under* him, to depend on him. Accordingly, the oppressed are emotionally dependent.

> The peasant is a dependent. He can't say what he wants. Before he discovers his dependence, he suffers. He lets off steam at home, where he shouts at his children, beats them, and despairs. He complains about his wife and thinks everything is dreadful. He doesn't let off steam with the boss because he thinks the boss is a superior being. Lots of times, the peasant gives vent to his sorrows by drinking.[23]

This total emotional dependence can lead the oppressed to what Fromm calls necrophilic behavior: the destruction of life—their own or that of their oppressed fellows.

It is only when the oppressed find the oppressor out and become involved in the organized struggle for their liberation that they begin to believe in themselves. This discovery cannot be purely intellectual but must involve action; nor can it be limited to mere activism, but must include serious reflection: only then will it be a praxis.

Critical and liberating dialogue, which presupposes action, must be carried on with the oppressed at whatever the stage of their struggle for liberation.[24] The content of that dialogue can and should vary in accordance with historical conditions and the level at which the oppressed perceive reality. But to substitute monologue, slogans, and communiqués for dialogue is to attempt to liberate the oppressed with the instruments of domestication. Attempting to liberate the oppressed without their reflective participation in the act of liberation is to treat them as objects which must be saved from a burning building; it is to lead them into the populist pitfall and transform them into masses which can be manipulated.

At all stages of their liberation, the oppressed must see themselves as women and men engaged in the ontological and historical vocation of becoming more fully human. Reflection and action become imperative when one does not erroneously attempt to dichotomize the content of humanity from its historical forms.

---

23. Interview with a peasant.

24. Not in the open, of course; that would only provoke the fury of the oppressor and lead to still greater repression.

The insistence that the oppressed engage in reflection on their concrete situation is not a call to armchair revolution. On the contrary, reflection—true reflection—leads to action. On the other hand, when the situation calls for action, that action will constitute an authentic praxis only if its consequences become the object of critical reflection. In this sense, the praxis is the new *raison d'être* of the oppressed; and the revolution, which inaugurates the historical moment of this *raison d'être,* is not viable apart from their concomitant conscious involvement. Otherwise, action is pure activism.

To achieve this praxis, however, it is necessary to trust in the oppressed and in their ability to reason. Whoever lacks this trust will fail to initiate (or will abandon) dialogue, reflection, and communication, and will fall into using slogans, communiqués, monologues, and instructions. Superficial conversions to the cause of liberation carry this danger.

Political action on the side of the oppressed must be pedagogical action in the authentic sense of the word, and therefore, action *with* the oppressed. Those who work for liberation must not take advantage of the emotional dependence of the oppressed—dependence that is the fruit of the concrete situation of domination which surrounds them and which engendered their unauthentic view of the world. Using their dependence to create still greater dependence is an oppressor tactic.

Libertarian action must recognize this dependence as a weak point and must attempt through reflection and action to transform it into independence. However, not even the best-intentioned leadership can bestow independence as a gift. The liberation of the oppressed is a liberation of women and men, not things. Accordingly, while no one liberates himself by his own efforts alone, neither is he liberated by others. Liberation, a human phenomenon, cannot be achieved by semihumans. Any attempt to treat people as semihumans only dehumanizes them. When people are already dehumanized, due to the oppression they suffer, the process of their liberation must not employ the methods of dehumanization.

The correct method for a revolutionary leadership to employ in the task of liberation is, therefore, *not* "libertarian propaganda." Nor can the leadership merely "implant" in the oppressed a belief in freedom, thus thinking to win their trust. The correct method lies in dialogue. The conviction of the oppressed that they must fight for their liberation is not a gift bestowed by the revolutionary leadership, but the result of their own *conscientização.*

The revolutionary leaders must realize that their own conviction of the necessity for struggle (an indispensable dimension of revolutionary wisdom) was not given to them by anyone else—if it is authentic. This conviction cannot be packaged and sold; it is reached, rather, by means of a totality of reflection and action. Only the leaders' own involvement in reality, within an historical situation, led them to criticize this situation and to wish to change it.

Likewise, the oppressed (who do not commit themselves to the struggle unless they are convinced, and who, if they do not make such a commitment, withhold the indispensable conditions for this struggle) must reach this conviction as Subjects, not as objects. They also must intervene critically in the situation which surrounds them and whose mark they bear; propaganda cannot achieve this. While the conviction of the necessity for struggle (without which the struggle is unfeasible) is indispensable to the revolutionary leadership (indeed, it was this conviction which constituted that leadership), it is also necessary for the oppressed. It is necessary, that is, unless one intends to carry out the transformation *for* the oppressed rather than *with* them. It is my belief that only the latter form of transformation is valid.[25]

The object in presenting these considerations is to defend the eminently pedagogical character of the revolution. The revolutionary leaders of every epoch who have affirmed that the oppressed must accept the struggle for their liberation—an obvious point—have also thereby implicitly recognized the pedagogical aspect of this struggle. Many of these leaders, however (perhaps due to natural and understandable biases against pedagogy), have ended up using the "educational" methods employed by the oppressor. They deny pedagogical action in the liberation process, but they use propaganda to convince.

It is essential for the oppressed to realize that when they accept the struggle for humanization they also accept, from that moment, their total responsibility for the struggle. They must realize that they are fighting not merely for freedom from hunger, but for

> . . . freedom to create and to construct, to wonder and to venture. Such freedom requires that the individual be active and responsible, not a slave or a well-fed cog in the machine. . . . It is not enough that men

---

25. These points are discussed at length in chapter 4 of *Pedagogy of the Oppressed*.

are not slaves; if social conditions further the existence of automatons, the result will not be love of life, but love of death.[26]

The oppressed, who have been shaped by the death-affirming climate of oppression, must find through their struggle the way to life-affirming humanization, which does not lie *simply* in having more to eat (although it does involve having more to eat and cannot fail to include this aspect). The oppressed have been destroyed precisely because their situation has reduced them to things. In order to regain their humanity they must cease to be things and fight as men and women. This is a radical requirement. They cannot enter the struggle as objects in order *later* to become human beings.

The struggle begins with men's and women's recognition that they have been destroyed. Propaganda, management, manipulation—all arms of domination—cannot be the instruments of their rehumanization. The only effective instrument is a humanizing pedagogy in which the revolutionary leadership establishes a permanent relationship of dialogue with the oppressed. In a humanizing pedagogy the method ceases to be an instrument by which the teachers (in this instance, the revolutionary leadership) can manipulate the students (in this instance, the oppressed), because it expresses the consciousness of the students themselves.

> The method is, in fact, the external form of consciousness manifest in acts, which takes on the fundamental property of consciousness—its intentionality. The essence of consciousness is being with the world, and this behavior is permanent and unavoidable. Accordingly, consciousness is in essence a 'way towards' something apart from itself, outside itself, which surrounds it and which it apprehends by means of its ideational capacity. Consciousness is thus by definition a method, in the most general sense of the word.[27]

A revolutionary leadership must accordingly practice *co-intentional* education. Teachers and students (leadership and people), co-intent on reality, are both Subjects, not only in the task of unveiling that reality, and thereby coming to know it critically, but in the task of re-creating that knowledge. As they attain this knowledge of reality through common reflection and

---

26. Fromm, *op. cit.*, pp. 52–53.

27. Álvaro Vieira Pinto, from a work in preparation on the philosophy of science. I consider the quoted portion of great importance for the understanding of a problem-posing pedagogy (to be presented in chapter 2), and wish to thank Professor Vieira Pinto for permission to cite his work prior to publication.

action, they discover themselves as its permanent re-creators. In this way, the presence of the oppressed in the struggle for their liberation will be what it should be: not pseudo-participation, but committed involvement.

Chapter 2: The "Banking" Concept of Education

A careful analysis of the teacher-student relationship at any level, inside or outside the school, reveals its fundamentally *narrative* character. This relationship involves a narrating Subject (the teacher) and patient, listening objects (the students). The contents, whether values or empirical dimensions of reality, tend in the process of being narrated to become lifeless and petrified. Education is suffering from narration sickness.

The teacher talks about reality as if it were motionless, static, compartmentalized, and predictable. Or else he expounds on a topic completely alien to the existential experience of the students. His task is to "fill" the students with the contents of his narration—contents which are detached from reality, disconnected from the totality that engendered them and could give them significance. Words are emptied of their concreteness and become a hollow, alienated, and alienating verbosity.

The outstanding characteristic of this narrative education, then, is the sonority of words, not their transforming power. "Four times four is sixteen; the capital of Pará is Belém." The student records, memorizes, and repeats these phrases without perceiving what four times four really means, or realizing the true significance of "capital" in the affirmation "the capital of Pará is Belém," that is, what Belém means for Pará and what Pará means for Brazil.

Narration (with the teacher as narrator) leads the students to memorize mechanically the narrated content. Worse yet, it turns them into "containers," into "receptacles" to be "filled" by the teacher. The more completely she fills the receptacles, the better a teacher she is. The more meekly the receptacles permit themselves to be filled, the better students they are.

Education thus becomes an act of depositing, in which the students are the depositories and the teacher is the depositor. Instead of communicating, the teacher issues communiqués and makes deposits which the students patiently receive, memorize, and repeat. This is the "banking" concept of education, in which the scope of action allowed to the students extends only as far as receiving, filing, and storing the deposits. They do, it is true, have the opportunity to become collectors or cataloguers of the things they store. But in the last analysis, it is the people themselves who are filed away through the lack of creativity, transformation, and knowledge in this (at best) misguided system. For apart from inquiry, apart from the praxis, individuals cannot be truly human. Knowledge emerges only through invention and reinvention, through the restless, impatient, continuing, hopeful inquiry human beings pursue in the world, with the world, and with each other.

In the banking concept of education, knowledge is a gift bestowed by those who consider themselves knowledgeable upon those whom they consider to know nothing. Projecting an absolute ignorance onto others, a characteristic of the ideology of oppression, negates education and knowledge as processes of inquiry. The teacher presents himself to his students as their necessary opposite; by considering their ignorance absolute, he justifies his own existence. The students, alienated like the slave in the Hegelian dialectic, accept their ignorance as justifying the teacher's existence—but, unlike the slave, they never discover that they educate the teacher.

The *raison d'être* of libertarian education, on the other hand, lies in its drive toward reconciliation. Education must begin with the solution of the teacher-student contradiction, by reconciling the poles of the contradiction so that both are simultaneously teachers *and* students.

This solution is not (nor can it be) found in the banking concept. On the contrary, banking education maintains and even stimulates the contradiction through the following attitudes and practices, which mirror oppressive society as a whole:

(a) the teacher teaches and the students are taught
(b) the teacher knows everything and the students know nothing
(c) the teacher thinks and the students are thought about
(d) the teacher talks and the students listen—meekly
(e) the teacher disciplines and the students are disciplined
(f) the teacher chooses and enforces his choice, and the students comply
(g) the teacher acts and the students have the illusion of acting through the action of the teacher
(h) the teacher chooses the program content, and the students (who were not consulted) adapt to it

(i) the teacher confuses the authority of knowledge with his or her own professional authority, which she and he sets in opposition to the freedom of the students

(j) the teacher is the Subject of the learning process, while the pupils are mere objects

It is not surprising that the banking concept of education regards men as adaptable, manageable beings. The more students work at storing the deposits entrusted to them, the less they develop the critical consciousness which would result from their intervention in the world as transformers of that world. The more completely they accept the passive role imposed on them, the more they tend simply to adapt to the world as it is and to the fragmented view of reality deposited in them.

The capability of banking education to minimize or annul the students' creative power and to stimulate their credulity serves the interests of the oppressors, who care neither to have the world revealed nor to see it transformed. The oppressors use their "humanitarianism" to preserve a profitable situation. Thus they react almost instinctively against any experiment in education which stimulates the critical faculties and is not content with a partial view of reality but always seeks out the ties which link one point to another and one problem to another.

Indeed, the interests of the oppressors lie in "changing the consciousness of the oppressed, not the situation which oppresses them";[1] for the more the oppressed can be led to adapt to that situation, the more easily they can be dominated. To achieve this end, the oppressors use the banking concept of education in conjunction with a paternalistic social action apparatus, within which the oppressed receive the euphemistic title of "welfare recipients." They are treated as individual cases, as marginal persons who deviate from the general configuration of a "good, organized, and just" society. The oppressed are regarded as the pathology of the healthy society, which must therefore adjust these "incompetent and lazy" folk to its own patterns by changing their mentality. These marginals need to be "integrated," "incorporated" into the healthy society that they have "forsaken."

The truth is, however, that the oppressed are not "marginals," are not people living "outside" society. They have always been "inside"—inside the structure which made them "beings for others." The solution is not to

---

1. Simone de Beauvoir, *La Pensée de Droite, Aujord'hui* (Paris); ST, *El Pensamiento político de la Derecha* (Buenos Aires, 1963), p. 34.

"integrate" them into the structure of oppression, but to transform that structure so that they can become "beings for themselves." Such transformation, of course, would undermine the oppressors' purposes; hence their utilization of the banking concept of education to avoid the threat of student *conscientização*.

The banking approach to adult education, for example, will never propose to students that they critically consider reality. It will deal instead with such vital questions as whether Roger gave green grass to the goat, and insist upon the importance of learning that, on the contrary, *Roger* gave green grass to the rabbit. The "humanism" of the banking approach masks the effort to turn women and men into automatons—the very negation of their ontological vocation to be more fully human.

Those who use the banking approach, knowingly or unknowingly (for there are innumerable well-intentional bank-clerk teachers who do not realize that they are serving only to dehumanize), fail to perceive that the deposits themselves contain contradictions about reality. But, sooner or later, these contradictions may lead formerly passive students to turn against their domestication and the attempt to domesticate reality. They may discover through existential experience that their present way of life is irreconcilable with their vocation to become fully human. They may perceive through their relations with reality that reality is really a *process*, undergoing constant transformation. If men and women are searchers and their ontological vocation is humanization, sooner or later they may perceive the contradiction in which banking education seeks to maintain them, and then engage themselves in the struggle for their liberation.

But the humanist, revolutionary educator cannot wait for this possibility to materialize. From the outset, her efforts must coincide with those of the students to engage in critical thinking and the quest for mutual humanization. His efforts must be imbued with a profound trust in people and their creative power. To achieve this, they must be partners of the students in their relations with them.

The banking concept does not admit to such partnership—and necessarily so. To resolve the teacher-student contradiction, to exchange the role of depositor, prescriber, domesticator, for the role of student among students would be to undermine the power of oppression and serve the cause of liberation.

Implicit in the banking concept is the assumption of a dichotomy between human beings and the world: a person is merely *in* the world, not *with* the world or with others; the individual is spectator, not re-creator. In this view, the person is not a conscious being *(corpo consciente)*; he or she is rather the possessor of *a* consciousness: an empty "mind" passively open to the reception of deposits of reality from the world outside. For example, my desk, my books, my coffee cup, all the objects before me—as bits of the world which surround me—would be "inside" me, exactly as I am inside my study right now. This view makes no distinction between being accessible to consciousness and entering consciousness. The distinction, however, is essential: the objects which surround me are simply accessible to my consciousness, not located within it. I am aware of them, but they are not inside me.

It follows logically from the banking notion of consciousness that the educator's role is to regulate the way the world "enters into" the students. The teacher's task is to organize a process which already occurs spontaneously, to "fill" the students by making deposits of information which he or she considers to constitute true knowledge.[2] And since people "receive" the world as passive entities, education should make them more passive still, and adapt them to the world. The educated individual is the adapted person, because she or he is better "fit" for the world. Translated into practice, this concept is well suited to the purposes of the oppressors, whose tranquility rests on how well people fit the world the oppressors have created, and how little they question it.

The more completely the majority adapt to the purposes which the dominant minority prescribe for them (thereby depriving them of the right to their own purposes), the more easily the minority can continue to prescribe. The theory and practice of banking education serve this end quite efficiently. Verbalistic lessons, reading requirements,[3] the methods for evaluating "knowledge," the distance between the teacher and the taught, the criteria for promotion: everything in this ready-to-wear approach serves to obviate thinking.

The bank-clerk educator does not realize that there is no true security in his hypertrophied role, that one must seek to live *with* others in solidarity. One cannot impose oneself, nor even merely co-exist with one's students.

---

2. This concept corresponds to what Sartre calls the "digestive" or "nutritive" concept of education, in which knowledge is "fed" by the teacher to the students to "fill them out." See Jean-Paul Sartre, "Une idée fundamentale de la phénoménologie de Husserl: L'intentionalité," *Situations I* (Paris, 1947).

3. For example, some professors specify in their reading lists that a book should be read from pages 10 to 15—and do this to "help" their students!

Solidarity requires true communication, and the concept by which such an educator is guided fears and proscribes communication.

Yet only through communication can human life hold meaning. The teacher's thinking is authenticated only by the authenticity of the students' thinking. The teacher cannot think for her students, nor can she impose her thought on them. Authentic thinking, thinking that is concerned about *reality,* does not take place in ivory tower isolation, but only in communication. If it is true that thought has meaning only when generated by action upon the world, the subordination of students to teachers becomes impossible.

Because banking education begins with a false understanding of men and women as objects, it cannot promote the development of what Fromm calls "biophily," but instead produces its opposite: "necrophily."

> While life is characterized by growth in a structured, functional manner, the necrophilous person loves all that does not grow, all that is mechanical. The necrophilous person is driven by the desire to transform the organic into the inorganic, to approach life mechanically, as if all living persons were things. . . . Memory, rather than experience; having, rather than being, is what counts. The necrophilous person can relate to an object—a flower or a person—only if he possesses it; hence a threat to his possession is a threat to himself; if he loses possession he loses contact with the world. . . . He loves control, and in the act of controlling he kills life.[4]

Oppression—overwhelming control—is necrophilic; it is nourished by love of death, not life. The banking concept of education, which serves the interests of oppression, is also necrophilic. Based on a mechanistic, static, naturalistic, spatialized view of consciousness, it transforms students into receiving objects. It attempts to control thinking and action, leads women and men to adjust to the world, and inhibits their creative power.

When their efforts to act responsibly are frustrated, when they find themselves unable to use their faculties, people suffer. "This suffering due to impotence is rooted in the very fact that the human equilibrium has been disturbed."[5] But the inability to act which causes people's anguish also causes them to reject their impotence, by attempting

> . . . to restore [their] capacity to act. But can [they], and how? One way is to submit to and identify with a person or group having power. By

---

4. Fromm, *op. cit.,* p. 41.
5. *Ibid.,* p. 31.

this symbolic participation in another person's life, [men have] the illusion of acting, when in reality [they] only submit to and become a part of those who act.[6]

Populist manifestations perhaps best exemplify this type of behavior by the oppressed, who, by identifying with charismatic leaders, come to feel that they themselves are active and effective. The rebellion they express as they emerge in the historical process is motivated by that desire to act effectively. The dominant elites consider the remedy to be more domination and repression, carried out in the name of freedom, order, and social peace (that is, the peace of the elites). Thus they can condemn—logically, from their point of view—"the violence of a strike by workers and [can] call upon the state in the same breath to use violence in putting down the strike."[7]

Education as the exercise of domination stimulates the credulity of students, with the ideological intent (often not perceived by educators) of indoctrinating them to adapt to the world of oppression. This accusation is not made in the naïve hope that the dominant elites will thereby simply abandon the practice. Its objective is to call the attention of true humanists to the fact that they cannot use banking educational methods in the pursuit of liberation, for they would only negate that very pursuit. Nor may a revolutionary society inherit these methods from an oppressor society. The revolutionary society which practices banking education is either misguided or mistrusting of people. In either event, it is threatened by the specter of reaction.

Unfortunately, those who espouse the cause of liberation are themselves surrounded and influenced by the climate which generates the banking concept, and often do not perceive its true significance or its dehumanizing power. Paradoxically, then, they utilize this same instrument of alienation in what they consider an effort to liberate. Indeed, some "revolutionaries" brand as "innocents," "dreamers," or even "reactionaries" those who would challenge this educational practice. But one does not liberate people by alienating them. Authentic liberation—the process of humanization—is not another deposit to be made in men. Liberation is a praxis; the action and reflection of men and women upon their world in order to transform it. Those truly committed to the cause of liberation can accept neither the mechanistic concept of consciousness as an empty vessel to be filled, nor

---

6. *Ibid.*
7. Reinhold Niebuhr, *Moral Man and Immoral Society* (New York, 1960), p. 130.

the use of banking methods of domination (propaganda, slogans—deposits) in the name of liberation.

Those truly committed to liberation must reject the banking concept in its entirety, adopting instead a concept of women and men as conscious beings, and consciousness as consciousness intent upon the world. They must abandon the educational goal of deposit-making and replace it with the posing of the problems of human beings in their relations with the world. "Problem-posing" education, responding to the essence of consciousness—*intentionality*—rejects communiqués and embodies communication. It epitomizes the special characteristic of consciousness: being *conscious of*, not only as intent on objects but as turned in upon itself in Jasperian "split"—consciousness as consciousness *of* consciousness.

Liberating education consists in acts of cognition, not transferrals of information. It is a learning situation in which the cognizable object (far from being the end of the cognitive act) intermediates the cognitive actors—teacher on the one hand and students on the other. Accordingly, the practice of problem-posing education entails at the outset that the teacher-student contradiction be resolved. Dialogical relations—indispensable to the capacity of cognitive actors to cooperate in perceiving the same cognizable object—are otherwise impossible.

Indeed, problem-posing education, which breaks with the vertical patterns characteristic of banking education, can fulfill its function as the practice of freedom only if it can overcome the above contradiction. Through dialogue, the teacher-of-the-students and the students-of-the-teacher cease to exist and a new term emerges: teacher-student with students-teachers. The teacher is no longer merely the-one-who-teaches, but one who is himself taught in dialogue with the students, who in turn while being taught also teach. They become jointly responsible for a process in which all grow. In this process, arguments based on "authority" are no longer valid; in order to function, authority must be *on the side of* freedom, not *against* it. Here, no one teaches another, nor is anyone self-taught. People teach each other, mediated by the world, by the cognizable objects which in banking education are "owned" by the teacher.

The banking concept (with its tendency to dichotomize everything) distinguishes two stages in the action of the educator. During the first, he cognizes a cognizable object while he prepares his lessons in his study or his laboratory; during the second, he expounds to his students about that object. The students are not called upon to know, but to memorize the contents narrated by the teacher. Nor do the students practice any act of cognition, since the object toward which the act should be directed is the property of the teacher rather than a medium evoking the critical reflection of both teacher and students. Hence in the name of the "preservation of culture and knowledge" we have a system which achieves neither true knowledge nor true culture.

The problem-posing method does not dichotomize the activity of the teacher-student: she is not "cognitive" at one point and "narrative" at another. She is always "cognitive," whether preparing a project or engaging in dialogue with the students. He does not regard cognizable objects as his private property, but as the object of reflection by himself and the students. In this way, the problem-posing educator constantly re-forms his reflections in the reflection of the students. The students—no longer docile listeners—are now critical co-investigators in dialogue with the teacher. The teacher presents the material to the students for their consideration, and re-considers her earlier considerations as the students express their own. The role of the problem-posing educator is to create, together with the students, the conditions under which knowledge at the level of the *doxa* is superseded by true knowledge, at the level of the *logos*.

Whereas banking education anesthetizes and inhibits creative power, problem-posing education involves a constant unveiling of reality. The former attempts to maintain the *submersion* of consciousness; the latter strives for the *emergence* of consciousness and *critical intervention* in reality.

Students, as they are increasingly posed with problems relating to themselves in the world and with the world, will feel increasingly challenged and obliged to respond to that challenge. Because they apprehend the challenge as interrelated to other problems within a total context, not as a theoretical question, the resulting comprehension tends to be increasingly critical and thus constantly less alienated. Their response to the challenge evokes new challenges, followed by new understandings; and gradually the students come to regard themselves as committed.

Education as the practice of freedom—as opposed to education as the practice of domination—denies that man is abstract, isolated, independent, and unattached to the world; it also denies that the world exists as a reality apart from people. Authentic reflection considers neither abstract man nor the world without people, but people in their relations with the world. In these relations consciousness and world are simultaneous: consciousness neither precedes the world nor follows it.

La conscience et le monde sont dormés d'un même coup: extérieur par essence à la conscience, le monde est, par essence relatif à elle.[8]

8. Sartre, *op. cit.*, p. 32.

In one of our culture circles in Chile, the group was discussing (based on a codification) the anthropological concept of culture. In the midst of the discussion, a peasant who by banking standards was completely ignorant said: "Now I see that without man there is no world." When the educator responded: "Let's say, for the sake of argument, that all the men on earth were to die, but that the earth itself remained, together with trees, birds, animals, rivers, seas, the stars . . . wouldn't all this be a world?" "Oh no," the peasant replied emphatically. "There would be no one to say: 'This is a world'."

The peasant wished to express the idea that there would be lacking the consciousness of the world which necessarily implies the world of consciousness. *I* cannot exist without a *non-I*. In turn, the *not-I* depends on that existence. The world which brings consciousness into existence becomes the world *of* that consciousness. Hence, the previously cited affirmation of Sartre: "*La conscience et la monde sont dormés d'un même coup.*"

As women and men, simultaneously reflecting on themselves and on the world, increase the scope of their perception, they begin to direct their observations towards previously inconspicuous phenomena:

> In perception properly so-called, as an explicit awareness [*Gewahren*], I am turned towards the object, to the paper, for instance. I apprehend it as being this here and now. The apprehension is a singling out, every object having a background in experience. Around and about the paper lie books, pencils, inkwell, and so forth, and these in a certain sense are also "perceived," perceptually there, in the "field of intuition"; but whilst I was turned towards the paper there was no turning in their direction, nor any apprehending of them, not even in a secondary sense. They appeared and yet were not singled out, were not posited on their own account. Every perception of a thing has such a zone of background intuitions or background awareness, if "intuiting" already includes the state of being turned towards, and this also is a "conscious experience," or more briefly a "consciousness of" all indeed that in point of fact lies in the co-perceived objective background.[9]

That which had existed objectively but had not been perceived in its deeper implications (if indeed it was perceived at all) begins to "stand out," assuming the character of a problem and therefore of challenge. Thus, men and women begin to single out elements from their "background awareness"

---

9. Edmund Husserl, *Ideas—General Introduction to Pure Phenomenology* (London, 1969), pp. 105–6.

and to reflect upon them. These elements are now objects of their consideration, and, as such, objects of their action and cognition.

In problem-posing education, people develop their power to perceive
critically *the way they exist* in the world *with which* and *in which* they
find themselves; they come to see the world not as a static reality, but as
a reality in process, in transformation. Although the dialectical relations of
women and men with the world exist independently of how these relations
are perceived (or whether or not they are perceived at all), it is also true
that the form of action they adopt is to a large extent a function of how
they perceive themselves in the world. Hence, the teacher-student and
the students-teachers reflect simultaneously on themselves and the world
without dichotomizing this reflection from action, and thus establish an
authentic form of thought and action.

Once again, the two educational concepts and practices under analysis
come into conflict. Banking education (for obvious reasons) attempts, by
mythicizing reality, to conceal certain facts which explain the way human
beings exist in the world; problem-posing education sets itself the task
of demythologizing. Banking education resists dialogue; problem-posing
education regards dialogue as indispensable to the act of cognition which
unveils reality. Banking education treats students as objects of assistance;
problem-posing education makes them critical thinkers. Banking education
inhibits creativity and domesticates (although it cannot completely destroy)
the *intentionality* of consciousness by isolating consciousness from the
world, thereby denying people their ontological and historical vocation of
becoming more fully human. Problem-posing education bases itself on
creativity and stimulates true reflection and action upon reality, thereby
responding to the vocation of persons as beings who are authentic only
when engaged in inquiry and creative transformation. In sum: banking
theory and practice, as immobilizing and fixating forces, fail to acknowledge
men and women as historical beings; problem-posing theory and practice
take the people's historicity as their starting point.

Problem-posing education affirms men and women as beings in the
process of *becoming*—as unfinished, uncompleted beings in and with a
likewise unfinished reality. Indeed, in contrast to other animals who are
unfinished, but not historical, people know themselves to be unfinished;
they are aware of their incompletion. In this incompletion and this awareness lie the very roots of education as an exclusively human manifestation.
The unfinished character of human beings and the transformational character of reality necessitate that education be an ongoing activity.

Education is thus constantly remade in the praxis. In order to *be*, it must *become*. Its "duration" (in the Bergsonian meaning of the word) is found in the interplay of the opposites *permanence* and *change*. The banking method emphasized permanence and becomes reactionary; problem-posing education—which accepts neither a "well-behaved" present nor a predetermined future—roots itself in the dynamic present and becomes revolutionary.

Problem-posing education is revolutionary futurity. Hence it is prophetic (and, as such, hopeful). Hence, it corresponds to the historical nature of humankind. Hence, it affirms women and men as beings who transcend themselves, who move forward and look ahead, for whom immobility represents a fatal threat, for whom looking at the past must only be a means of understanding more clearly what and who they are so that they can more wisely build the future. Hence, it identifies with the movement that engages people as beings aware of their incompletion—a historical movement which has its point of departure, its Subjects and its objective.

The point of departure of the movement lies in the people themselves. But since people do not exist apart from the world, apart from reality, the movement must begin with the human-world relationship. Accordingly, the point of departure must always be with men and women in the "here and now," which constitutes the situation within which they are submerged, from which they emerge, and in which they intervene. Only by starting from this situation—which determines their perception of it—can they begin to move. To do this authentically they must perceive their state not as fated and unalterable, but merely as limiting—and therefore challenging.

Whereas the banking method directly or indirectly reinforces men's fatalistic perception of their situation, the problem-posing method presents this very situation to them as a problem. As the situation becomes the object of their cognition, the naive or magical perception which produced their fatalism gives way to perception which is able to perceive itself even as it perceives reality, and can thus be critically objective about that reality.

A deepened consciousness of their situation leads people to apprehend that situation as an historical reality susceptible of transformation. Resignation gives way to the drive for transformation and inquiry, over which men feel themselves to be in control. If people, as historical beings necessarily engaged with other people in a movement of inquiry, did not control that movement, it would be (and is) a violation of their humanity. Any situation in which some individuals prevent others from engaging in the process of inquiry is one of violence. The means used are not important; to alienate human beings from their own decision-making is to change them into objects.

This movement of inquiry must be directed towards humanization—the people's historical vocation. The pursuit of full humanity, however, cannot be carried out in isolation or individualism, but only in fellowship and solidarity; therefore it cannot unfold in the antagonistic relations between oppressors and oppressed. No one can be authentically human while he prevents others from being so. Attempting *to be more* human, individualistically, leads to *having more*, egotistically, a form of dehumanization. Not that it is not fundamental *to have* in order *to be* human. Precisely because it *is* necessary, some men's *having* must not be allowed to constitute an obstacle to others' *having*, must not consolidate the power of the former to crush the latter.

Problem-posing education, as a humanist and liberating praxis, posits as fundamental that the people subjected to domination must fight for their emancipation. To that end, it enables teachers and students to become Subjects of the educational process by overcoming authoritarianism and an alienating intellectualism; it also enables people to overcome their false perception of reality. The world—no longer something to be described with deceptive words—becomes the object of their transforming action by men and women which results in their humanization.

Problem-posing education does not and cannot serve the interests of the oppressor. No oppressive order could permit the oppressed to begin to question: Why? While only a revolutionary society can carry out this education in systematic terms, the revolutionary leaders need not take full power before they can employ the method. In the revolutionary process, the leaders cannot utilize the banking method as an interim measure, justified on grounds of expediency, with the intention of *later* behaving in a genuinely revolutionary fashion. They must be revolutionary—that is to say, dialogical—from the outset.

Translated by Myra Bergman Ramos; revised by the publisher (1993)

· 2 ·

EDUCATION FOR
CRITICAL CONSCIOUSNESS

Education and Conscientização

My concern for the democratization of culture, within the context of fundamental democratization, required special attention to the quantitative and qualitative deficits in our education. In 1964, approximately four million school-age children lacked schools; there were sixteen million illiterates of fourteen years and older. These truly alarming deficits constituted obstacles to the development of the country and to the creation of a democratic mentality.

For more than fifteen years I had been accumulating experiences in the field of adult education, in urban and rural proletarian and subproletarian areas. Urban dwellers showed a surprising interest in education, associated directly to the transitivity of their consciousness; the inverse was true in rural areas. (Today, in some areas, that situation is already changing.) I had experimented with—and abandoned—various methods and processes of communication. Never, however, had I abandoned the conviction that only by working with the people could I achieve anything authentic on their behalf. Never had I believed that the democratization of culture meant either its vulgarization or simply passing on to the people prescriptions formulated in the teacher's office. I agreed with Mannheim that "as democratic processes become widespread, it becomes more and more difficult to permit the masses to remain in a state of ignorance."[1] Mannheim would not restrict his definition of ignorance to illiteracy, but would include the masses' lack of experience at participating and intervening in the historical process.

---

1. Karl Mannheim, *Freedom, Power, and Democratic Planning* (New York, 1950).

Experiences as the Coordinator of the Adult Education Project of the Movement of Popular Culture in Recife led to the maturing of my early educational convictions. Through this project, we launched a new institution of popular culture, a "culture circle," since among us a school was a traditionally passive concept. Instead of a teacher, we had a coordinator; instead of lectures, dialogue; instead of pupils, group participants; instead of alienating syllabi, compact programs that were "broken down" and "codified" into learning units.

In the culture circles, we attempted through group debate either to clarify situations or to seek action arising from that clarification. The topics for these debates were offered us by the groups themselves. Nationalism, profit remittances abroad, the political evolution of Brazil, development, illiteracy, the vote for illiterates, democracy, were some of the themes which were repeated from group to group. These subjects and others were schematized as far as possible and presented to the groups with visual aids, in the form of dialogue. We were amazed by the results.

After six months of experience with the culture circles, we asked ourselves if it would not be possible to do something in the field of adult literacy which would give us similar results to those we were achieving in the analysis of aspects of Brazilian reality. We started with some data and added more, aided by the Service of Cultural Extension of the University of Recife, which I directed at the time and under whose auspices the experiment was conducted.

The first literacy attempt took place in Recife, with a group of five illiterates, of which two dropped out on the second or third day. The participants, who had migrated from rural areas, revealed a certain fatalism and apathy in regard to their problems. They were totally illiterate. At the twentieth meeting, we gave progress tests. To achieve greater flexibility, we used an epidiascope. We projected a slide on which two kitchen containers appeared. "Sugar" was written on one, "poison" on the other. And underneath, the caption: "Which of the two would you use in your orangeade?" We asked the group to try to read the question and to give the answer orally. They answered, laughing, after several seconds, "Sugar." We followed the same procedure with other tests, such as recognizing bus lines and public buildings. During the twenty-first hour of study, one of the participants wrote, confidently, "I am amazed at myself."

From the beginning, we rejected the hypothesis of a purely mechanistic literacy program and considered the problem of teaching adults how to read in relation to the awakening of their consciousness. We wished to design a project in which we would attempt to move from naïveté to a critical attitude at the same time we taught reading. We wanted a literacy program which would be an introduction to the democratization of culture, a program with men and women as its Subjects rather than as patient recipients,[2] a program which itself would be an act of creation, capable of releasing other creative acts, one in which students would develop the impatience and vivacity which characterize search and invention.

We began with the conviction that the role of men and women was not only to be in the world, but to engage in relations with the world—that through acts of creation and re-creation, we make cultural reality and thereby add to the natural world, which we did not make. We were certain that people's relation to reality, expressed as a Subject to an object, results in knowledge, which men and women could express through language.

This relation, as is already clear, is carried out by men whether or not they are literate. It is sufficient to be a person to perceive the data of reality, to be capable of knowing, even if this knowledge is mere opinion. There is no such thing as absolute ignorance or absolute wisdom.[3] But men and women do not perceive those data in a pure form. As they apprehend a phenomenon or a problem, they also apprehend its causal links. The more accurately men and women grasp true causality, the more critical their understanding of reality will be. Their understanding will be magical to the degree that they fail to grasp causality. Further, critical consciousness always submits that causality to analysis; what is true today may not be so tomorrow. Naive consciousness sees causality as a static, established fact, and thus is deceived in its perception.

Critical consciousness represents "things and facts as they exist empirically, in their causal and circumstantial correlations . . . naïve consciousness considers itself superior to facts, in control of facts, and thus free to understand them as it pleases."[4]

---

2. In most reading programs, the students must endure an abysm between their own experience and the contents offered for them to learn. It requires patience indeed, after the hardships of a day's work (or of a day without work), to tolerate lessons dealing with "wing." "Johnny saw the wing." "The wing is on the bird." Lessons talking of Graces and grapes to men who never knew a Grace and never ate a grape. "Grace saw the grape."

3. No one ignores everything, just as no one knows everything. The dominating consciousness absolutizes ignorance in order to manipulate the so-called "uncultured." If some men are "totally ignorant," they will be incapable of managing themselves, and will need the orientation, the "direction," the "leadership" of those who consider themselves to be "cultured" and "superior."

4. Álvaro Vieira Pinto, *Consciência e Realidade Nacional* (Rio de Janeiro, 1961).

Magic consciousness, in contrast, simply apprehends facts and attributes to them a superior power by which it is controlled and to which it must therefore submit. Magic consciousness is characterized by fatalism, which leads men to fold their arms, resigned to the impossibility of resisting the power of facts.

Critical consciousness is integrated with reality; naïve consciousness superimposes itself on reality; and fanatical consciousness, whose pathological naïveté leads to the irrational, adapts to reality.

It so happens that to every understanding, sooner or later an action corresponds. Once man perceives a challenge, understands it, and recognizes the possibilities of response, he acts. The nature of that action corresponds to the nature of his understanding. Critical understanding leads to critical action; magic understanding to magic response.

We wanted to offer the people the means by which they could supersede their magic or naïve perception of reality by one that was predominantly critical, so that they could assume positions appropriate to the dynamic climate of the transition. This meant that we must take the people at the point of emergence and, by helping them move from naïve to critical transitivity, facilitate their intervention in the historical process.

But how could this be done?

The answer seemed to lie:

(a) in an active, *dialogical*, critical and criticism-stimulating *method;*

(b) in changing the *program content* of education;

(c) in the use of *techniques* like thematic "breakdown" and "codification."[5]

Our method, then, was to be based on dialogue, which is a horizontal relationship between persons.

DIALOGUE

A with B = communication

intercommunication

Relation of "empathy" between two "poles" who are engaged in a joint search.

MATRIX: Loving, humble, hopeful, trusting, critical.

Born of a critical matrix, dialogue creates a critical attitude (Jaspers). It is nourished by love, humility, hope, faith, and trust. When the two "poles"

---

5. "Breakdown": a splitting of themes into their fundamental nuclei. See *Pedagogy of the Oppressed*, p. 101ff. "Codification": the representation of a theme in the form of an existential situation. See *Pedagogy*, pp. 95–96 and pp. 102–3.—Translator's note.

of the dialogue are thus linked by love, hope, and mutual trust, they can join in a critical search for something. Only dialogue truly communicates.

> Dialogue is the only way, not only in the vital questions of the political order, but in all the expressions of our being. Only by virtue of faith, however, does dialogue have power and meaning: by faith in man and his possibilities, by the faith that I can only become truly myself when other men also become themselves.[6]

And so we set dialogue in opposition with the anti-dialogue which was so much a part of our historical-cultural formation, and so present in the climate of transition.

ANTI-DIALOGUE

A

over

B = communiqué

Relation of "empathy" is broken.
MATRIX: Loveless, arrogant, hopeless, mistrustful, acritical.

It involves vertical relationships between persons. It lacks love, is therefore acritical, and cannot create a critical attitude. It is self-sufficient and hopelessly arrogant. In anti-dialogue the relation of empathy between the "poles" is broken. Thus, anti-dialogue does not communicate, but rather issues communiqués.[7]

Whoever enters into dialogue does so with someone about something; and that something ought to constitute the new content of our proposed education. We felt that even before teaching the illiterate to read, we could help him to overcome his magic or naïve understanding and to develop an increasingly critical understanding. Toward this end, the first dimension of our new program content would be the anthropological concept of culture—that is, the distinction between the world of nature and the world of culture; the active role of men *in* and *with* their reality; the role of mediation which nature plays in relationships and communication among people; culture as the addition made by men and women to a world they

---

6. Karl Jaspers, *op. cit.*
7. See Jaspers, *op. cit.*

did not make; culture as the result of people's labor, of their efforts to create and re-create; the transcendental meaning of human relationships; the humanist dimension of culture; culture as a systematic acquisition of human experience (but as creative assimilation, not as information-storing); the democratization of culture; the learning of reading and writing as a key to the world of written communication. In short, the role of man and woman as Subject in the world and with the world.

From that point of departure, the illiterate would begin to effect a change in his or her former attitudes, by discovering himself or herself to be a maker of the world of culture, by discovering that he or she, as well as the literate person, has a creative and re-creative impulse. He or she would discover that culture is just as much a clay doll made by artists who are his or her peers as it is the work of a great sculptor, a great painter, a great mystic, or a great philosopher; that culture is the poetry of lettered poets and also the poetry of his or her own popular songs—that culture is all human creation.

To introduce the concept of culture, first we "broke down" this concept into its fundamental aspects. Then, on the basis of this breakdown, we "codified" (i.e., represented visually) ten existential situations. These situations are presented in the Appendix, together with a brief description of some of the basic elements contained in each. Each representation contained a number of elements to be "decoded" by the group participants, with the help of the coordinator. Francisco Brenand, one of the greatest contemporary Brazilian artists, painted these codifications, perfectly integrating education and art.

It is remarkable to see with what enthusiasm these illiterates engage in debate and with what curiosity they respond to questions implicit in the codifications. In the words of Odilon Ribeiro Coutinho, these "detemporalized men begin to integrate themselves in time." As the dialogue intensifies, a "current" is established among the participants, dynamic to the degree that the content of the codifications corresponds to the existential reality of the groups.

Many participants during these debates affirm happily and self-confidently that they are not being shown "anything new, just remembering." "I make shoes," said one, "and now I see that I am worth as much as the Ph.D. who writes books."

"Tomorrow," said a street-sweeper in Brasília, "I'm going to go to work with my head high." He had discovered the value of his person. "I know now that I am cultured," an elderly peasant said emphatically. And when he was asked how it was that now he knew himself to be cultured, he answered with the same emphasis, "Because I work, and working, I transform the world."[8]

Once the group has perceived the distinction between the two worlds—nature and culture—and recognized the individual's role in each, the coordinator presents situations focusing on or expanding other aspects of culture.

The participants go on to discuss culture as a systematic acquisition of human experience, and to discover that in a lettered culture this acquisition is not limited to oral transmission, as is the case in unlettered cultures which lack graphic signs. They conclude by debating the democratization of culture, which opens the perspective of acquiring literacy.

All these discussions are critical, stimulating, and highly motivating. The illiterate perceives critically that it is necessary to learn to read and write, and prepares himself to become the agent of this learning.

To acquire literacy is more than to psychologically and mechanically dominate reading and writing techniques. It is to dominate these techniques in terms of consciousness; to understand what one reads and to write what one understands; it is to *communicate* graphically. Acquiring literacy does not involve memorizing sentences, words, or syllables—lifeless objects unconnected to an existential universe—but rather an attitude of creation and re-creation, a self-transformation producing a stance of intervention in one's context.

Thus the educator's role is fundamentally to enter into dialogue with the illiterate about concrete situations and simply to offer him the instruments with which he can teach himself to read and write. This teaching cannot be done from the top down, but only from the inside out, by the illiterate himself or herself, with the collaboration of the educator. That is why we searched for a method which would be the instrument of the learner as well as of the educator, and which, in the lucid observation of a young Brazilian sociologist,[9] "would identify learning *content* with the learning *process.*"

Hence, our mistrust in primers,[10] which set up a certain grouping of graphic signs as a gift and cast the illiterate in the role of the *object* rather

---

8. Similar responses were evoked by the programs carried out in Chile.

9. Celso Beisegel, in an unpublished work.

10. I am not opposed to reading texts, which are in fact indispensable to developing the visual-graphic channel of communication and which in great part should be elaborated by the participants themselves. I should add that our experience is based on the use of multiple channels of communication.

than the *Subject* of his learning. Primers, even when they try to avoid this pitfall, end by *donating* to the illiterate words and sentences which really should result from his own creative effort. We opted instead for the use of "generative words," those whose syllabic elements offer, through recombination, the creation of new words. Teaching men and women how to read and write a syllabic language like Portuguese, means showing them how to grasp critically the way its words are formed, so that they themselves can carry out the creative play of combinations. Fifteen or eighteen words seemed sufficient to present the basic phonemes of the Portuguese language. The seventeen generative words used in the State of Rio are presented in the Appendix.

The program is elaborated in several phases:

Phase 1: Researching the vocabulary of the groups with which one is working. This research is carried out during informal encounters with the inhabitants of the area. One selects not only the words most weighted with existential meaning (and thus the greatest emotional content), but also typical sayings, as well as words and expressions linked to the experience of the groups in which the researcher participates. These interviews reveal longings, frustrations, disbeliefs, hopes, and an impetus to participate. During this initial phase the team of educators form rewarding relationships and discover often unsuspected exuberance and beauty in the people's language.

The archives of the Service of Cultural Extension of the University of Recife contain vocabulary studies of rural and urban areas in the Northeast and in southern Brazil full of such examples as the following:

"The month of January in Angicos," said a man from the backlands of Rio Grande do Norte, "is a hard one to live through, because January is a tough guy who makes us suffer." (*Janeiro em Angicos é duro de se viver, porque janeiro é cabra danado para judiar de nós.*)

"I want to learn to read and write," said an illiterate from Recife, "so that I can stop being the shadow of other people."

A man from Florianópolis: "The people have an answer."

Another, in an injured tone: "I am not angry (*não tenho paixão*) at being poor, but at not knowing how to read."

"I have the school of the world," said an illiterate from the southern part of the country, which led Professor Jomard de Brito to ask in an essay, "What can one presume to 'teach' an adult who affirms 'I have the school of the world'?"[11]

11. "Educação de Adultos e Unificação de Cultura," Estudos Universitários, *Revista de Cultura,* Universidade de Recife, 2–4, 1963.

"I want to learn to read and to write so I can change the world," said an illiterate from São Paulo, for whom to *know* quite correctly meant *to intervene* in his reality.

"The people put a screw in their heads," said another in somewhat esoteric language. And when he was asked what he meant, he replied in terms revealing the phenomenon of popular emergence: "That is what explains that you, Professor, have come to talk with me, the people."

Such affirmations merit interpretation by specialists, to produce a more efficient instrument for the educator's action.[12] The generative words to be used in the program should emerge from this field vocabulary research, not from the educator's personal inspiration, no matter how proficiently he might construct a list.

Phase 2: Selection of the generative words from the vocabulary which was studied. The following criteria should govern their selection:

(a) phonemic richness;

(b) phonetic difficulty (the words chosen should correspond to the phonetic difficulties of the language, placed in a sequence moving gradually from words of less to those of greater difficulty);

(c) pragmatic tone, which implies a greater engagement of a word in a given social, cultural, and political reality.

Professor Jarbas Maciel has commented that "these criteria are contained in the semeiotic criterion: the best generative word is that which combines the greatest possible 'percentage' of the syntactic criteria (phonemic richness, degree of complex phonetic difficulty, 'manipulability' of the groups of signs, the syllables, etc.), the semantic criteria (greater or lesser 'intensity' of the link between the word and the thing it designates), the greater or lesser correspondence between the word and the pragmatic thing designated, the greater or lesser quality of *conscientização* which the word potentially carries, or the grouping of sociocultural reactions which the word generates in the person or group using it."[13]

Phase 3: The creation of the "codifications:" the representation of typical existential situations of the group with which one is working. These representations function as challenges, as coded situation-problems containing elements to be decoded by the groups with the collaboration of the coordinator. Discussion of these codifications will lead the groups toward a more

---

12. Luis Costa Lima, Professor of Literary Theory, has analyzed many of these texts by illiterate authors.

13. "A Fundamentação Teórica do Sistema Paulo Freire de Educação," Estudos Universitários, *Revista de Cultura*, Universidade do Recife, No. IV, 1963.

critical consciousness at the same time that they begin to learn to read and write. The codifications represent familiar local situations—which, however, open perspectives for the analysis of regional and national problems. The generative words are set into the codifications, graduated according to their phonetic difficulty. One generative word may embody the entire situation, or it may refer to only one of the elements of the situation.

Phase 4: The elaboration of agendas, which should serve as mere aids to the coordinators, never as rigid schedules to be obeyed.

Phase 5: The preparation of cards with the breakdown of the phonemic families which correspond to the generative words.

A major problem in setting up the program is instructing the teams of coordinators. Teaching the purely technical aspect of the procedure is not difficult; the difficulty lies rather in the creation of a new attitude—that of dialogue, so absent in our own upbringing and education. The coordinators must be converted to dialogue in order to carry out education rather than domestication. Dialogue is an I–Thou relationship, and thus necessarily a relationship between two Subjects. Each time the "thou" is changed into an object, an "it," dialogue is subverted and education is changed to deformation. The period of instruction must be followed by dialogical supervision, to avoid the temptation of anti-dialogue on the part of the coordinators.

Once the material has been prepared in the form of slides, filmstrips, or posters, once the teams of coordinators and supervisors have been instructed in all aspects of the method and have been given their agendas, the program itself can begin. It functions in the following manner:

The codified situation is projected, together with the first generative word, which graphically represents the oral expression of the object perceived. Debate about its implications follows.

Only after the group, with the collaboration of the coordinator, has exhausted the analysis (decoding) of the situation, does the coordinator call attention to the generative word, encouraging the participants to visualize (not memorize) it. Once the word has been visualized, and the semantic link established between the word and the object to which it refers, the word is presented alone on another slide (or poster or photogram) without the object it names. Then the same word is separated into syllables, which the illiterate usually identifies as "pieces." Once the "pieces" are recognized, the coordinator presents visually the phonemic families which compose the word, first in isolation and then together, to arrive at the recognition of the vowels. The card presenting the phonemic families has been called the "discovery card."[14] Using this card to reach a synthesis, men discover the mechanism of word formation through phonemic combinations in a syllabic language like Portuguese. By appropriating this mechanism critically (not learning it by rote), they themselves can begin to produce a system of graphic signs. They can begin, with surprising ease, to create words with the phonemic combinations offered by the breakdown of a trisyllabic word, on the first day of the program.[15]

For example, let us take the word *tijolo* (brick) as the first generative word, placed in a "situation" of construction work. After discussing the situation in all its possible aspects, the semantic link between the word and the object it names is established. Once the word has been noted within the situation, it is presented without the object: *tijolo*.

Afterward: *ti-jo-lo*. By moving immediately to present the "pieces" visually, we initiate the recognition of the phonemic families. Beginning with the first syllable, *ti*, the group is motivated to learn the whole phonemic family resulting from the combination of the initial consonant with the other vowels. The group then learns the second family through the visual presentation of *jo*, and finally arrives at the third family.

When the phonemic family is projected, the group at first recognizes only the syllable of the word which has been shown:

(ta-te-*ti*-to-tu), (ja-je-ji-*jo*-ju), (la-le-li-*lo*-lu)

When the participants recognize *ti*, from the generative word *tijolo*, it is proposed that they compare it with the other syllables; whereupon they discover that while all the syllables begin the same, they end differently. Thus, they cannot all be called *ti*.

The same procedure is followed with the syllables *jo* and *lo* and their families. After learning each phonemic family, the group practices reading the new syllables.

The most important moment arises when the three families are presented together:

---

14. Aurenice Cardoso, "Conscientização e Alfabetização—Visão Prática do Sistema Paulo Freire de Educação de Adultos," Estudos Universitários, *Revista de Cultura,* Universidade do Recife, No. II, 1963.

15. Generally, in a period of six weeks to two months, we could leave a group of twenty-five persons reading newspapers, writing notes and simple letters, and discussing problems of local and national interest.

Each culture circle was equipped with a Polish-made projector, imported at the cost of about $13. Since we had not yet set up our own laboratory, a filmstrip cost us bout $7–$8. We also used an inexpensive blackboard. The slides were projected on the wall of the house where the culture

ta-te-ti-to-tu
ja-je-ji-jo-ju   THE DISCOVERY CARD
la-le-li-lo-lu

After one horizontal and one vertical reading to grasp the vocal sounds, the group (*not* the coordinator) begins to carry out oral synthesis. One by one, they all begin to "make" words with the combinations available:[16] *tatu* (armadillo), *luta* (struggle), *lajota* (small flagstone), *loja* (store), *jato* (jet), *juta* (jute), *lote* (lot), *lula* (squid), *tela* (screen), etc. There are even some participants who take a vowel from one of the syllables, link it to another syllable, and add a third, thus forming a word. For example, they take the *i* from li, join it to *le* and add *te: leitre* (milk).

There are others, like an illiterate from Brasília, who on the first night he began his literary program said, *"tu já lê"* ("you already read").[17]

The oral exercises involve not only learning, but recognition (without which there is no true learning). Once these are completed, the participants begin—on that same first evening—to write. On the following day they bring from home as many words as they were able to make with the combinations of the phonemes they learned. It doesn't matter if they bring combinations which are not actual words—what does matter is the discovery of the mechanism of phonemic combinations.

The group itself, with the help of the educator (*not* the educator with the help of the group), should test the words thus created. A group in the state of Rio Grande do Norte called those combinations which were actual words "thinking words" and those which were not, "dead words."

Not infrequently, after assimilating the phonemic mechanism by using the "discovery card," participants would write words with complex phonemes (*tra, nha,* etc.), which had not yet been presented to them. In one of the Culture Circles in Angicos, Rio Grande do Norte, on the fifth day of discussion, in which simple phonemes were being shown, one of the participants went to the blackboard to write (as he said) "a thinking word." He wrote: *"o povo vai resouver os poblemas do Brasil votando conciente"*[18]

---

circle met or, where this was difficult, on the reverse side (painted white) of the blackboard.

The Education Ministry imported 35,000 of the projectors, which after the military coup of 1964 were presented on television as "highly subversive."

16. In a television interview, Gilson Amado observed lucidly, "They can do this, because there is no such thing as oral illiteracy."

17. In correct Portuguese, *tu já lês.*

18. *Resouver* is a corruption of *resolver; poblemas* a corruption of *problemas;* the letter *s* is lacking from the syllable *cons.*

("the people will solve the problems of Brazil by informed voting"). In such cases, the group discussed the text, debating its significance in the context of their reality.

How can one explain the fact that a man who was illiterate several days earlier could write words with complex phonemes before he had even studied them? Once he had dominated the mechanism of phonemic combinations, he attempted—and managed—to express himself graphically, in the way he spoke.[19]

I wish to emphasize that in educating adults, to avoid a rote, mechanical process one must make it possible for them to achieve critical consciousness so that they can teach themselves to read and write.

As an active educational method helps a person to become consciously aware of his context and his condition as a human being as Subject, it will become an instrument of choice. At that point he will become politicized. When an ex-illiterate of Angicos, speaking before President João Goulart and the presidential staff,[20] declared that he was no longer part of the *mass*, but one of the *people*, he had done more than utter a mere phrase; he had made a conscious option. He had chosen decisional participation, which belongs to the people, and had renounced the emotional resignation of the masses. He had become political.

The National Literary Program of the Ministry of Education and Culture, which I coordinated, planned to extend and strengthen this education work throughout Brazil. Obviously we could not confine that work to a literacy program, even one which was critical rather than mechanical. With the same spirit of a pedagogy of communication, we were therefore planning a post-literacy stage which would vary only as to curriculum. If the National Literacy Program had not been terminated by the military coup, in 1964 there would have been more than 20,000 culture circles functioning throughout the country. In these, we planned to investigate the themes of the Brazilian people. These themes would be analyzed by specialists and broken down into learning units, as we had done with the concept of culture and with the coded situations linked to the generative words. We

---

19. Interestingly enough, as a rule the illiterates wrote confidently and legibly, largely overcoming the natural indecisiveness of beginners. Elza Freire thinks this may be due to the fact that these persons, beginning with the discussion of the anthropological concept of culture, discovered themselves to be more fully human, thereby acquiring an increasing emotional confidence in their learning which was reflected in their motor activity.

20. I wish to acknowledge the support given our efforts by President Goulart, by Ministers of Education Paulo de Tarso and Júlio Sambaquy, and by the Rector of the University of Recife, Professor João Alfredo da Costa Lima.

would prepare filmstrips with these breakdowns as well as simplified texts with references to the original texts. By gathering this thematic material, we could have offered a substantial post-literacy program. Further, by making a catalog of thematic breakdowns and bibliographic references available to high schools and colleges, we could widen the sphere of the program and help identify our schools with our reality.

At the same time, we began to prepare material with which we could carry out concretely an education that would encourage what Aldous Huxley has called the "art of dissociating ideas"[21] as an antidote to the domesticating power of propaganda.[22] We planned filmstrips, for use in the literacy phase, presenting propaganda—from advertising commercials to ideological indoctrination—as a "problem-situation" for discussion.

For example, as men through discussion begin to perceive the deceit in a cigarette advertisement featuring a beautiful, smiling woman in a bikini (i.e., the fact that she, her smile, her beauty, and her bikini have nothing at all to do with the cigarette), they begin to discover the difference between education and propaganda. At the same time, they are preparing themselves to discuss and perceive the same deceit in ideological or political propaganda;[23] they are arming themselves to "dissociate ideas." In fact, this has always seemed to me to be the way to defend democracy, not a way to subvert it.

---

21. *Ends and Means* (New York and London, 1937), p. 252.

22. I have never forgotten the publicity (done cleverly, considering our acritical mental habits) for a certain Brazilian public figure. The bust of the candidate was displayed with arrows pointing to his head, his eyes, his mouth, and his hands. Next to the arrows appeared the legend:

> *You don't need to think he thinks for you!*
> *You don't need to see, he sees for you!*
> *You don't need to talk, he talks for you!*
> *You don't need to act, he acts for you!*

23. In the campaigns carried out against me, I have been called "ignorant" and "illiterate," "the author of a method so innocuous that it did not even manage to teach him how to read and write." It was said that I was not "the inventor" of dialogue (as if I had ever made such an irresponsible affirmation). It was said that I had done "nothing original," and that I had "plagiarized European or North-American educators," as well as the author of a Brazilian primer. (On the subject of originality, I have always agreed with Dewey, for whom originality does not lie in the "extraordinary and fanciful," but "in putting everyday things to uses which had not occurred to others." *Democracy and Education*, New York, 1916, p. 187.)

None of these accusations has ever wounded me. What does leave me perplexed is to hear or read that I intended to "Bolchevize the country" with my method. In fact, my actual crime was that I treated literacy as more than a mechanical problem, and linked it to *conscientização*, which was "dangerous." It was that I viewed education as an effort to liberate men, not as yet another instrument to dominate them.

One subverts democracy (even though one does this in the name of democracy) by making it irrational; by making it rigid in order "to defend it against totalitarian rigidity"; by making it hateful, when it can only develop in a context of love and respect for persons; by closing it, when it only lives in openness; by nourishing it with fear when it must be courageous; by making it an instrument of the powerful in the oppression of the weak; by militarizing it against the people; by alienating a nation in the name of democracy.

One defends democracy by leading it to the state Mannheim calls "militant democracy"—a democracy which does not fear the people, which suppresses privilege, which can plan without becoming rigid, which defends itself without hate, which is nourished by a critical spirit rather than irrationality.

Postscript

Today, the task of overcoming our lack of democratic experience through experiences in participation still awaits us, as does the task of superseding the irrational climate which prevails in Brazil.

It is too soon to say to what extent this climate can be overcome without provoking larger explosions and even more severe forms of retreat. Possibly the intense emotionality generated by irrational sectarianism can open a new way within the historical process which will lead less rapidly to more authentic and human forms of life for the Brazilian people.

Appendix

The following drawings represent the "situations" discussed in the cultural circles. The originals, by Francisco Brenand, were taken from me; these were done by another Brazilian artist, Vicente de Abreu, now in exile.

FIRST SITUATION
People in the World and with the World, Nature and Culture

Through the discussion of this situation (page 96)—man or woman as a being of relationships—the participants arrive at the distinction between two worlds: that of nature and that of culture. They perceive the normal situation of man as a being in the world and with the world, as a creative and re-creative being who, through work, constantly alters reality. By means of simple questions, such as, "Who made the well? Why did he do it? How did he do it? When?" which are repeated with regard to the other "elements" of the situation, two basic concepts emerge: that of *necessity* and that of *work;* and culture becomes explicit on a primary level, that of subsistence. The man made the well because he needed water. And he did it because, relating to the world, he made the latter the object of his knowledge. By work, he submitted the world to a process of transformation. Thus, he made the house, his clothes, his work tools. From that point, one discusses with the group, in obviously simple but critically objective terms, the relations among men, which unlike those discussed previously cannot be either of domination or transformation, because they are relations among Subjects.

SECOND SITUATION
Dialogue Mediated by Nature

In the first situation, we reached the analysis of relationships among men, which, because they are relations among Subjects, cannot be those of domination. Now, confronted by this second situation, the group is motivated to analyze dialogue, interpersonal communication, the encounter of consciousnesses; motivated to analyze the mediation of the world—as transformed and humanized by men and women—in this communication; motivated to analyze the loving, humble, hopeful, critical, and creative foundation of dialogue.

The three situations which follow constitute a series, the analysis of which validates the concept of culture at the same time in which other aspects of real interest are discussed.

THIRD SITUATION
Unlettered Hunter

The debate is initiated by distinguishing in this situation (page 98) what belongs to nature and what belongs to culture. "Culture in this picture," the participants say, "is the bow, it is the arrow, it is the feathers the Indian wears." And when they are asked if the feathers are not nature, they always answer, "The feathers are nature, while they are on the bird. After man kills the bird, takes the feathers, and transforms them with work, they are not nature any longer. They are culture." (I had the opportunity to hear this reply innumerable times, in various regions of the country.) By distinguishing the historical-cultural period of the hunter from their own, the participants arrive at the perception of what constitutes an unlettered culture. They discover that when man prolongs his arms five to ten yards by making an implement and therefore no longer needs to catch his prey with his hands, he has created culture. By transferring not only the use of the implement, but the incipient technology of its manufacture, to younger generations, he has created education. The participants discuss how education occurs in an unlettered culture, where one cannot properly speak of illiterates. They then perceive immediately that to be illiterate is to belong to an unlettered culture and to fail to dominate the techniques of reading and writing. For some, this perception is dramatic.

FOURTH SITUATION
Lettered Hunter (Lettered Culture)

When this situation is projected, the participants identify the hunter as a man of their culture, although he may be illiterate. They discuss the technological advance represented by the rifle as compared with the bow and arrow. They analyze men's and women's increasing opportunity, because of his or her work and his or her creative spirit, to transform the world. They discuss the fact that this transformation, however, has meaning only to the extent that it contributes to the humanization of man and woman, and is employed toward his or her liberation. They finally analyze the implications of education for development.

FIFTH SITUATION
The Hunter and the Cat

With this situation, the participants discuss the fundamental aspects which characterize the different forms of being in the world—those of men and of animals. They discuss man as a being who not only knows, but knows that he knows; as a conscious being *(corpo consciente)* in the world; as a consciousness which in the process of becoming an authentic person emerges reflective and intent upon the world.

In regard to the preceding series, I will never forget an illiterate from Brasília who affirmed, with absolute self-confidence, "Of these three, only two are hunters—the two men. They are hunters because they make culture before and after they hunt." (He failed only to say that they made culture while they hunted.) "The third, the cat, does not make culture, either before or after the 'hunt.' He is not a hunter, he is a pursuer." By making this subtle distinction between hunting and pursuing, this man grasped the fundamental point: the creation of culture.

The debate of these situations produced a wealth of observations about men and animals, about creative power, freedom, intelligence, instinct, education, and training.

SIXTH SITUATION
Man and Woman Transform the Material of Nature by His or Her Work

"What do we see here? What are the men doing?" the coordinator asks. "They are working with clay," all the participants answer. "They are changing the materials of nature with work," many answer.

After a series of analyses of work (Some participants even speak of the "pleasure of making beautiful things," as did one man from Brasília), the coordinator asks whether the work represented in the situation will result in an object of culture. They answer yes: "A vase." "A jug." "A pot," etc.

SEVENTH SITUATION
A Vase, the Product of Man's and Woamn's Work upon the Material of Nature

During a discussion of this situation in a Culture Circle of Recife, I was moved to hear a woman say with emotion, "I make culture. I know how to make that." Many participants, referring to the flowers in the vase, say, "As flowers, they are nature. As decoration, they are culture." The esthetic dimension of the product, which in a sense had been awakened from the beginning, is now reinforced. This aspect will be discussed fully in the following situation, when culture is analyzed on the level of spiritual necessity.

EIGHTH SITUATION
Poetry

First the coordinator reads, slowly, the text which has been projected. "This is a poem," everyone usually says.[24] The participants describe the poem as popular, saying that its author is a simple man of the people. They discuss whether or not the poem is culture. "It is culture, just as the vase is," they say, "but it is different from the vase." Through the discussion they perceive, in critical terms, that poetic expression, whose material is not the same, responds to a different necessity. After discussing aspects of popular and erudite artistic expression in various fields, the coordinator rereads the text and submits it to a group discussion.

24. "THE BOMB: The terrible atomic bomb / And radioactivity / Signify terror, / Ruin and calamity. / If war were ended, / And everything were united, / Our world / Would not be destroyed."

NINTH SITUATION
Patterns of Behavior

In this situation, we wish to analyze patterns of behavior as a cultural manifestation, in order subsequently to discuss resistance to change.

The picture presents a *gaucho* from the south of Brazil and a cowboy from the Brazilian northeast, each dressed in his customary fashion. Starting with the subject of their clothing, the discussion moves on to some of their forms of behavior. Once, in a Culture Circle in the south of Brazil, I heard the following: "We see here traditions of two Brazilian regions—the south and the northeast. Traditions of clothing. But before the traditions were formed, there was a need to dress like that—one with warm clothing, the other with thick leather clothing. Sometimes the need passes but the tradition goes on."

TENTH SITUATION
A Culture Circle in Action—Synthesis of the Previous Discussions

On seeing this situation (page 107), the Culture Circle participants easily identify themselves. They discuss culture as a systematic acquisition of knowledge, and also the democratization of culture within the general context of fundamental democratization. "The democratization of culture," one of these anonymous illiterate teachers once said, "has to start from what we are and what we do as a people, not from what some people think and want for us." In addition to discussing culture and its democratization, the participants analyze the functioning of a Culture Circle, its dynamic significance, the creative power of dialogue and the clarification of consciousness.

The proceeding situations are discussed in two sessions, strongly motivating the group to begin on the third night their literacy program, which they now see as a key to written communication.

Literacy makes sense only in these terms, as the consequence of men's beginning to reflect about their own capacity for reflection, about the world, about their position in the world, about their work, about their power to transform the world, about the encounter of consciousness—about literacy itself, which thereby ceases to be something external and becomes a part of them, comes as a creation from within them. I can see validity only in a literacy program in which men understand words in their true significance: as a force to transform the world. As illiterate men and women discover the relativity of ignorance and of wisdom, they destroy one of the myths by which false elites have manipulated them. Learning to read and write has meaning in that, by requiring men and women to reflect about themselves and about the world they are in and with, it makes them discover that the world is also theirs, that their work is not the price they pay for being citizens but rather a way of loving—and of helping the world to be a better place.

The following are the seventeen generative words selected from the "vocabular universe" gathered in the State of Rio de Janeiro and applicable also to Guanabara. I have not included the visual representations within which these words were presented, but have indicated some of the dimensions of reality which were analyzed in the discussion of those situations.

Generative Words

(1) SLUM (*favela*)—fundamental necessities:
Housing
Food
Clothing
Health
Education

I will repeat here, with the generative word *favela*, a breakdown similar to that of the word *tijolo*. After analyzing the existential situation (a photograph showing a slum), in which the group discusses the problems of housing, food, clothing, health, and education in a slum and in which the group further perceives the slum as a problem situation, the coordinator proceeds to present visually the word *favela* with its semantic links.

(a) First a slide appears showing only the word:
FAVELA

(b) Immediately afterward, another slide appears with the word separated into syllables:
FA-VE-LA

(c) Afterward, the phonemic family:
FA-FE-FI-FO-FU

(d) On another slide:
VA-VE-VI-VO-VU

(e) Then:
LA-LE-LI-LO-LU

(f) Now, the three families together:
FA-FE-FI-FO-FU
VA-VE-VI-VO-VU *Discovery card*
LA-LE-LI-LO-LU

The group then begins to create words with the various combinations.

(2) RAIN (*chuva*)
Aspects for discussion: The influence of the environment on human life.
The climate factor in a subsistence economy.
Regional climatic imbalances in Brazil.

(3) PLOW (*arado*)
Aspects for discussion: The value of human labor. Men and women, and techniques: the process of transforming nature. Labor and capital. Agrarian reform.

(4) LAND (*terreno*)

Aspects for discussion: Economic domination. The latifundium. Irrigation. Natural resources. Defense of the national patrimony.

(5) FOOD (*comida*)

Aspects for discussion: Malnutrition. Hunger (from the local to the national sphere). Infant mortality and related diseases.

(6) AFRO-BRAZILIAN DANCING (*batuque*)

Aspects for discussion: Popular culture. Folklore. Erudite culture. Cultural alienation.

(7) WELL (*poço*)

Aspects for discussion: Health and endemic diseases. Sanitary education. Water supply.

(8) BICYCLE (*bicicleta*)

Aspects for discussion: Transportation problems. Mass transportation.

(9) WORK (*trabalho*)

Aspects for discussion: The process of transforming reality. Man's value through work. Manual, intellectual, and technological work. Craftsmanship. The dichotomy between manual and intellectual labor.

(10) SALARY (*salário*)

Aspects for discussion: The economic sphere.

Man's situation

(a) remuneration: salaried and non-salaried labor

(b) the minimum wage

(c) *salário móvel* (adjustment of wages to changes in the cost of living)

(11) PROFESSION (*profissão*)

Aspects for discussion: The social sphere. The problem of business. Social classes and social mobility. Trade unionism. Strikes.

(12) GOVERNMENT (*govêrno*)

Aspects for discussion: The political sphere. Political power (the three powers). The role of the people in the organization of power. Popular participation.

(13) SWAMPLANDS (*mangue*)

Aspects for discussion: The population of the swamplands. Paternalism. Assistencialism. Ascent by these populations from the position of object to that of Subject.

(14) SUGAR MILL (*engenho*)

Aspects for discussion: The economic formation of Brazil. Monoculture. Latifundium. Agrarian reform.

(15) HOE *(enxada)*

Aspects for discussion: Agrarian reform and banking reform. Technology and reforms.

(16) BRICK *(tijolo)*

Aspects for discussion: Urban reform—fundamental aspects. Planning. The relationship between various reforms.

(17) WEALTH *(riqueza)*

Aspects for discussion: Brazil and the universal dimension. The confrontation between wealth and poverty. Rich person vs. poor person. Rich nations vs. poor nations. Dominant nations and dominated nations. Developed and underdeveloped nations. National emancipation. Effective aid among nations and world peace.

Translated by Myra Bergman Ramos

PEDAGOGY IN PROCESS

Introduction

PART 1

This introduction is, above all, a letter-report that I make to the reader. It will be as informal as the letters contained in the body of the book. I shall attempt, as though in conversation with the reader, to emphasize this or that significant aspect that has impressed me in my working visits to Guinea-Bissau, ingloriously called by the Portuguese colonialists until very recently an "overseas province." With this pompous name they tried to mask their presence as invaders in those lands and their relentless exploitation of the people.

My first encounter with Africa was not, however, with Guinea-Bissau but with Tanzania, to which, for a variety of reasons, I feel very closely related. I make this reference to underline how important it was for me to step for the first time on African soil, and to feel myself to be one who was returning and not one who was arriving. In truth, five years ago, as I left the airport of Dar es Salaam, going toward the university campus, the city opened before me as something I was seeing again and in which I reencountered myself. From that moment on, even the smallest things, like old acquaintances, began to speak to me of myself. The color of the skies; the blue-green of the sea; the coconut, the mango, and the cashew trees; the perfume of the flowers; the smell of the earth; the bananas and, among them, my very favorite, the apple-banana; the fish cooked in coconut oil; the locusts hopping in the dry grass; the sinuous body movements of the people as they walked in the streets, their smiles so ready for life; the drums sounding in the depths of night; bodies dancing and, as they did so, "designing the world"; the presence among the people of expressions of their culture that the colonialists, no matter how hard they tried, could not stamp out—all of this took possession of me and made me realize that I was more African than I had thought.

Naturally, it was not only these aspects, considered by some people merely sentimental, that affected me. There was something else in that encounter: a reencounter with myself.

There is much I could say of the impressions that continue and of the learning I have done on successive visits to Tanzania. It is not this, however, that makes me refer now to this country to which I am so attached. I speak of Tanzania only to emphasize the importance for me of stepping on African soil and feeling as though I were returning somewhere, rather than arriving.

This sense of being at home on African soil was repeated, sometimes accentuated, when, in September of 1975, accompanied by the team from the Institute for Cultural Action (IDAC), I visited Guinea-Bissau for the first time, that is, when I "returned" to Guinea-Bissau.

In this introduction, I shall speak of what it has come to mean, not only to me but to the members of the team, as we participate in this rich and challenging experience in the field of education in general and, particularly, adult education, in which we are working *with* Guinean learners and educators, not working either *on* them, or simply *on their behalf*.

Before I do that, however, I should explain what led me to publish now, rather than later, the few letters I have written thus far to the Commissioner on Education and to the Coordinating Commission responsible for literacy education in Bissau. My basic intention is to offer readers, by means of the letters and of the introduction that precedes them, a dynamic vision of the activities being developed in that country and of the theoretical problems that underlie them. From this concept comes the title of the book, *Pedagogy in Process: The Letters to Guinea-Bissau.*

Between revealing the work as it progresses and publishing a book two or three years later as a final report, I prefer the former. If I should attempt another publication on the same experience, which I really hope to do, it will not be made up of the letters which I will continue to write. I prefer to feel as spontaneous in writing future letters as I did in preparing those now being published. This spontaneity—not a kind of neutrality—could be affected if, in writing future letters, I felt that I were working on a second volume of letters to Guinea-Bissau.

Background and Assumptions of the Education Project

Given this explanation, let us begin to talk, without too much preoccupation with didactics, about the activities in Guinea. In doing this, I want to emphasize the satisfaction with which we, in the Department of Education of the World Council of Churches and the team of IDAC, received, in May of 1975, the official invitation of the government through the Commission on Education to make a first visit in order to discuss the bases of our collaboration in the field of literacy education for adults.

The struggle of the people of Guinea-Bissau and the Cape Verde Islands, under the extraordinary leadership of Amilcar Cabral and the comrades of PAIGC,[1] to expel the Portuguese colonizers was not in any way strange to us. We knew what this struggle had meant both for the formation of the political consciousness of the majority of the people and their leaders and also as a basic factor explaining the twenty-fifth of April in Portugal.[2]

We knew that we would be working not with cold, objective intellectuals, nor with neutral specialists, but with militants engaged in a serious effort at reconstruction of their country. I use the term "reconstruction" because Guinea-Bissau does not start from zero. Her cultural and historical roots are something very much her own, in the very soul of her people, which the violence of the colonialists could not destroy. She does, however, start from zero with reference to the material conditions left by the invaders when, politically and militarily defeated in an impossible war, they had to abandon the country definitively after April twenty-fifth, leaving behind a legacy of problems and scarcities which spoke so eloquently of the "civilizing power" of colonialism.

For all of these reasons, we received the invitation with great satisfaction. It offered us an opportunity to participate, even minimally, in responding to the challenge posed by reconstruction.

We knew that we had something with which to meet that challenge. If that had not been true, there would be no explanation for our acceptance of the invitation. But, fundamentally, we knew that the help for which they asked would be true help only to the degree to which, in the process of offering it, we never pretended to be the exclusive Subjects of it, thus reducing the national leaders and people to being simply objects. Authentic help means that all who are involved help each other mutually, growing together in the common effort to understand the reality which they seek to transform. Only through such praxis—in which those who help and those who are being helped help each other simultaneously—can the act of helping become free from the distortion in which the helper dominates the helped. For this reason there can be no real help between dominating and dominated classes, nor between "imperial" and so-called "dependent"

---

1. The African Party for the Independence of Guinea and the Cape Verde Islands (PAIGC).

2. On April 25, 1974, a military coup overthrew the rightist dictatorship of the National Popular Action Party that had ruled Portugal for forty years.—Translator's note.

societies. These relationships can never be understood except in the light of class analysis.

It is for this reason that only as militants could we become true collaborators, even in a very small way—never as neutral specialists or as members of a foreign technical assistance mission. Our own political choices, and our praxis which is coherent with these choices, have kept us from even thinking of preparing in Geneva a project for the literacy education of adults with all of its points worked out in fine detail, to be taken to Guinea-Bissau as a generous gift. This project, on the contrary, together with the basic plans for our collaboration, would have to be born there, thought through by the national educators in harmony with the social situation in the country. Our cooperation in the design and practical application of the project would depend upon our ability to understand national reality; to deepen what we already knew about the liberation struggle and the experiments carried out by PAIGC in the older liberated zones, we began to read everything we could find, especially the works of Amilcar Cabral. These studies of ours, begun in Geneva, would be carried further in our first visit to the country and continued in subsequent visits if we should enter into a prolonged relationship. It would be in subsequent visits that we would think with the national educators in evaluation seminars about their own praxis. We would start, in any case, from a radical position, refusing to accept packaged or prefabricated solutions and avoiding every kind of cultural invasion, whether it be open or cleverly hidden.

Our political choice and its praxis also keeps us from even thinking that we could teach the educators and learners of Guinea-Bissau anything unless we were also learning with and from them. If the dichotomy between teaching and learning results in the refusal of the one who teaches to learn from the one being taught, it grows out of an ideology of domination. Those who are called to teach must first learn how to continue learning when they begin to teach.

Elza and I had had this experience—of learning first in order to continue learning—later as we were teaching. In our first meetings with Chilean educators, we listened much more than we spoke. When we did speak, it was in order to describe the praxis which was ours in Brazil—not to prescribe for Chilean educators but simply to present the negative and positive aspects of our experience. In learning with them and with the workers in the fields and factories, it became possible for us also to teach. If there was anything that we discovered in Brazil that we were able to repeat exactly in Chile, it was not to separate the act of teaching from the act of learning. We also learned not to attempt to impose on the Chilean context what we had done in different circumstances in Brazil. Experiments cannot be transplanted; they must be reinvented. One of our most pressing concerns when we were preparing as a team for our first visit to Guinea-Bissau was to guard against the temptation to overestimate the significance of some aspect of an earlier experience, giving it universal validity.

We tried to analyze our own experiences and those of others in different settings, giving increasing critical attention to the politics and ideology of literacy education for adults and of education in general. We also analyzed carefully the relation between literacy education, post-literacy and production within the total plan for the society. We looked at the relation between literacy education and general education. We sought a critical comprehension of the role that literacy education for adults might play in a society like that of Guinea, where people's lives had all been touched directly or indirectly by the war for liberation, "a cultural fact and a factor of culture," to use Amilcar Cabral's expression. The political consciousness of the people had been born of the struggle itself. While ninety percent of the people were illiterate, in the literal sense of the term, they were politically highly literate—just the opposite of certain communities which possess a sophisticated kind of literacy but are grossly illiterate about political matters.

These, then, were the central themes in our seminars during all of the time that we were preparing for our first visit to the country; they were also part of the concern of each one of us individually in our hours of personal reflection about our work in Guinea-Bissau. We never spent very long studying adult literacy methods and techniques for their own sake, but looked at them in relation to and in the service of a specific theory of knowledge, applied in practice, which in its turn must be consonant with a particular political stance. If the educator has a revolutionary stance and if his practice is coherent with that stance, then the learner in adult literacy education is one of the Subjects of the act of knowing. It becomes the duty of the educator to search out appropriate paths for the learner to travel and the best assistance that can be offered so that the learner is enabled to exercise the role of Subject in relation to learning during the process of literacy education. The educator must constantly discover and rediscover these paths that make it easier for the learner to see the object to be revealed, and finally learned, as a problem. The educator's task is not to use these means and these paths to uncover the object himself and to offer it, paternalistically, to the learner, thus denying him the effort of searching that is so indispensable to the act of knowing. Rather, in the connection between the educator and the learner, mediated by the object to be revealed, the most important factor is the development of a critical attitude *in relation to* the object and not a discourse by the educator *about* the object. And even when, in the midst of these relations, the educator and the learner come close to the object of their analysis and become curious about its meaning, they need the kind of solid information that is indispensable to accurate analysis. To know is not to guess; information is useful only when a problem has been posed. Without this basic problem-statement, the furnishing of information is not a significant moment in the act of learning and becomes simply the transfer of something from the educator to the learner.

From the beginning of my work in the field of adult literacy education, I have tried to get rid of little primers. Let me emphasize that it is the primers that I object to and not the other materials which help learners in their process of firming up and deepening their studies. I have always defended materials that help learners conquer language through the breaking up of generative words in order to construct other words through the various combinations of syllables. These materials involve a creative act and reinforce learning.

Unfortunately, this is not what happens, even with those primers whose authors, trying their best to go beyond the role of "donors," offer the learners opportunities to create words and short texts. Actually, much of the effort of the learners, especially in creating their own words, has already been programmed in the primers by their author. And so, instead of stimulating learners' curiosity, the primers reinforce a passive, receptive attitude which contradicts the creative act of knowing.

It seems to me that this is one of the problems in the field of education that a revolutionary society needs to address, that is, the meaning of the act of knowing. A revolutionary society should look at the roles that the act of knowing demands of its Subjects—creators, recreator, and reinventor. It should examine, also, the role of curiosity in relation to the object to be known: whether curiosity is related to the search for existing knowledge or to the attempt to create new knowledge. Such moments are, really, indivisible. The separation between these moments reduces the act of learning existing knowledge to mere bureaucratic transference. In such circumstances, the school, whatever its level, becomes a knowledge market; the professor, a sophisticated specialist who sells and distributes "packaged knowledge"; the learner, a client, who purchases and "consumes" this knowledge.

If the educator, on the other hand, is not bureaucratized in this process, but keeps his curiosity alive, the object is unveiled again for him or her, while the learner is in the process of unveiling it. Very often, the educator thus perceives a new dimension of that object which had, until now, been hidden.

It is essential that educators learning and learners educating make a constant effort to refuse to be bureaucratized. Bureaucracy annihilates creativity and transforms persons into mere repeaters of clichés. The more bureaucratized they become, the more likely they are to become alienated adherents of daily routine, from which they can never stand apart in order to understand their reason for being.

Coherence between the political-revolutionary stance of the educator and his/her action is the only way to avoid bureaucratization. The more vigilant the educator in living out this coherence, the more authentically militant s/he becomes, refusing, at the same time, the role of technician or specialist in some particular field.

It was, then, as militants, not as neutral specialists or cold technicians, that we accepted the invitation from the government of Guinea-Bissau. We left Geneva ready to see and hear, to inquire and to discuss. In our baggage we carried no saving plans or reports semiprepared.

As a team, we had talked in Geneva about the best way to see and hear, inquire and discuss so that the plan for our contribution might result—a plan for a program that would be born there, in dialogue with people of the country, about their own reality, their needs, and the possibility of our assistance. We could not design such a plan for them in Geneva.

We have never understood literacy education of adults as a thing in itself, as simply learning the mechanics of reading and writing, but, rather, as a political act, directly related to production, to health, to the regular system of instruction, to the overall plan for the society still to be realized. Therefore the process of seeing and hearing, questioning and discussing, would have to extend beyond the Commission on Education to other Commissions, to the Party, including the mass organizations. And so, our work plan for the first visit, merely outlined in Geneva, and actually developed in dialogue with national leaders in Guinea, had envisaged three major points of emphasis, never, of course, rigidly divided from each other.

The First Emphasis: Learning History from the Commission on Education and Other Leaders

In the first phase of our visit, we entered into contact not only with the recently created Department of Adult Education, but with various teams of the Commission on Education.

We needed to know the central issues in primary and secondary schooling and the manner in which they were being addressed. We were interested in the modifications which had already been introduced in the general educational system inherited from the colonialists and in their potential for stimulating its gradual transformation. A new educational praxis, expressing different concepts of education consonant with the plan for the society as a whole, would be created by the Party with the people.

The inherited colonial education had as one of its principal objectives the de-Africanization of nationals. It was discriminatory, mediocre, and based on verbalism. It could not contribute anything to national reconstruction because it was not constituted for this purpose. Each level of the colonial system—primary, lycée, and technical—was separated from the preceding one. Schooling was antidemocratic in its methods, in its content, and in its objectives. Divorced from the reality of the country, it was, for this very reason, a school for a minority, and thus against the majority. It selected out only a very few of those who had access to it, excluded most of them after a few years and, due to continued selective filtering, the number rejected constantly increased. A sense of inferiority and of inadequacy was fostered by this "failure."

This system could not help but reproduce in children and youth the profile that colonial ideology itself had created for them, namely, that of inferior beings, lacking in all ability; their only salvation lay in becoming "white" or "black with white souls." The system, then, was not concerned with anything related closely to nationals (called "natives"). Worse than the lack of concern was the actual negation of every authentic representation of national peoples—their history, their culture, their language. The history of those colonized was thought to have begun with the civilizing presence of the colonizers. The culture of the colonized was a reflection of their barbaric way of seeing the world. Culture belonged only to the colonizers. The music of the colonized, their rhythm, their dance, the delicacy of their body movements, their general creativity—none of these had any value for the colonizers. And so these gifts were all repressed, and in their place the taste of the dominant metropolitan class was imposed. The alienating experience of colonial education was only counteracted for the colonized at those moments when, in an urge for independence, they rejected some of its aspects. At these times, the people "assumed their own history," inserting themselves into a process which could be called "the decolonizing of mentality" to which Aristides Pereira makes reference. Amilcar Cabral called it the "re-Africanization of mentality."

All of this implies a radical transformation of the educational system inherited from the colonizers. Such transformation can never be done mechanically. It requires a political decision coherent with the plan for the society to be created, and must be based on certain material conditions that also offer incentives for change. It demands increased production. At the same time it requires a reorientation of production through a new concept of distribution. A high degree of political clarity must underlie any discussions of what to produce, how to produce it, for what and for whom it is to be produced. Any change, even a change initiated timidly, in the interest of new material conditions in any significant aspect of society (such as, for example, in the dichotomy between manual and intellectual labor) necessarily provokes resistance from the old ideology that survives in the face of forces to create a new society.

Obviously these ideological resistances are the same ones that oppose the destruction of the incorrect notion that knowledge is something concluded, assuming for the educator the role of "possessor" of this completed knowledge that must be transferred to the learner who needs it. What is worse, the resistance is often not to the intellectual understanding of a concept of knowledge but to the action coherent with it. For this reason, the radical transformation of the educational system inherited from the colonizers requires an infrastructural effort. That is, it requires an effort toward massive change at the level of infrastructures and simultaneous action of an ideological nature. It implies the reorganization of the means of production and the involvement of workers in a specific form of education, through which they are called to become more than skilled production workers, through an understanding of the process of work itself.

In transforming the educational system inherited from the colonizers one of the necessary tasks is the training of new groups of teachers and the retraining of old ones. Among these teachers, and especially among those who have taught before, there will always be those who perceive themselves to be "captured" by the old ideology and who will consciously continue to embrace it; they will fall into the practice of undermining, either in a hidden or an open way, the new practice. From such persons one cannot hope for any positive action toward the reconstruction of society. But there will be others who, also perceiving themselves to be captive to the old ideology, will nonetheless attempt to free themselves from it through the new practice to which they will adhere. It is possible to work with these persons. They are the ones who "commit class suicide." The others refuse to do so.

Referring to the role of the middle class in the general picture of the struggle for national liberation, Amilcar Cabral affirmed: "If they are not to betray these objectives (of the liberation struggle), the middle class has only one possible road: that is, to strengthen their revolutionary conscience, to repudiate all that draws them toward middle-class standards and the natural attraction of that kind of class mentality, and to identify themselves with the working class by not opposing, in any way, the normal unfolding of the process of the revolution. This means that, in order to fulfill their specific revolutionary role in the struggle for national liberation, the revolutionary members of the middle class must be capable of committing suicide as a class in order to rise again as revolutionary workers, completely committed to the deepest aspirations of the people to which they belong.

"This alternative," Cabral goes on, "to betray the revolution or to commit class suicide, constitutes the real option of the middle class in the general picture of the struggle for national liberation." The same alternatives exist today in the movement for national liberation which is the natural continuation of the liberation struggle.

These discussions about the subject of literacy education for adults cannot be understood apart from the problems to which we have just alluded briefly. This should not, of course, be taken to mean that literacy activities cannot begin until after the radical transformation of the system inherited from the colonizers has taken place. It does mean, however, that radical transformation, and not simply reform, is the objective to be pursued with clarity and speed.

The debate surrounding this fundamental problem—that of an educational system inherited from the colonial era—led us, necessarily, in our conversations with the team from the Commission on Education, to an analysis of another inheritance—that of the liberation war itself. This latter inheritance can be seen in the excellent experiments conducted in the older liberated zones, as they are now called, in areas of production and distribution, in the establishment of the new "peoples' markets" as well as in the fields of health, education and justice.

We wanted to know, above all, how those teams that were preoccupied with the transformation of the inherited colonial system viewed this other inheritance, the war itself. The new system that would come into being could not be merely a fortuitous synthesis of the two inheritances but it must improve on and address at greater depth all that had been accomplished in the liberated zones, where an education, no longer elitist but eminently popular, had been developed.[3] In these areas, the local population had taken the matter of education into their own hands, just as they had done in supporting the guerilla fighters. A work school, closely linked to production and dedicated to the political education of the learners, had come into being in response to the real requirements of the liberation struggle. The children even had to learn what to do in order to live through the devastating attacks of enemy planes.

This was an education that not only expressed the climate of solidarity induced by the struggle itself, but also deepened it. Incarnating the dramatic present of the war, it both searched for the authentic past of the people and offered itself for their present.

Here, as in all of the dimensions of the liberation process, one can appreciate the prophetic vision of Amilcar Cabral. He had a capacity to analyze the reality of the country, never to deny it. He began always with what was actually true and not with what he might wish were true as he both denounced and announced. Denunciation and annunciation in Amilcar Cabral were never disassociated from each other, just as they were never outside the revolutionary praxis. From the midst of the struggle beside his comrades he denounced the oppressive reality of the exploitative colonialist farce that sought always to cover up its exploitation. In the same way he announced the new society that was being formed, deep in the heart of the old, through the revolutionary changes that were taking place. As with every person who truly lives out the coherence between political choice and actions, the word, for Cabral, was always a dialectical unity between

---

3. "This educational work in the interior of the country had obtained important results, offering schooling for children over ten years of age. (Because of the war conditions, this had to be the minimum age for admission to primary schools.) In the academic year 1971–72, PAIGC had a total of 164 schools in the liberated zones where 258 teachers taught 14,531 students. Later, the best students were selected to attend live-in schools set up in neighboring countries by the Party. In addition, PAIGC was always very conscious of the requirements of national reconstruction and not merely of those created by the war with its need for young people in military service. Therefore particular attention was given to offering middle school and higher education to many groups of students. They were able to count on the support of nearby countries for this purpose and the result has been that a far larger number of Guinean students completed advanced courses during the war years than during the whole period of Portuguese occupation. In ten years under PAIGC more classes graduated than in five centuries of Portuguese domination. (In the ten years from 1963–73, the following cadres were graduated under PAIGC: 36 in higher education; 46 with the middle-level technical course; 241 with professional and specialized courses; and 174 with political and union courses. In comparison, from 1471 to 1961 only 14 Guineans finished higher education courses and 11 the technical level.)": Luiza Teotonio Pereira and Luis Motta, *Guiné Bissau—Trés anos de Independência* (Lisbon, 1976), pp. 106–7.

action and reflection, practice and theory. He never allowed himself to be tempted on the one hand by empty words, nor on the other by activism.

His political clarity, the coherence between his choices and his practice, is at the root both of his refusal to be drawn into making undisciplined responses and of his rejection of manipulation. He dismissed any idea of the masses divided, following their own inclinations, marching in response to whatever happened, without a revolutionary party or leaders who could mobilize, organize and orient. In the same way he also rejected a leadership which felt that it "owned" the masses. Unlimited freedom and bureaucratic authoritarianism were equally abhorrent. Neither a leadership which followed the masses so far behind that they got lost in the dust stirred up by the people, nor leaders so far out in front that they left the people enshrouded in their dust, but leaders always *with* the people, teaching and learning mutually in the liberation struggle—this was his way. Like Guevara and like Fidel, Cabral was in constant communion with the people, whose past he knew so well and in whose present he was so deeply rooted, a present filled with struggle, to which he gave himself without restriction. He could thus see the future before others did. In each of the days that he lived so intensely, there was always a possible dream, a viable history that could begin to be forged on that very day.

Once when he was discussing the magical powers of amulets with some soldiers, he said, "We will not die if we do not make war or if we do not attack the enemy at the point of his vulnerability. But if we make mistakes, if we find ourselves in a position of weakness, we will die; there is no other way out. You will say to me: 'Cabral does not know, but we have seen various cases in which it was an amulet that saved one of our comrades from death. The bullets came and were deflected.' You may say that. I hope that the sons of our sons, when they hear such stories and when they rejoice that PAIGC was able to direct the struggle in accord with the reality of the country, will say, 'Our fathers struggled hard but they believed in some very strange things.' What I am saying to you perhaps does not make sense now. I will speak again tomorrow. . . ."

Amilcar Cabral knew that cannons alone do not make a war and that the resolution of a war only comes when the vulnerability of the oppressed becomes strength, capable of transforming the power of the oppressor into weakness. This was the source of his constant concern, the patient impatience with which he invariably gave himself to the political and ideological formation of militants, whatever their level of the sector in which they were active. This was also the source of the special attention which he dedicated to the work of education in the liberated zones and also of the tenderness he showed when, before going into battle, he visited the children in the little schools, sharing in their games and always having just the right word to say to them. He called them the "flowers of our revolution."

We were not really surprised, therefore, at the clarity with which the national teams analyzed all of these points. The Commissioner on Education was present in these sessions and felt himself very much part of the process in which everyone was conscious of the significance of recreating a society. They knew well the obstacles that confronted them daily—from the lack of the most minimal material things, a typewriter for instance, to the overwhelming need to train leadership groups in the most diverse fields in order to put all of their projects in practice.

We were able to observe Commissioner Mário Cabral's lucid comprehension of the rich educational experience developed during the war as well as the positive way in which he faced the radical transformation of the inherited system. He knew all the time that the change could not take place through magic. Mário Cabral was aware, as a result of his militant leadership of the Commission on Education, that the relations between the educational system and the total society are dialectic in nature and not mechanical. Recognizing the limits of formal education as a subsystem within a larger system, he also recognized its fundamental role in the formation of a new mentality, coherent with the objectives of the new society to be created. He knew, further, that this fundamental role could not be realized if, instead of dealing with the social practice in the country, he tried to create an education to fit the future society now being formed. Such an attempt would be highly idealistic and could not, for that very reason, become a reality. Between the alternatives of abruptly closing all the schools inherited from the colonial era, at both the primary and middle-school levels, while the educational system was being entirely reoriented, and that of introducing into the old system some fundamental reforms capable of accelerating the future radical transformation consistent with the changes operating in the material bases of the society, he preferred the latter.

It was imperative to reformulate the programs of geography, history and the Portuguese language, changing all the reading texts that were so heavily impregnated with the colonialist ideology. It was an absolute priority that Guinean students should study their own geography and not that of Portugal, the inlets of the sea and not the Rio Tejo. It was urgent that they study their history, the history of the resistance of their people to the invader and the struggle for their liberation which gave them back the right to make their own history, and not the history of the kings of Portugal and the intrigues of the court. It was necessary that Guinean students be called to participate in the efforts toward national reconstruction and not to "exercises in clay modeling of the blind poet crowned in laurels." And it was also important to begin, perhaps timidly at first, to bring about the first steps toward a closeness between the middle-school students of Bissau and productive work.

"The school in the country" was one of the projects about which Mário Cabral spoke to us. It involved temporarily moving urban schools with their teachers and students to rural areas where, living in camps, they might learn with the peasants through participation in productive activities and also teach them some things, without in any way eliminating their regular school activities.

Thus experiments were begun in 1975 which would later be extended in 1976, to integrate productive labor with the normal school activities, with the intention of combining work and study so that, as far as possible, the former might provide direction for the latter and that, together, they might form a unity.

To the degree to which these experiments are systematized and deepened, it is possible, increasingly, to derive from productive activities the programmatic content of the different disciplines which, in the traditional system, were "transferred" verbally to the students, if anything happened at all.

In a certain moment it becomes true that one no longer studies in order to work nor does one work in order to study; one studies in the process of working. There comes about, thus, a true unity between practice and theory. We must be clear, however, that what is eliminated is not that study which is critical reflection on practice completed or in process (theory), but the separation between the two. The unity of theory and practice thus establishes the unity, also, between the school, whatever its level, and productive activity as a dimension of the concrete context.

In spite of the difficulties that the Commission has faced, some of an ideological nature, such as the resistance of students who did not accept the idea of working with their hands, and some of a material nature, such as the lack of transportation, it is possible to list a number of very positive experiences, such as: the work, on Sunday mornings in the state granaries, of 120 students who were just completing their middle-school course; the participation of students from the second and third years of middle school in Bissau in the productive work in the gardens of the Institute of Friendship; two months of work by the second-year students of the Salvador Allende School in the area of cattle raising; and the gardens planted by a very large number of primary school children in the capital.

It is important to point out that before and after these trips to the country, the middle-school students met with agricultural technicians to discuss various aspects of the activities in which they would be engaged. The technicians also accompanied them on these trips. In evaluation seminars on their return, their understanding of the points addressed in the preparatory meetings was either confirmed, deepened or corrected.

The openness of the peasants who received the visiting urban students and their readiness both to teach and to learn are also very significant. Basically, however, it was probably the urban students who learned most from their first experience of intimate relationship with the hard work of tilling the soil, harvesting and producing.

These experiments took place not only in Bissau where the difficulties are greater, but in other parts of the country with more favorable conditions. At the present time these experiments have been extended to include almost the whole country. Some schools, like the middle-school in Bafatá, have two fields of agriculture. The schools of the older liberated zones continue to be self-sufficient through the productive work of their teachers and students. Actually, in the Batafá region 96 of the 106 schools have some agricultural work.

Measures such as these are the precursors of much more profound change. The Commission on Education has allied itself with these efforts, avoiding, however, any attempt at rigid centralization. At the time of our visit, two Cuban educators were closely related to the work which had just begun in the area of training and retraining of teachers. I shall be speaking more later of all of these transformations, which are now taking place.

Activities Already Taking Place in the Field of Adult Literacy

Two basic initiatives have already been undertaken in the field of adult literacy education—one related to the Armed Forces of the People (FARP) and the other to the Commission on Education which has just created a Department of Adult Education.

There is evident a movement toward the unification of these two efforts, indispensable for the efficiency of a national program. However, the unique characteristics of each will be respected.

It is interesting to note that literacy education, whether from the point of view of FARP or of the Commission on Education, has been seen as a political act in which the learners, with the help of enablers, engage in a critical approach to reading and writing and not in an alienating and mechanical memorization of syllables, words and sentences which are given to them. This position, of course, is in complete accord with our own. The problem is not at the level of conceptualization but, rather, in making the process concrete.

The most important factor in the literacy education of adults is not the learning of reading and writing, which may result in the reading of texts without any critical comprehension of the social context to which they refer. This is the kind of literacy which interests the dominant classes when, for different reasons, they see some need to stimulate among the dominated classes "their first entry into the world of letters." The more "neutral" this "entry," the better it pleases those with power.

In a revolutionary context, on the contrary, it is important that the learners perceive, or deepen their perception, that the most important thing for them is to make history and to be made and remade by it, and not to read alienating stories. Running the risk of appearing schematically symmetrical, I would say that, in the first case, the learners are never called to think critically about the conditioning of their own thought process; to reflect on the reason for their own present situation; to make a new "reading" of the reality that is presented to them simply as something to which they should adapt themselves. The thought-language, absurdly separated from objectivity, and the mechanisms used to interject the dominant ideology, are never discussed. They learn that knowledge is something to be "consumed" and not made and remade. Illiteracy is sometimes thought of as a harmful weed and, at other times, as an illness. Thus people speak of its "eradication" or refer to it as a "plague."

Existing as objects in the general context of class society, oppressed and forbidden to *be*, illiterates continue as objects in the process of learning to read and write. They are brought to the learning process, not as persons invited to know the knowledge of the past so that, recognizing its limitations, they can know more. On the contrary, what is proposed for them is the passive acceptance of packaged knowledge.

In the revolutionary perspective, the learners are invited to think. Being conscious, in this sense, is not simply a formula or a slogan. It is a radical form of being, of being human. It pertains to beings that not only know, but know that they know. The act of learning to read and write, in this instance, is a creative act that involves a critical comprehension of reality. The knowledge of earlier knowledge, gained by the learners as a result of analyzing praxis in its social context, opens to them the possibility of new knowledge. The new knowledge, going far beyond the limits of the earlier knowledge, reveals the reason for being behind the facts, thus demythologizing the false interpretations of these same facts. And so, there is now no more separation between thought-language and objective reality. The reading of a text now demands a "reading" within the social context to which it refers.

In this sense, literacy education for adults becomes an introduction to the effort to systematize the knowledge that rural and urban workers gain in the course of their daily activity—a knowledge that is never self-explanatory but must always be understood in terms of the ends that it serves. This process of systematization deepens in the stages that follow literacy.

Parallel with the reorganization of the means of production, an essential task for critical understanding and attention in a revolutionary society is the valorization—and not the idealization—of popular wisdom that includes the creative activity of a people and reveals the levels of their knowledge regarding reality. What is implied is not the transmission to the people of a knowledge previously elaborated, a process that ignores what they already know, but the act of returning to them, in an organized form, what they have themselves offered in a disorganized form.[4] In other words, it is a process of knowing with the people how they know things and the level of that knowledge. This means challenging them, through critical reflection, regarding their own practical experience and the ends that motivate them in order, in the end, to organize the findings, and thus to replace mere opinion about facts with an increasingly rigorous understanding of their significance. This is the challenge to which Amilcar Cabral gave so much attention when, analyzing the liberation struggle as both "a cultural fact and a factor of culture," he emphasized the necessity for this culture to

---

4. "We must teach the masses with precision what we receive from them with confusion," said Mao in an interview with André Malraux (*Antimémoires* [Paris, 1967], p. 531).

become increasingly more scientific, in the truest sense of that term, thus overcoming what he called the "weaknesses of culture."

A work such as this, based always on the practice of thinking about practice, through which practice is perfected, might give rise to true study centers which, although they revolved around certain specific themes such as agriculture or health, for example, could develop global analyses of these themes. Such centers, through their ongoing task of systematizing and deepening knowledge, might become units of a future university—a type of university that grows from and with the working classes and is not imposed on them, which, in the end, always means that it is *against* them.

The most important feature of such work with the people is the exercise of a critical stance in the face of reality. Reality itself thus becomes the object of knowledge—understood by means of analysis of the action that transforms it. Every day, practical activity becomes a permanent object of study. The understanding that results is far more significant than the immediate utilitarian purpose of the activity itself. Thus, activity becomes not only a source of knowledge about itself and its own rationale, but also a means of comprehending other matters related to it.

The question posed for a revolutionary society is not only one of how to train workers in the skills considered necessary to increase production—skills that in a capitalist society are increasingly more limited in scope—but one of enlarging the workers' horizons through an understanding of the productive process itself.

But let us speak now of what was actually happening in the field of literacy education for adults at the time of our first visit.

As might be expected, the high level of political clarity among the members of the People's Armed Forces (FARP) had already meant that their work met with extremely positive results in spite of the innumerable difficulties that had to be overcome. Some of these difficulties were material in nature. Others arose from a lack of efficiency among certain literacy workers who expected immediate permanent change and perfection as a result of their efforts.

In July 1975, two months before our first visit to the country and following a training course that had been, initially, under the direction of one leader,[5] eighty-two literary workers and seven supervisors from FARP were already

---

5. This leader had participated in a seminar in Lisbon, coordinated by Professor Cintra, in which the fundamental aspects of the author's work in Brazil were analyzed.

active in the military installations in Bissau while 150 others were completing their training.

The FARP project, conceived by the Political Commissioner of the Armed Forces, Júlio de Carvalho, and his assistants, included three integrated phases. The first was an intensive effort at literacy by means of which they sought to overcome the problem of illiteracy among the military in the Bissau zone as rapidly as possible. In the second phase, parallel with the initiation of post-literacy work in Bissau, literacy education was to be extended to all of the military units in the country. In the third and final phase, FARP would "overflow its own borders" in order to, in the words of Júlio de Carvalho, reach the whole civilian population. This "overflowing" would be carried out by military personnel who, although they were engaged in productive labor and no longer officially in the army, would remain linked to FARP, and by some still in the military especially assigned to literacy work among civilians.

At the time of writing this introduction, I can verify that the first two phases are under way. Post-literacy work has begun in the military installations in Bissau—where there is practically no illiteracy remaining—and the expansion of literacy education has reached 80 percent of the total armed forces in the rest of the country. The third phase is in its beginning stages. All of these efforts are in addition to the collaboration of representatives of FARP with the Coordinating Commission for Adult Literacy of which they are also members. This is the commission that, in accordance with the policies of the Government and of the Party, plans and supervises adult literacy work in the civilian population.

Obviously it was necessary that the five members of our team[6] should be divided in order to visit at least some of the Culture Circles in action. At the stage at which we found ourselves—that of seeing and listening, asking and discussing, it was essential for us to observe how things were going in the Circles, among the participants and the literacy workers. We wanted to see both the creative aspects of their work and those instances where, on the contrary, they might be engaged merely in repetition and memorization. We were eager to know whether the learners had been able to appropriate for themselves their own "word," developing an ability to express themselves as conscious participants in a political act, or whether they were simply learning to read and write.

---

6. At the time of the visit, the team was made up of Miguel D'Arcy de Oliveira, Claudius Ceccon, Marcos Arruda, Elza Freire, and Paulo Freire. Later, two persons living in Bissau, José Barbosa and Gisèle Ouvray, and another in Geneva, Rosisca D'Arcy de Oliveira, were added.

It is important to note that our attitude in visiting the Culture Circles was neither that of persons inclined to overestimate what we were seeing, nor were we like those so attached to ideal models that they cannot see the distance between those ideals and concrete reality. We felt neither uncontained euphoria in the face of good work nor negativity regarding the mistakes that we might encounter. What was important was to see what might really be happening under the limited material conditions we knew existed. We wanted to discover what could be done better under these conditions and, if this were not possible, to consider ways to improve the conditions themselves.

What we discovered in the Culture Circles was that, in spite of some difficulties and errors, the learners and workers were engaged in an effort that was preponderantly creative. Much more than the mastery of the mechanics of reading and writing was going on. This was the important fact.

Among the most obvious errors, we might note the impatience of some of the workers that led them to create the words instead of challenging the learners to do so for themselves; the tendency of some to rely on the repetition of syllables in chorus; or the lack of vivacity on the part of some of the workers as they participated in discussions of the themes related to the generative words.

The lack of such mistakes would really have surprised us, especially since the time given to training and theoretical formation of the workers had been so short. The ongoing process of the evaluation seminars would be a powerful force in overcoming these mistakes. Effective practices would be reinforced and errors eliminated.

We want to note the creative imagination that we were able to observe in many of the workers. One of them, for example, arrived at the meeting place of the Culture Circle, greeted the learners and immediately began to sweep the classroom with an old broom. Patiently he moved from one corner of the room to the other, stopping sometimes to look under the benches on which the learners, already beginning to show signs of impatience, were seated. They could not understand their teacher's behavior, nor the thoroughness with which he pursued his task of sweeping what seemed to them an already clean room. Finally, one of them, expressing what all were wondering, asked, "Comrade, when will we begin our class?"

"The class began as soon as you arrived," replied the teacher, asking immediately, "What have I been doing?"

"Cleaning the room," they replied.

"Exactly," said the teacher. Going to the improvised blackboard, he wrote: CLEAN. "That is the word that we will study today, CLEAN."

The educator is a politician and an artist who must use the science of techniques but must never become a cold, neutral technician.

If our attitude in visiting the Culture Circles had been one of the two referred to above—easy euphoria in the face of what was effective or negativity in the face of mistakes—we might have idealized all that we saw or decreed the whole experiment invalid. In either case, we would have been wrong.

In the most populous sections of Bissau, in the experiments in work with civilians, the situation was completely different, but, at the same time, completely understandable. It is one thing to work with FARP, where the militants possess great clarity about the significance of national reconstruction and the continuation of the struggle because of their participation in the long pursuit of liberation. It is quite another to work in crowded areas of the city where the people were not touched in any direct way by the war but, rather, were deeply influenced by the colonialist ideology. Thus, while there were eighty-two functioning Culture Circles among the military in Bissau at the time of our first visit, everything among the civilians still remained to be started, or, in many cases, to be done over.

What both of these experiments—within FARP and in the populous neighborhoods of Bissau—made very clear was the need for establishing priorities in the literacy program for adults. Although the objectives were national in scope, the program must start in certain predetermined areas on the basis of the clearest possible criteria. If literacy efforts were to achieve their primary objective, that of contributing effectively to national reconstruction, then it would also be necessary to establish a dynamic relation between them and all of the other forms of social intervention in any way related to or dependent upon literacy. Literacy education for adults, like all other forms of education, cannot be imposed on the social practice of a society but must emerge from this practice as one of its dimensions.

There would be no sense in transforming the emerging National Literacy Program for Adults into just one more campaign of the traditional type that we all know so well. Either through ingenuousness or artifice, all of these campaigns idealize literacy and give it a power that it does not, in itself, possess. The question facing the Guineans is not that of whether to do literacy education for its own sake or to do it as a means of transformation but, rather, how to put it at the service of national reconstruction.

For these reasons, literacy education should become concrete through projects in areas where, in accordance with the policies of the Party carried out by the government, certain changes in the social relations of production are either already taking place or about to be initiated. The second important area is within the various administrative organs of the State—hospitals, postal services, public works agencies—where literacy education might enable employees to engage in other new tasks demanded by national reconstruction.[7] Mário Cabral emphasized the great need for close relations between the Commission on Education and those responsible for planning, for agriculture and for health. Cooperation with the mass organizations of the Party, such as African Youth Amilcar Cabral (JAAC) whose members are already doing valuable work in the area of literacy, can also contribute to joint efforts in behalf of national reconstruction.

We made contact with all of these organizations and commissions in the first phase of our visit, as well as with the Political Commission of FARP to which we have already made reference. We were received in a visit that was more for work than for protocol by Comrade Francisco Mendes, the Chief Commissioner, and by the President of the Council of State Luíz Cabral.

We were particularly interested in the possible contribution of the Commission on Information in future programs of literacy education. They clearly understand information in the dynamic sense of developing communication rather than simply the transmission of messages. Through the use of radio, newspapers and other channels they could assist in the important task of mobilizing large numbers of people for active participation in literacy efforts.

Our conversations with responsible persons in the Commissions on Health and Agriculture were naturally more brief than those with the Commission on Education, but they helped us to see the necessary interdependence of literacy and health and agricultural production. Preventive medicine and the encouragement of mutual help in the development of cooperatives and on State farms appeared as significant educational concerns that were basic to all of the Commissions in their dedication to the goals of development for the country.

Therefore, a major question confronting the Commission on Education, as the Commissioner so lucidly pointed out, is the inclusion of all of these

---

7. While these matters were discussed briefly on our first visit, they were more central to our discussions in the second visit, in February of 1976 when they became more clearly defined.

concerns in adult-literacy projects. At the same time that students are learning reading and writing, they can, for example, consider their own practices with regard to the mosquito and the battle against malaria. Militant workers in production cooperatives, when they serve as literacy workers, can share their own experience regarding the advantages of mutual assistance in the accomplishment of work over individual efforts as the basis for establishing new cooperatives. In effective adult literacy education there is no place for exclusive categories of working and learning. The concerns of all of the different Commissions meet in the life of the people and can be incorporated into their process of learning and growing.

Visual materials based on the experience of other African countries and accompanied by analyses that transcend geographical barriers can also be used to give people a broader vision of reality. To consider the fight against mosquitoes in a rural area of Guinea-Bissau, and then to see the same situation in a rural community in Mozambique, Tanzania, or São Tomé e Principe, would offer an opportunity not only to think about this problem itself but to consider other problems in relation to the experience of these countries.

The Second Emphasis: Visits to the Older Liberated Zones

The second phase of our first stay in Guinea-Bissau was dedicated to rapid visits to some of the older liberated zones. It was here that PAIGC, as I mentioned earlier, had carried out some highly important experiments in education, health, justice, production and distribution, the latter through the "People's Markets" that succeeded, in the space of only one year after the total independence of the country, in gaining control of commerce.

Although in part influenced by bad weather, these visits were able to give us many important contacts with local political commissions. We heard of their experiences during the struggle and of the things they had learned from them, leading not only to their survival and the defeat of the enemy forces but to that commitment to apply that learning in the continuation of that same struggle in the movement for national reconstruction. We made contact also with many technicians, both national and foreign, and with a number of primary-school teachers participating in a first training seminar based on the teaching principles of Freinet.[8]

It was, however, not until our second visit to the country in February 1976 that we were able to deepen our understanding of the situation in

---

8. Celestin Freinet, a French educator, born in 1896.

the interior, both through more extensive travels in rural areas and through conversations with students and peasants.

In any case, I would like to record here at least one of the incidents that occurred in one of those visits, touching us very deeply. Elza and I had a remarkable conversation with the young director of a live-in school. He spoke softly, coolly and objectively. He told pieces of a history that, in one sense, he had made, and by which he had also been shaped. Without rhetoric or the exaggerated use of adjectives, and also without cold impartiality, he described to us, in a profoundly human manner, the work of his school in a liberated zone. He spoke of the way that the school and the community were integrated in the common task of sustaining the struggle, the task assigned to them by PAIGC, to conquer and drive out the invader and to liberate the country. He referred to Amilcar Cabral, neither sentimentally nor as a mythological figure to be worshipped, but as a symbol, a significant presence in the history of his people.

It was not necessary for him to use the terms "symbol" or "significant presence" for me to realize that it was in this way that he saw Cabral. This feeling is general in Guinea-Bissau and the Cape Verde Islands, the result of the authenticity of the great leader's witness and of the intensity of his communion with the people, without which he could not have accomplished what he did nor been what he was and continues to be for his people. No one can live completely alone. Long before Cabral became the "Father of the Nation," he was the "Son of the People" who learned with them and taught them in the revolutionary praxis.[9]

While the young worker was talking with Elza and me of the experience of the school, of the students and teachers working and learning together, including how to defend themselves against the cruel enemy bombardments, the role that that experience has played and continues to play in the struggle for national reconstruction became increasingly clear to us. We could also discern its role in replacing the old educational system inherited from the colonizers.

During the whole time that we were together, waiting out a severe rainstorm on the narrow porch of a tiny house, we listened much more

---

9. In this connection we remember an incident referred to by President Luiz Cabral. At the time of Amilcar Cabral's assassination by the colonialists, a militant who stood beside his fallen body said, "I do not cry for Comrade Cabral. He has not died. The one who speaks now is not I, but he. He speaks through me. Comrade Cabral will continue to speak through his people, calling us for the battle and for the victory against the oppressor."

than we spoke. Once in a while we asked a question that enabled the young educator to clarify what he had said or to remember some other incident.

"We always had, not far from the school, shelters where we could accommodate the children and people from the surrounding area in case of enemy attack," he said. "As soon as they began to hear the sound of the planes, everyone began to organize, rapidly and almost instinctively, to abandon the area. Everyone knew what to do—and did it—on those occasions. One time," he continued, "when we returned from hiding, after an attack, we found three of our comrades lying in the courtyard of the school, their stomachs cut open. Two were already dead. One was dying. With them were three fetuses, pierced through with a bayonet."

I did not ask him how the authors of such a crime had arrived in the liberated zone. I did not care whether they had come by a plane landing in a field after the bombing or whether they were soldiers of one of the advance guards of the colonialist army. None of this interested me at that moment. I could only ask, as my hands trembled, what they did when they succeeded in capturing so depraved an assassin.

I had the impression that the young man perceived in my tone of voice, in my trembling hands, in my face, in my whole being, and in Elza's look and her silence which cried aloud, the immense sense of revulsion which had come over us.

His voice still soft and gentle, his reply was a teaching in itself. "Evil persons like that," he said, "when they are caught, are punished in accord with the people's judgment. The revolution punishes but it does not torture. Comrade Cabral always spoke of the respect that we should show to the enemy. That was a rule of our party and of PAIGC."

And this is a radical difference between the violence of the oppressor and the violence of the oppressed. That of the former is exercised in order to express the violence implicit in exploitation and domination. That of the latter is used to eliminate violence through the revolutionary transformation of the reality that makes it possible.

The political maturity revealed by that young militant and brought about by the liberation struggle as a "cultural fact and a factor of culture" is a constant in Guinea-Bissau with the exception of a few sectors of the population in certain areas less affected by the struggle itself. In Guinea-Bissau they speak of the struggle without oratorical tirades or excesses. They speak of what it taught, of what it required; of what it continues to teach and to demand as part of an ongoing process. They speak of the engagement it implies and of the vigilance it demands.

In truth, this simplicity and absence of triumphalism reveal, on the one hand, a deeply rooted sense of security; on the other, a true humility that, for this very reason, does not spend itself in false modesty. Security and humility were formed in the difficult struggle overcoming obstacles, and in the victory over the enemy. It is because the people are so deeply rooted in this security and humility that one perceives the firm commitment of both the people and their leaders to make concrete the dream that they have pursued since the beginning of the struggle—to reinvent their society, banishing the exploitation of some by others, and overcoming injustices.

Discreetly, with revolutionary modesty and, coherent with this modesty, absolute assurance of the historic role of his people, the young militant spoke to Elza and me of the praxis in which he had been remade and continued to be remade, together with his comrades. And he spoke of the joy of having participated in the hardships of the struggle, of the joy in his involvement in the reconstruction of his country.

On the return trip to Bissau, looking from the window of the helicopter piloted by two Soviet citizens together with two young nationals learning from them, I saw spread below us the foliage of the trees burned by napalm.

I looked intently and with curiosity. There was not one animal. A few large birds flew calmly by. I remembered what President Luíz Cabral had said to us in our first meeting when he spoke, with the same seriousness displayed by the young school director, about different incidents in the struggle. "There was a time," said the President, "when the animals of Guinea all sought 'asylum' in neighboring countries. Only the small monkeys stayed behind, taking refuge in the liberated zones. They were deathly afraid of the 'tuga.'[10] In the end the poor things feared us, too. That was because we found ourselves forced to eat them. I hope that very soon all of our animals will return, convinced that the war is over."

From the window of the helicopter, I looked intently, curiously. There was not yet a sign, at least in that part of the country, of that return.

Back in Bissau, while our team prepared for the last phase of the visit, there was an event that affected us profoundly. Since I have referred to it so many times since then, I cannot omit it here.

It was a warm September morning. The heat was almost suffocating. The celebration of the anniversary of independence was in progress.

Deep inside a large park was a huge platform on which the national authorities, the foreign diplomats, special guests, and delegations from foreign countries were seated.

---

10. A term used in Guinea-Bissau to refer to "white-faced" people.—Translator's note.

A wide variety of groups were in the parade, representing popular organizations from the different sections of Bissau. Children, young people, women and men were all colorfully dressed. They sang and danced. All was in movement. They came and went, curving and recurving in an extraordinary richness of rhythm. The whole multitude along the avenue that opened into the park participated actively in the parade. They were not there only to see and hear, but to express, consciously, the joy of being there as a people who had won the right to *be*.

The multitude sang and moved together. This was not, in any sense, a folkloric spectacle watched by a few people at a distance. Rather, it was a festival. Everyone was living a very important day.

The parade concluded with the review of units of FARP and then the President, Luíz Cabral, began his discourse. Directly in front of the platform where he stood, a group from the military band was drawn up at attention. At a certain moment, one of the soldiers in the band, as though he were falling on top of himself, fainted. The President stopped his speech. He looked fixedly at the soldier who was being supported by his comrades. The crowd perceived what was happening. They opened a path for a car that approached and, in a moment, took the soldier to the hospital. The President watched the car until it disappeared. Only then did he continue to speak.

At my side, in a very low voice, Elza said, "This was the most beautiful moment of our visit to this country. We really have much to learn from a people who live so intensely the unity between word and deed. The individual here is valued as a person. The human person is something concrete and not an abstraction."

The President continued with his discourse. Everything about him was authentic. His word was for the people. How coherent his action was with his word in the face of the incident which had occurred! It had taken only a few seconds, yet many years of struggle explained it. That was certainly not the first time that Luíz Cabral, the militant, expressed, in whatever form, his solidarity with a companion in difficulty. Luíz Cabral, the President, stopped his speech and, very worried, accompanied with his eyes the comrade who had fainted on that hot September morning; Luíz Cabral, the soldier, must have stopped innumerable times to attend a comrade fallen in the common struggle for the liberation of their people.

Incidents like this, whose profound meaning is indisputable, are not isolated or extraordinary events in Guinea-Bissau. They constitute a way of life for the people. It would have been strange if the President, "distant and cold," had continued his discourse when his comrade of FARP had been taken ill.

What seems of fundamental importance to me is that the values born in the duress of struggle continue to prevail. The more conscious that PAIGC, as the vanguard of the people, is of the necessity of preserving its communion with the people, in whose hearts their very position as vanguard is sealed, the more surely the revolution will be safe from threats of distortion. The degree to which it seeks to preserve and develop its oneness with the working classes will determine the understanding of "class suicide" born so long ago in the thought of Amilcar Cabral. If this "suicide" gets lost, it will open the way for the return to power of a "bureaucratized bourgeoisie" separated from the working classes even when it claims to speak in their name.

The Third Emphasis: Making Plans for Future Collaboration

I said in the beginning of this introduction that our work plan, outlined in Geneva and fully elaborated with our colleagues in Guinea-Bissau, had divided our time in the country into three basic phases, never really separate one from the other. The first two, which I sought to characterize as times of seeking to see and hear, question and discuss, were actually analytical in nature. The third phase—synthesis—grew naturally from them. In fact, this latter activity was taking place all the time even in the midst of analysis, from which it can never really be separated. It is for this reason that much of what happened in the third phase of the visit has already been described, although somewhat tentatively, in what I have said about the first two analytical phases. During these, taking as far as possible the reality of the country as a whole as the object of our curiosity, we tried to separate it into its several parts in order to know it better.

During the synthesis, being formed, as I said before, within the analysis itself, our effort was to bring together again the separated parts. Basically, the two actions are integrated in one dynamic movement that includes taking the object apart and putting it back together again.

In the first two phases, we looked on reality as a code that we were trying to decipher, sometimes with the national groups and sometimes among ourselves as a visiting team during our evaluation meetings while the work was in process. In this latter instance, we sometimes were engaged in a double task. Sometimes we took reality itself as the object of our analysis, attempting to "read it" critically. At other times, the object of our reflection was the process in which we had been engaged with the national teams when, with them, we had sought to analyze reality. In this way, we were analyzing the earlier analysis, trying to recapture critically the way in which we had perceived the same reality as the object of our curiosity.

Naturally, while we were participants in the same process of decoding reality in dialogue with the national teams, we could not, on the one hand, be mere silent spectators nor, on the other, be the exclusive Subjects of the act of decoding. It would have been contradictory to the basic principles underlying our trip to Guinea-Bissau to assume that we were the exclusive Subjects of the decoding of reality while living out the role of receivers of the decoding (carried out, in this case, by the national teams) and then, at the last moment of synthesis, to offer our interpretation, almost mysteriously, as a kind of zealously guarded, secret revelation.

Actually, we found ourselves involved with the national teams in an act of knowing in which we, as much as they, had to assume the role of knowing Subjects. The dialogue between us and the national teams, mediated by the reality that we were seeking to know, was the seal of that act of knowing. It would be through knowing and reknowing together that we would begin to learn and to teach together also.

I underline this point not only as something that should be said in the sequence of this introduction, but in order that, once again, I can make clear my position—not always clearly understood—that dialogue authenticates both the act of knowing and the role of the knowing Subject in the midst of the act.

This was, moreover, a rich theme that we debated and sought to deepen at the very beginning of our visit, principally in our study meetings with Mário Cabral and his teams from the Commission on Education. It was one to which we returned in our successive visits to the country. This theme was referred to, often rather fully, at the beginning of this essay and, for that very reason, it could not be omitted here.

Dividing the third phase of our visit in two parts, we saved the first part to work with Mário Cabral and his assistants on the recapitulation of our earlier effort, carried out together, to analyze reality—the decoding of which we had been able to accomplish.

The recapitulation, which it was our task to initiate, meant that we must make clear the "reading" which we had made of national reality. Our "reading," in its turn, was put before the teams of the Commission on Education as a new challenge to which they must respond—either accepting it or rejecting it, totally or in part, improving it or deepening it. In the synthesis, we thus returned to the analysis, in order to reach a new synthesis.

At the conclusion of the final phase of our visit, we discussed with the national leaders the bases for our continuing contribution to the work since this had been requested by the Commissioner, Mário Cabral, on behalf of the government and with the agreement of the Party. We were able at this point to base our discussions on what we had seen and heard firsthand, on the replies made to our inquiries, and on our common understanding of the role of education in general and of literacy education in particular in the process of national reconstruction.

In essence, the project that we outlined called for some activities to be carried out in Geneva and others that we would accomplish in Guinea-Bissau. Three visits were agreed to for 1976—all of which were realized. It was also agreed that a member of the IDAC team would be located in Bissau, without any expense to the government, to work full time for the Coordinating Commission for Adult Literacy. This plan has also been in effect since February 1976. The Commission itself was created by Mário Cabral as a result of our meetings during the first visit.

It was further agreed that we would evaluate the activities going on in the field of adult literacy on the basis of reports to be sent during the intervals between our visits to the country. As part of this process, we would continue to probe more deeply some of the aspects central to our discussions during the first visit.

The methods of work in subsequent visits to the country would be substantially the same as those adopted in the first visit: a period of analysis, in the dynamic sense of the term as I described it above, and a period of synthesis from which would result the need for new analysis.

In Geneva we would continue to deepen our understanding as a team of the educational problems of the country, particularly in the field of literacy education in its most global sense—about which I have been so insistent in this essay. We would prepare teaching materials in Geneva, as requested, with the understanding that they would be tested before they were put into general use. We would also give our opinion about other materials prepared in Bissau that might be sent to us for our evaluation.

In this manner, the project was born on which we are working jointly today: on the one side, the Commission on Education of Guinea-Bissau; on the other, the Commission on the Churches' Participation in Development which finances it, the Institute for Cultural Action and the Development of Education of the World Council of Churches. The first year has been a common learning process that has enriched all of us.

PART 2

This introduction would be even more incomplete than it now is if I did not describe some of the principal activities that have taken place since September 1975.

The Educational System of Guinea-Bissau

The first of my comments is about the changes that have taken place or are going to be introduced into the educational system of the country. These modifications are in addition to those to which I referred earlier. Mário Cabral, faithful to the objectives of the Party and the orientation of the government, is preparing, through them, for the radical transformation of the system inherited from the colonizers.

I start with these changes because they will necessarily have repercussions on the education of adults—which, as I observed earlier, cannot be separated from the whole educational plan contained in the regular system of education of the country.

Conflict between an effort in the sector of informal education for adults and the educational system of a given society comes about when that effort, antagonistic to the overall social system, is the instrument that a movement or a revolutionary party seeks to use in the tactical organization of the dominated classes in order to achieve power. In the case of Guinea-Bissau, which is quite different, the important thing is the harmony between what is intended with the education of adults and what is being sought through the regular system of education in the country.

The first source of information about the changes that are taking place is Commissioner Mário Cabral. In our working meetings in Bissau, he spoke with increasing clarity about the way in which he and his associates were confronting the transformation of education in the country. I shall also refer to an interview that Cabral gave to *Nô Pintcha,* one of the newspapers in Bissau, and from which I shall quote several passages.

The new system will be constituted dialogically in relation to the infrastructure of society. The changes being introduced are never mechanical. They are part of a larger process.

Completely coherent with this vision is the concern for replacing the concept and practice that sees each part of the system as a separate entity. When each segment of the system is isolated from the others, the learner's own development is forgotten and each stage becomes an alienating and alienated moment, merely a preparation for the next stage.

The plan in which the Commission on Education of Guinea-Bissau is engaged is realistic, consonant with the country's situation. The plan recognizes the relation between the different educational levels, but it is planned so that, in each one, a particular learning task will be realized as fully as possible. Thus the relationship between Basic Instruction and the General Equivalency Course or the Middle-Level Technical School does not reduce Basic Instruction to a corridor through which a few pass with the objective of reaching the next course which, in its turn, leads only to the "elite landscape" of the university.

"Our instruction," says Mário Cabral, "will be divided into three levels: (1) Basic Instruction, with six years broken into two cycles, one of four years and the other of two; (2) General Equivalency, of three years; and (3) Middle-Level Polytechnical, which varies according to the specific requirements of the material and will be from two to three years."

Basic Instruction will become universal as soon as the Party and the State are able to bring this about. Fundamental background necessary for the full participation of any citizen in the development of the new society will be included in Basic Instruction.

We are not talking about instruction in a school that simply prepares the learners for another school, but about a real education where the content is in a constant dialectical relation with the needs of the country. In this kind of education, knowledge, resulting in practical action, itself grows out of the unity between theory and practice. For this reason, it is not possible to divorce the process of learning from its own source within the lives of the learners themselves.

The values that this education seeks are empty if they are not incarnated in life. They are only incarnated if they are put into practice. Thus, from the earliest cycle of instruction, the first four grades, participation in common experiences stimulates social solidarity rather than individualism. The principle of mutual help, practical creativity in the face of actual problems, and the unity of mental and manual labor are experienced daily. The learners begin creating new forms of behavior in accordance with the responsibility they must take within the community.

The second cycle of Basic Education, the fifth and sixth grades, involves the learners at a deeper level of the same act of learning that they experienced earlier: working and searching together not only to extend the areas of their knowledge but also to probe them more deeply. In the process, they, together with their teachers, assume the role of Subjects of their own learning.

An education that envisages making concrete such values as solidarity, social responsibility, creativity, discipline in the service of the common good, vigilance and a critical spirit—values by which PAIGC has been forged through the whole liberation process—would not be possible if, in that education, the learners continued to be what they were in the colonial educational system, mere recipients of packaged knowledge, transferred to them by their teachers. This latter process reduces them to mere "incidents" of the "educational" action of the educators.

To be identified with the reality of the country also requires that education be centered in rural reality.

"We know," says Mário Cabral, "that ninety percent of our population, at the very least, are peasants. The instruction that we are organizing must take this fact into consideration and will be, therefore, directed toward the countryside. The learner, through this education, must be able to participate as a Subject, in the necessary transformation in the local community," Cabral emphasized.

Later, referring to the necessity for extending the areas of knowledge in the second cycle of Basic Education, Mário Cabral continued, "We can say that, beginning now, we are going to introduce at this level basic notions of physics, chemistry and biology as the basis for understanding the processes of nature." Later he referred to the study of history as indispensable to the formation of militants, saying that it would be part of a basic social-science course.

"Within the courses that we are going to introduce at this level, including geography, and with the orientation that will be given for these studies, any students who finish the course will have the kind of knowledge they need to be farmers, mechanics or progressive medical workers."

At the second level, that of General Equivalency Instruction, the goal of preparing students to respond to the most pressing needs of the country will still allow us to offer them options within the various sectors. Their scientific formation will be intensified, parallel with their general, integrated training. Militant action and social responsibility as part of a permanent process of critical reflection are, of course, indispensable. "But, above all," said the Commissioner, "practical activities will follow the characteristics and needs of each region. And we cannot leave out general skills in carpentry, electricity and agriculture that the learners will acquire through practice."

The plan also calls for the establishment of professional schools where specialization will never be distorted to become "specialism." Schools for the training of primary-school teachers, nurses' helpers, agronomists, carpenters and metal workers will be created in accord with the needs of the country. These schools will have strong ties not only to the Commission on Education but also to the other Commissions that have interest in the skills being developed.

The training offered in the General Equivalency Level schools will be continued, deepened and diversified in the Middle-Level Polytechnical Institutes. Their principal objective will be to train technicians in different fields with sufficient background to make their contribution indispensable to the transformation of the country. That training will be broad enough to avoid turning them into technocrats with such narrow, focused vision of their specialty that they are alienated from everything else.

Among the Institutes desired at this level are those dedicated to professional development, pedagogy (to prepare teachers for primary and secondary schools); nursing and the social sciences. The creation of an institute for administration as well as one for agricultural sciences is also being considered.

In all of these Institutes, young persons will be trained who, in relation to the real needs of the country, would be able to enter universities abroad. Many, of course, will be needed for continued direct engagement in national reconstruction.

In any case, to go from one of these Institutes directly into a foreign university means that certain requirements must be fulfilled. Commissioner Mário Cabral has also affirmed that only those who are most competent in their work, most committed and capable, will be chosen for courses outside the country.

There will inevitably also be criteria governing the passing of students from one level of instruction to another—from Basic Instruction to General Equivalency to Middle Polytechnical. Students will pass from one to the other "in accordance with the qualities revealed in the earlier level." Proof of seriousness in their studies, scientific and technical qualifications at the level completed, as well as indication of their moral qualities and social initiative will be considered.

One of the most important aspects of the plan, as I remarked earlier, is that it does not reduce the educational system to a funnel between the different levels of instruction. One level is not simply "preparation" for the other. Thus, students who do not go beyond Basic Instruction and who have no opportunity to broaden their knowledge in some systematic way will not have been deprived of the chance to take part in a fundamental formative experience that will enable them to contribute to the reconstruction of the country as conscious militants.

To put all this into practice requires the preparation of teachers capable of multiplying themselves through the training of others. Mário Cabral has emphasized this and gone on to say, "We will not be able to do anything in the development of different sectors of national reconstruction if we do not have sufficient teachers, both in quantity and quality. We already have funds for the creation of an Institute with this objective. We are thinking of locating it in the center of the country, perhaps at Mansabá."

The intention of the Commission is to graduate, initially, 250 lead-teachers who, after a year's experience in the field, will participate in a seminar for continuing education, based on the evaluation of their own experience. The Institute will prepare teachers for the different levels of instruction. Admission to the courses will depend on different criteria depending on the level at which the candidate intends to teach. Thus, those who want to teach in Basic Instruction will have to have completed six years. The duration of their course will be three years. Those aspiring to teach in the second level of Basic Instruction must have completed nine years and will undergo three years' additional training.

To teach in the General Equivalency level, students will have to have completed 11 years. Their course will also be three years.

"We can say," affirms Mário Cabral, "that this Institute will be, in embryonic form, the first university of the country. For those who intend to become professors in a teacher-training school, 11 years of schooling will be required, and they will have a four-year training course at the Institute of Pedagogy."

And now I shall speak in a kind of parenthesis: I believe that I will not be betraying the spirit of the Commission on Education in Guinea-Bissau when I affirm the importance it is giving to the gradual scientific formation of their students. This will result in increasing understanding of reality as the students act on that reality. It has nothing to do with "scientism," which mythologizes science and distorts reason. In the same way, as they come to recognize the necessary relation between education and production, they will not fall into the error of glorifying production and, with it, consumerism.

One of the basic aspects of the Guinean system that is being created, it seems to me, is the invitation being offered to students to develop solidarity and social responsibility through their practice of service. They come to see work as the source of knowledge and, in the production of what is socially necessary, they discover an authentic camaraderie instead of the competition engendered by individualism. This is in addition to their necessary scientific formation.

"The real objective of the new system," says Mário Cabral emphatically, "is to eliminate the remains of the colonial system in order to contribute to the objectives of PAIGC to create new persons, workers aware of their historical responsibilities and of avenues of creative, effective participation in the process of social transformation. We hope to make this desire real through the ever-growing understanding of the concrete necessities of the country, through the definition of our plan for development, and through the work itself, realized at the level of the schools as well as through discussions in all the collective organizations. These discussions would include not only the technical aspects but also the needs of life itself."

Later, however, he warns, "The whole plan for the transformation of the national instructional system will not be worth anything if there are not similar transformations in all of the other sectors of activity.

"It is possible," said Mário Cabral in the last meeting we had with him in Bissau in September of 1976, "that, in a certain sense, education initiates the challenge. It is necessary, moreover, that structural transformations be made, giving support to the challenge, so that the practice implied in the challenge may become concrete."

Following the normal practice of Guinea-Bissau—that of open discussions always encouraged by PAIGC and the Government—Commissioner Mário Cabral held a great public meeting that brought together students and their families, professors, educational functionaries and other interested persons. He assessed the activities in the year that had just ended, and spoke of the Commission's principal tasks for the next school year, designated as the Second Year of Organization (*Nô Pintcha*, November 1976).

The first part of his address focused clearly and directly on the difficulties that they had confronted, beginning in October 1974 when PAIGC, entering Bissau, took over the government of the whole country. He spoke of the mass withdrawal of secondary-school teachers. Most of them were "members of the military, here to oppress our people and to put obstacles in the way of our progress." He noted the lack of experienced leadership in the Commission on Education in regard to the tasks of planning, organizing and reorganizing the curriculum and the uncertainty about what to do in the face of the educational inheritance from colonial times. It was clear that it would be impossible to make changes from one day to the next. The Commissioner told us that it was at this time that the idea of the systematic closing of all the schools was suggested and discarded. "Some wanted us to close our schools in order to reorganize the Commission and be able to have the kind of instruction and the means of education that we, in fact, needed. This was only a dream. If we had done that, we would still not be ready to begin our classes today because we have not even yet achieved the perfect conditions required by such ideal forms of instruction."

He then referred to certain positive achievements and to some of the mistakes made, the dedication of some, and the failures of others. Highlighting what happened between September 1974 and September 1975 as a learning period for everyone dedicated to the educational task, he called this period the "Year of Experimentation" from which emerged the need to constitute the following year as the "First Year of Organization."

In analyzing the accomplishments of the year just ended, the First Year of Organization, and criticizing again the failures that should never be hidden, he stressed the accomplishments and the strong spirit of the majority of the comrades in the Commission on Education; he spoke of the effort expended in the structuring of the Commission. He told of the results obtained through this structure, with the creation, for example, of bodies such as the Policy Council, the Technical Teaching Council, and the Administrative Council, all of them bodies that function in a dynamic manner, facilitating constant discussions regarding the educational reality in the country.

The importance of these Councils is, obviously, not in their mere existence, since they also exist within other ministries of education. The important thing is the practice that has evolved, coherent with the objectives that they serve, and the climate of search and dialogue that characterizes them. "Their activity is, in fact, what allows us to advance in our work," said Cabral.

Later in his address as he spoke of the praxis about which he is constantly thinking, Cabral said that one of his principal preoccupations was the relation between the school at whatever level and the local, regional and national reality. "One of our principal objectives is to make the connection between the school and life—to relate it to the community in which it exists, to the small village or to the neighborhood. We strive, as well, to link the school to productive labor in the area and, especially, to agriculture; to bring it closer to the mass organizations, to JACC, to the Young Pioneers, the labor unions, and the women's organizations. Much of this task has already been achieved and, in some regions, extremely efficiently. In the Bafatá region, for example, of 106 schools, 96 are producing from their fields. In Bissau, even though we have not achieved the same results, a lot has happened also.

"It has been," continued Mário Cabral, "in the school at Có that we have achieved the maximum linkage between the school and productive work and between the school and the local population, with the integration of the people in the area in the cultural activities of the school. We can consider the school at Có as the best in the whole country during the year that has just ended."

Elza and I feel a particular closeness to this school at Có—the Maxim Gorki Center for the Formation of Teachers. It has assumed great importance not only in the educational efforts of the whole country but has made particular contributions to the development of models for adult literacy education. We have visited it on each of our trips to Guinea-Bissau and we are always deeply impressed by the dedication of the teachers, whose critical optimism penetrates everything they do to carry out their tasks.

The Commissioner's report highlighted the following achievements of the academic year 1975–76: (1) the participation of middle-school students from Bissau in productive activities; (2) the creation of a Party committee to work with primary-school teachers, both in their cultural work and in the social and political activities that support it; (3) the exceptional contributions of children and their teachers in celebrating the twentieth anniversary of PAIGC, especially their gymnastic exhibition; (4) the seminars in which those responsible for education in various parts of the country came together to discuss their experience, "brigades" trained and supervised by the Coordinating Commission on Literacy.

"This year we went out into the regions. Next year we need far greater participation of our students, not only from Bissau but from all areas of the country."

As part of the second task, the government, through the Commission on Education, will sponsor the first international seminar to be held in Bissau. This will be coordinated by the Ministers of Education in Guinea-Bissau and the Cape Verde Islands, São Tomé e Principe, Angola, and Mozambique. Delegations from these countries will come together to evaluate the praxis in their own countries in the field of education with special concern for adult literacy education.

The results of such a meeting should provide an opportunity for rich learning on the part of participants and also a practical impetus for collaboration among them despite the uniqueness of each country. The same basic struggle for national reconstruction engages all.

The third task emphasizes the relation between the school and productive work, attempting on the one hand to improve these relations and, on the other, to extend them, as far as possible, throughout the nation.

"Comrade Amilcar Cabral used to say, 'I am a simple African who wishes only to pay his debt to his own people and to live to the full his own epoch.' May we all pay our debts to our people and live fully our own time. Our historical epoch demands total liberation, total independence, and our total engagement in overcoming illiteracy and combating underdevelopment in national reconstruction," concluded Mário Cabral.

I do not know whether, without afflicting my readers too much. I have accomplished what I intended in this introduction. From the beginning, I have wanted to offer a picture—that could never, of course, be complete—of what is happening in Guinea-Bissau. All of the achievements have interested us intensely; from them we have learned a great deal. Our effort has often taken the form of active involvement rather than a narrowly professional contribution.

The richness of the Guinean experience has been such that it has been impossible to speak of it in a few words. And thus I must still prolong my observations in spite of necessary omissions regarding certain details that I know to be of great importance.

The Maxim Gorki Center at Có

We visited the Maxim Gorki Training Center for the first time in February 1976. Elza and I went with the team from IDAC, with Mário Cabral himself as our guide.

Early in the morning on our way to Có, a tiny rural settlement near Cacheu, about fifty kilometers north of Bissau, Mário Cabral spoke with enthusiasm of the Center and told us something of its history.

In November 1975 a group of educators had sought out the Commissioner. Without any preliminaries, they laid before him their plan to create a training center for teachers in an old military installation vacated by the colonial army at the time of independence. The installation was like so many others that the colonial army had spread throughout the countryside, surrounded by barbed wire and mines. Like the others, this one had been a fortification for the invaders and had also served as a site where they tortured nationals, sometimes to the point of death. On many occasions the Portuguese themselves, terrified by the strong determination of their prisoners, had increasingly become imprisoned within their own camps.

Much needed to be done to clean and improve the installation. In a strange way, without wanting to, the Portuguese had made this a natural location for a future political-pedagogical training center. Just as the people had seen those who were tortured as heroes, they were ready to see the educators who came to transform the barracks as new heroes, inheritors of the earlier ones. I visited an early hero's grave that had recently been identified by the people of the community. He and his comrades had paid a price for their rebellion and their desire to stand on the side of their own people.

At the time of our visit, four months had passed since the group of educators had begun the process of installing the center. Reflecting their vivid experiences in education in the liberated zones, they had dedicated themselves completely to cleaning the barracks, razing unnecessary small buildings, improving sanitary conditions, planting trees, and restoring the well that now furnishes excellent water. With equal dedication they had begun to plan for the administration of the center and its effective integration into the life of the surrounding community. They designed the political-pedagogical activities to be undertaken and prepared to receive the first group of students.

Just as those who fought side by side with Amilcar Cabral understood that their dream must be incarnated in the people in order to become a reality, in the same way, the educators at Có involved the neighboring populations in the development of their dream for a training center. They interpreted the project and mobilized the population around both the idea and the necessary practical activities. People came from all around to clear the land, bringing their own work tools. The team and the local people worked side by side. The growing dialogue between them was sealed in their mutual activity on behalf of the center.

With each day that passes, the center resembles more closely a people's university, born at the heart of the life of working people, based on their productive labor, and dedicated to systematizing knowledge resulting from practical experience. The Center at Có is seeking to overcome the dichotomies that exist between mental and manual labor and between learning and teaching.

The activities of the very first class of students have also been in accord with this principle. They have devoted themselves to productive labor, closely associated with their intellectual work. The patterns established in the liberated zones have been faithfully adapted and expanded at Có. Last September I saw their cultivated fields—wheat, corn, potatoes, fruit, vegetables. In cooperation with the Ministry on Agriculture, they have also begun to raise chickens, ducks, pigs and sheep. Through these efforts, the center is becoming self-sufficient.

The participation of the students in productive work is highly Literacy Education of Adults, this experiment was actually carried out by students resident at Có for training. It has produced a remarkable socio-economic, cultural census—the best done in any area of the country. On the basis of the census, appropriate generative words were chosen and a dynamic approach to literacy education began.

Little by little the Center extended and intensified its activities. "We have done our best," said the Director, Jorge Ampa, "to fulfill the objective of our school in relating it to the life of the population. A team of three students trained in first aid operate a clinic. It is open daily and has sometimes attended more than 100 persons in a month. Between April and July of this year 294 were treated."

Preventive medicine has a high priority. The Center has sponsored with the local committee a series of meetings to discuss certain popular beliefs regarding health care and to analyze aspects of "magic" in those beliefs—the "weaknesses of culture" referred to by Amilcar Cabral.

These meetings are really seminars on health problems. They are held in clearings under the shade of a tree or under woven straw shelters constructed by the people. They focus on social practice in the community and serve to increase the people's comprehension of the world around them just as PAIGC has so characteristically done. In the final analysis, to overcome the "weaknesses of culture" as these are found in social practice, the practices themselves must be completely transformed. And this, of course, requires social change in relation to production. Since the change cannot be mechanical but, rather, dialectical, political-pedagogical activity is necessary. Health education seminars are, therefore, tied not only to an analysis of health but to a critical understanding of overall goals for national reconstruction. Health is seen in relation to production and to the social implications of any given mode of production. The discussions in the seminars often become political debates.

Whatever activity gives rise to political consciousness raising—whether it be health education, means of production, or adult literacy efforts—there is a basic unity of approach. The Director stressed that all of the activities are planned and carried out in cooperation with the local committee in every village.

It is my conviction that the permanent teaching staff of the Center needs to consider the basic relations between health, education and the means of production in ongoing seminars in addition to their more specific interests in discrete fields. The relationship underlies everything they do with the students who come to the Center to study. Amilcar Cabral was referring to the significance of the underlying relationship when he said, "The means of production represents at every stage in history the result of incessant search for a dynamic equilibrium between the forces of production and the political system governing the social utilization of these forces." Seminars on cultural alienation induced in certain sectors of the population by the presence of the colonial forces would also be extremely useful to the teaching staff.

The first class at Có had 30 students; the second 60. In 1977–78 they will be able to take 100 students. To the degree that they are able to intensify their political-pedagogical work with the population of the villages, their understanding of the reality that conditions village life will become increasingly clear.

As the teams are involved more and more deeply in a process of mutual learning, they will discover that, on the one hand, they are the Subjects of that learning and, on the other hand, that the popular groups with whom they enter into dialogue are themselves the Subjects. Learning from and with these groups, the teams from the Center have a task from which they cannot escape and for which they must be well prepared: that of helping, in the authentic sense of this word, the groups to analyze their praxis and to systematize their learning derived from this praxis. Thus they go beyond mere opinion about the facts to the critical comprehension of those same facts.

It is on the basis of such a task that the Center is becoming a true university of the people. Both the teams and the group take their own daily lives as the object of their reflection in process of this nature. They are required to stand at a distance from the daily lives in which they are generally immersed and to which they often attribute an aura of permanence. Only at a distance can they get a perspective that permits them to emerge from that daily routine and begin their own independent development. The necessary precondition to taking a distance from "dailiness" is the analysis of past and present practice and the extension of this analysis into their possible future, remembering always that every practice is social in character.

When people are able to see and analyze their own way of being in the world of their immediate daily life, including the life of their villages, and when they can perceive the rationale for the factors on which their daily life is based, they are enabled to go far beyond the narrow horizons of their own village and of the geographical area in which it is located, to gain a global perspective on reality.

Political-pedagogical activity such as this—one that puts a dialectical theory of knowledge in practice—becomes, in itself, a fundamental dimension of the task of national reconstruction. Out of such an understanding of national reconstruction, a new society can evolve and a new type of intellectual emerge. The unity between manual and intellectual work and between practice and theory becomes real.

I am absolutely convinced that if the school at Có continues its practice of organizing with the people the systematic knowledge derived from their own daily experience, it can contribute to the formation of the new intellectual and become the university center of which I spoke earlier. Activity in response both to the growing curiosity of the people and to local, regional and national needs perceived by them will make it possible for the school to develop community nurses, agricultural specialists, mechanics, electricians and persons knowledgeable in raising poultry. Ongoing evaluation of practice will increase the skills and overall ability of the people in specific fields.

These future specialists will be educated in a school that is as broad as life itself and will develop a critical comprehension—neither narrow nor ingenuous—regarding their own praxis within the larger praxis of the society in which they participate. Both the specific and the social practice of this critical comprehension demand a political formation as thorough as their technical and professional training.

In the face of everything this school stands for, it would be a contradiction if the administration were controlled entirely by its director. In fact the director, the permanent teaching staff, and the teachers who come there to study participate equally in the school's governance. Each week the governing body meets to make an evaluation of what has occurred in the past week. In an unpressured atmosphere, they discuss ideas and problems. As far as possible they avoid the necessity of taking a vote. "When we vote," says Jorge Ampa, "it is because there is disagreement."

In these meetings of the governing body, general directions for the life of the Center are outlined and carefully considered. All plans for activities in the community are discussed. These matters are again debated in an assembly that includes all of the students. It is not rare for new ideas and proposals that enrich the thinking done by the governing body and benefit the whole community to come out of these assemblies.

It would be similarly contradictory if this school, linked as it is to the Commission on Education—fifty kilometers away and with very difficult conditions for communication—depended upon that central body for the solution of its routine problems and for the development and implementation of its work plans. The only requirement placed upon the school is that its plans be in harmony with the objectives for education in the nation. In the final analysis, the Commission on Education operates at a national level as the school at Có operates at its level, openly and democratically. Instead of asphyxiating initiative with bureaucratic requirements, the Commission stimulates and even requires initiative and creativity, without allowing its action to get lost in a world of papers coming and going, filling a vacuum with bureaucratic uselessness. There are no inoperative vacant spots "filled" with people, either in the Commission on Education or in the school at Có. The latter has become an example of creativity and activism modelled after the experimental work of PAIGC in the liberated zones.

"Within the Second Year of Organization," says its director, "we will work harder and better, concentrating our action on the Third Party Congress that will be meeting very soon. We intend to celebrate the event by intensifying our practical and theoretical activities at the Center. If we received one hundred percent approval in this past year, we are going to do our best to achieve the same result in the year to come."

It was not without reason that the Maxim Gorki Center for Teacher Training in the town of Có was considered the model school for the whole country during the academic year 1975–76.

A Visit to a Rural Area

In February 1976, in a place a few kilometers to the north of Có, I attended a meeting between a significant group of peasants of the community and the Commissioner on Education. Political leaders of the area were also present.

In the process of our learning about the reality of Guinea-Bissau, this was the first time that we had come in contact with a group of peasants. It was intensely interesting to us, obviously, to discover how they saw themselves in relation to the Party and the government and in the general picture of national reconstruction. What did this struggle mean to them as a continuation of that other struggle for national liberation? It had been a struggle to which they had given their full support—as far as they could in the face of the colonialist repression to which they had been forced to submit.

The meeting did not take place in a formal hall but in the shade of an enormous and very ancient tree. The people demonstrated their hospitality by receiving the delegation in the inviting shade of that tree, in intimate relation with their own natural world.

My impression was that the shaded area beneath that tree was a kind of political-cultural center—a place for informal conversation—where they made their work plans together. I also thought how such a place, taking advantage of the shade, might be used for the programs of nonformal education.

As I went toward the tree, admiring its thick foliage, I remembered that it had been in the shade of just such trees that Amilcar Cabral met with armed militants during the struggle to evaluate their action against the colonialist armies. At such times, military and tactical analyses never failed to be accompanied by political discussions and debates about culture. Through this means the permanent leadership squadrons were formed.

I remembered also other things that a militant had said to me about the many meetings that Amilcar Cabral had had with peasants. Cabral, while directing some research regarding agrarian reality in Guinea-Bissau, had traveled throughout the country. He took advantage of the opportunity to talk discreetly with those whom he met about the oppressive reality in which the people found themselves. In these conversations he was able to identify future leaders for PAIGC. Three years after the initiation of the census, on September 19, 1956, PAIGC was founded.[11]

Once, during a conversation with peasants in the shade of a tree, Cabral arose, holding the seed of a dende palm in his hand. He chose a good

11. This census was determined by the then Ministry for Overseas Affairs of Portugal. It was carried out in 1953 to fulfill the obligation of the Portuguese delegation to an FAO (Food and

place, dug a hole and planted the seed. Afterwards, looking at the peasants gathered about him, he said, "We, the people of Guinea-Bissau, will accomplish many things before the palm tree that grows from this seed will bear fruit."

"Years later," the young man told me, "there was a meeting of the committee of PAIGC in that region beside the palm tree that had just borne its first fruit."

In making that speech Cabral spoke a language of hope. He did not confine himself to the spoken word but dramatized the idea by planting the seed. This was not the false hope of one who hopes for the sake of hoping and lives on the basis of vain hope. Hope is true and well founded only when it grows out of the unity between action that transforms the world and critical reflection regarding the meaning of that action.

As he spoke that language of hope with the peasants, Cabral began putting down his own roots in the midst of the people. With the formation of PAIGC, the process of re-Africanization associated with "class suicide," so necessary for African intellectuals, was intensified.

As our own meeting in the shade of the tree began, Mário Cabral, in very few words, explained our presence in Guinea-Bissau and the work that we were carrying on together with national leaders in the field of education. He ended by saying that he was there as the person ultimately responsible for education in the country, to hear and to talk with them freely about their most pressing needs.

Immediately, then, the five oldest members of the group gathered together in a small circle within the larger circle, talking among themselves in low voices, while all the rest remained silent. A Western educator, insensitive to other cultures and convinced of the efficacy of his own ways, would probably see in all of this signs of inefficiency, as though they had not "made serious plans for this meeting."

A youth near me said, "They are talking among themselves in order to establish the order in which they will speak, as well as to define the points about which they will speak. This is their custom."

At a given point the five began to speak, one by one. They were exceedingly rich in their use of metaphors and gestures, with which they underlined their affirmations and their meanings.

Agricultural Organization conference of the United Nations) in 1947 when, through the delegates, Portugal had agreed to carry out an agricultural census of all of its overseas possessions.

Referring to the violence of the colonialists, one of them bowed low and bowed again, curving his body, living the word with which he described the terrible treatment received. He walked from one side to the other within the circle of the shade in which we stood, using the movements of his body to express some aspect of the story he told. None of them spoke ecstatically, disassociating his body from the words he spoke. None spoke only to be heard. In Africa the word is also to be seen, part of the necessary gesture. No one in Africa, with the exception of the de-Africanized intellectuals, denies his roots, or reveals fear or shame in using his body to express his meaning.

And while we saw and heard them speaking, with the force of their metaphors, and the easy movements of their bodies, we thought of the innumerable possibilities that were opened for a liberating education by these wellsprings of African culture.

They spoke also of the present moment, of their desire to participate in the struggle for national reconstruction. They spoke, at the same time, of the difficulties that they confronted.

The oldest among them, the one who spoke last in the shade of that enormous tree, spoke to all of us in the language of hope.

"The PAIGC," he said, "for all of its 20 years, is still a child. Twenty years are many in the life of a person, but not in the life of a people, or of a Party. The good thing about PAIGC is that it has learned to walk with the people. I will not see the great things that the people of Guinea-Bissau, PAIGC and the government will do. But the children of our children will see these things. For this very reason, it is necessary that I who will not see that time, and all of us, do now what is necessary for our time."

Every time we come to Guinea-Bissau, we reserve time not only for reencounters and return visits but for new encounters and new visits. These make us more and more aware, in a very intimate way, of reality. New encounters and visits are absolutely fundamental to our praxis with the national teams. They are part of the method of work that we adopted and through which we attempt to see and hear, to question and discuss. In these visits and encounters, we are always attentive to the smallest detail that attracts our attention and challenges our curiosity to some new reflection with our national colleagues.

In our trips to the country we could not participate efficiently in the evaluation seminars with the Coordinating Commission on Literacy if (1) we remained only in Bissau and did not observe the practice in other areas of the country, or (2) we did not try to understand what was going on in other sectors of activity aside from adult literacy education.

Activities in Adult Literacy Education in 1975–76

In the following considerations with which I will conclude this introduction, I shall attempt a synthesis of the activities that have taken place recently in the field of adult literacy education in Guinea-Bissau.

There is one point that it seems to me necessary to underline above all others. That is the "mass line" that characterizes the literacy work in the country. What is intended, fundamentally, is to see the literacy education of adults as a political act, coherent with the principles of PAIGC. It is an act that informs the action of the government and is based on a real involvement of the people. Whenever programs of adult literacy are initiated, in accordance with the priorities established by the Party and the government, they are taken over, as far as possible, by the local population. In this way, an indispensable relation is established between the adult literacy programs and the political committees of the villages or city neighborhoods. Through these committees, the educators and local teachers, themselves activists, are put directly in touch with the people. What really characterizes the "mass line" and defines it as such is its revolutionary anti-elitism, its anti-paternalism, and the way in which local people assume the role of Subjects through their participation in programing the campaign. A dynamic relation between tactics and strategy is maintained. The strategy is to integrate the campaign into the overall plan for the society. The tactics are to initiate the campaign only in areas where conditions are already favorable for such activity. To say the campaign is national does not mean that it must begin everywhere at once. If conditions are right or are at least partially favorable, the efforts toward literacy move more rapidly. Something concrete results. If the conditions do not exist or are very far from being favorable, literacy efforts have no meaning. For this reason, there is no way to confuse the "mass line" with the voluntarist approach to literacy that depends on generalized planning rather than on careful tactics consistent with local reality.

A literacy campaign that follows the "mass line" will sooner or later be generalized to include the whole society. Although this is true, it does not necessarily follow that every literacy campaign that is aimed at the whole of the society is part of the "mass line." The establishment of priority zones in Guinea-Bissau for the launching of the literacy campaign is not a negation of the "mass line" but a means of realizing it.

In contrast with what happens in the usual voluntarist literacy campaign, the "mass line" demands of those involved that they live in permanent tension between patience and impatience. Voluntarist literacy campaigns, on the contrary, result in the negation of the tension, leaving those involved in a constant state of impatience. In order to break the tension, they tend to accelerate the process whether or not conditions are right. This results in teaching without learning and the "transfer" of knowledge because "there is no time to lose."

Breaking the tension between patience and impatience, under such circumstances, inevitably leads to teaching without dialogue. No matter what the intention, knowledge is presented as something finished, already concluded. There is often an unperceived contradiction between one's perception of the learning process and one's practice. The impatient educator often transfers knowledge like a package while discoursing volubly on the dynamic nature of knowledge.

When there is a rupture in the tension between patience and impatience, the opposite situation might also exist: impatience might also disappear. In this case educators may fall into passivity. "Let everything stay as it is so that we can see what will happen" is an attitude that has nothing in common with the militantly revolutionary "mass line." Patience is not conformity. The best way to accomplish those things that are impossible today is to do today whatever *is* possible.

Amilcar Cabral kept this tension. In his revolutionary praxis and in his reflections on it that he left us in his writings, the tension was always apparent: "We must walk rapidly but not run," he said. "We must not be opportunists, nor allow our enthusiasms to make us lose the vision of concrete reality. It is more important to begin an armed struggle with apparent delays but with the guarantee of continuity than to begin too early or in any moment when we do not have conditions that guarantee continuity and victory for our people." And, later, he goes on, "To know our strengths means to have at every instant complete consciousness of what we are able to do. It means also to evaluate our possibilities in every area, in every unit of the armed forces, to act always in accord with these possibilities and to do our best to increase our strength and our capability, in both men and material. It means never to do less than we can or ought to do, but not to pretend, ever, to do things that we are really not ready to do."

It is on the basis of these principles, valid not only for the liberation struggle yesterday but for national reconstruction today, that the government of Guinea-Bissau, through its Commission on Education, is working in the field of adult literacy education. And it is for this reason that, as I stressed earlier, although the campaign is national in scope, it is beginning in those areas that make a valid experience possible, offering those who participate the rich, dynamic opportunities for learning on which they can build in the future.

This aspect of the preparation of cadres able to put into practice a pedagogy that coincides with these basic principles cannot help becoming a fundamental factor in the general picture of a literacy campaign such as the one in which the government of Guinea-Bissau is now engaged. The necessary competence results from a unity of practice and theory. It does not come from "training" in a certain number of technical skills, as is the case in the advanced capitalist societies where more and more training in a limited number of skills takes place.

This aspect of the program is the direct responsibility of the Coordinating Commission for Adult Literacy[12] working in close cooperation with the Commissioner Mário Cabral.

None of the activities of the Coordinating Commission is easy to carry out, nor do the results always correspond with the hopes placed in them. The mistakes that have occurred at one time or another, resulting from poor planning or lack of adequate understanding of local reality, are analyzed by the Commission—a process that, in itself, is not without difficulties. In the exercise of self-criticism, the Commission members are also learning how to overcome the problems encountered. The important thing is to be convinced once again, with Amilcar Cabral, that "the errors we commit should not discourage us, just as the victories should not make us forget the mistakes."

In 1975–76 the principal task of the Commission at the national level has been to foster closer working relations with the Commissions on Health, Agriculture, Internal Services and Information. They have also tried to cooperate fully with local party committees, with the mass organizations

---

12. This Commission is increasingly operating as an intercommissional entity. It reports through the Commission on Education to the National Commission on Literacy in which all of the Commissioners whose responsibilities relate at all to literacy participate. The President of the Council of State himself serves as the President of the National Commission on Literacy. Their task is to outline the general policies and lines of action to be followed by the Coordinating Commission for Adult Literacy. We have participated in two meetings of this national commission and were impressed by the quality of their discussions.

like those for youth and labor, and they have worked closely with the Center at Có. Major attention has been directed toward the training of leadership cadres. Culture Circles have been created wherever continuity could be assured, and small nucleus programs have been organized in all the priority areas. In addition to these activities, brigades organized by the Commission have traveled widely in Bissau and in other priority zones. Their task has been to interpret the role of literacy education as integral to national reconstruction. Public opinion has been mobilized.

In full recognition of the errors committed in their first year, the Commission is now preparing for participation in the Second Year of Organization within which the national literacy campaign has been designated as one of the government's three principal tasks.

In its report made during the month of May 1976 the Commission said, "We want to refer especially to the tremendous support we have received from the leaders of the Party and the State that attests to the importance being given to literacy." This support was proven many times in the contacts that preceded the sending of one of the brigades into some area of the country. The President, Luíz Cabral, the different Commissions that are part of the National Commission on Literacy, all of the Commissioners, mass organizations and state organizations have all provided valuable contacts.

During a recent visit in September 1976 to the school at Có, we included trips to four small villages in the region. We were able to observe in the Culture Circles, held in the straw-roofed shelters, the extraordinary literacy work that was in progress there, growing out of the political-pedagogical presence of the school at Có.

We also dedicated eight days of that trip to a seminar to evaluate all the work of the Commission. The evaluation, as mentioned earlier, does not consist of a process in which we take the Coordinating Commission and its work as the object of our analysis, discussing them with "professional airs." Rather, we and the Commission members together engage in dialogue about what is being done. We are active Subjects in the evaluation as we try to analyze together the cause of whatever failures there have been and to study alternative means of overcoming them.

The programs carried out in the armed forces, through FARP, revealed a high index of efficiency. It was not pure coincidence that the most positive efforts in the civilian area were those in the villages around the school at Có.

One conclusion of the evaluation seminar was that the Commission should try, as far as possible, to establish a relation (in addition to its normal linkage to the local party committee) with whatever service facility it could find locally—whether that be a health clinic, a school, a production cooperative or other service group—so that the deep communication with the people enjoyed by these activities might also become a real source of support for literacy education programs.

Of one thing we are sure: moving ahead in "patient impatience" and, therefore, with confidence, the work of adult literacy education in Guinea-Bissau is more than a promise. It is a reality.

In concluding this introduction, there are two points that must not be omitted. First, I must express deep gratitude, not only my own but that of the team from IDAC and of the Department of Education of the World Council of Churches, to the people, to PAIGC, and to the government of Guinea-Bissau, for the opportunity they have given us both to learn so much and to teach, and, in this way, to participate in the effort to reconstruct the country.

Second, in my own name, and Elza's, I wish to speak of how much our involvement in Guinea-Bissau has called forth a nostalgia for Brazil—a deep longing that is both calm and "well behaved"—and for those now-distant years in Culture Circles, as lively as the ones at Có, where we learned so much from our own people.

Translated by Carmen St. John Hunter

LITERACY: READING THE WORD AND THE WORLD

Literacy in Guinea-Bissau Revisited

Donaldo Macedo: Why did you become interested and, later, involved in the illiteracy problem in Guinea-Bissau?

Paulo Freire: Let me begin by saying that even before my interest in the literacy campaign in Guinea-Bissau, I was extremely interested in the struggle for liberation of the African people in general. With great curiosity and even greater happiness, I closely followed the struggle of liberation in Mozambique, Angola, Cape Verde, São Tomé and Príncipe, and Guinea-Bissau, keeping in mind the distinct nature of these struggles. The differences in these struggles were conditioned obviously by the different historical and geographical contexts. Even before the independence of Guinea-Bissau, then, I already had an attachment—both political and affective to that country and its heroic people.

It was precisely these cultural, political, and affective links with Africa that fueled my interest in the literacy campaign in Guinea-Bissau. As a man from northeastern Brazil, I was somewhat culturally tied to Africa, particularly to those countries that were unfortunate enough to be colonized by Portugal, as was Brazil.

In 1970 or 1971, I made my first trip to Africa, to Tanzania and Zambia. After my arrival in Zambia, while I was waiting at the airport for a domestic flight to take me to my final destination, where I was to work with an educational team, I was paged and asked to report to the information counter. There I was met by a North American couple who represented MPLA (the Popular Movement for the Liberation of Angola), a group that included Lara, an important political figure not only in Angola but also throughout all of Africa.

The North American couple came with a proposal from the leaders of the MPLA, asking me if I would change my flight so I could spend a day meeting with some representatives of the MPLA who were most interested in talking to me. I immediately accepted. I looked forward to meeting with a group whose work for the freedom of their people I had admired and closely followed. We went to the North Americans' house where Lara, along with five more MPLA militants, was waiting.

Lara greeting me by saying: "Comrade Paulo Freire, if you knew my country as well as we know your work, you would know Angola extremely well!" We talked most of the afternoon about the ongoing struggle (at that time the fight for liberation in Angola was experiencing some setbacks) and, most important, we discussed at great length the role of literacy work in the struggle for liberation. We also discussed the literacy difficulties in Mozambique and Guinea-Bissau.

(Incidentally, the World Council of Churches, where I worked, had lent strong support to many African liberation movements even before my participation. I was not the one who initiated the involvement of the World Council with these movements. What I did was try to reinforce the already existing relationships.)

In addition to political and military concerns of the moment, Lara and I analyzed the nature of the new educational process taking place during the struggle, particularly in the areas that were being liberated. We discussed the practice of the struggle as a pedagogical praxis. At night, after supper, the MPLA members showed me documentary films about the liberation struggle and the pedagogical experience taking place during the struggle. This encounter with African liberation leaders preceded my involvement, and that of the team of educators I worked with, in Guinea-Bissau. In certain respects, it prepared me for what would later become our educational contribution to both Guinea-Bissau and Angola.

After Zambia, I went to Tanzania. I witnessed many of the same things there as in Zambia. At the University of Tanzania I was approached by a Tanzanian who was deeply involved with FRELIMO (the Liberation Front of Mozambique). He asked me if I would accept an invitation to meet with representatives of FRELIMO in Dar Es Salaam. I accepted. Among those present was the widow of Mondlame, the assassinated leader of FRELIMO. The present minister of education of Mozambique was also there. As in Zambia with the MPLA, we had conversations about education, its role and processes during the struggle for liberation.

I was then invited to visit the training camp that the president of Tanzania had set up for the FRELIMO fighters. Intensive training was preparing literacy teachers, who would later go into Mozambique to work in the literacy campaigns under way at the same time as the war for liberation. An important highlight of this training was the emphasis on not dichotomizing the struggles for freedom and literacy. In the training camp I met with educational leaders, including many Europeans committed to the Liberation struggle who were there to help.

I was happy to see that what was important for the European and African youths was the ideological strength informing the struggle to restore self-respect and dignity, which had been usurped by a cruel and vicious colonial machinery. It was clear to me that these European youths were on the side of the popular masses from Mozambique, who were fighting for their freedom. During that meeting we discussed the techniques and literacy methods they were using.

Then, in January 1975, while in Geneva, I received a long letter from Jose Maria Nunes Pereira, a Brazilian professor from the Catholic University of Rio de Janeiro, who was then serving as coordinator of African and Asian Studies at Cândido Mendes University, also in Rio de Janeiro. Professor Pereira wrote that as coordinator of Africa and Asian Studies, he had recently returned from Guinea-Bissau, where he had had a long meeting with the minister of education, Mário Cabral, and with the president of Guinea-Bissau, Luís Cabral, brother of Amilcar Cabral, the founder of PAIGC. In his letter, Pereira stressed that both the president and minister of education had urged him to ask me if I would accept an invitation to coordinate a team of educators in the literacy campaign in Guinea-Bissau. This campaign focused on adult literacy, but it also included other areas of education. If I was interested, I was to contact Mário Cabral.

After I received Pereira's letter, I organized a meeting at my house with other members of IDAC (Institute for Cultural Action) to discuss the letter and the possibility of establishing a collaborative program with Guinea-Bissau. Everybody from IDAC showed great interest in helping the Guinea-Bissau program. The next day I also discussed the invitation with the World Council of Churches. My intentions were to devise a plan in which the World Council and IDAC would work together, studying and planning ways to best contribute and meet the challenges of eradicating illiteracy in Guinea-Bissau. Both IDAC and the World Council accepted my proposal, and that January I wrote Mário Cabral. The first few lines of that letter mentioned that I received a letter from someone who had been in Guinea-

Bissau. Why did I not mention Professor Pereira's name in this letter? At the time, Brazil had in place an extremely repressive political machine. My own exile taught me to be careful about citing names because under the Brazilian dictatorship, I might endanger people's positions, or even their lives.

Continuing, I wrote: "The individual who wrote me from Brazil has discussed with you and the president the possibility of organizing a team of educators in which I would contribute to the adult literacy program already in place in Guinea-Bissau. He further suggested that I write you to begin a conversation on how to get started."

In April 1975, two and a half months after I wrote Mário Cabral, he answered my letter. That April I wrote him a second letter, which begins:

"Dear Comrade Mário Cabral: I just received your letter, in which you confirm the government's interest in our collaboration. I do not think it necessary to expand on our satisfaction in receiving this confirmation, satisfaction not only on the part of members of IDAC but also of the World Council of Churches."

In this second letter I proposed some guidelines, including the possibility of sending someone to Geneva to begin discussion on the general educational situation of Guinea-Bissau. We had proposed that Mário Cabral come to Geneva. I realize now that he was probably too busy to accept our invitation.

Macedo: Did you and your team of educators support your own educational activities in Guinea-Bissau?

Freire: In responding to this question, I can put to rest some small-minded criticism some have harbored against me. Some have said I offered huge grants to Guinea-Bissau and bought my way through Guinea-Bissau. In other words, Guinea-Bissau was not really interested in our contribution to the literacy campaign, but could not refuse the money. This type of criticism not only offends those of us who genuinely wanted to contribute to the reconstruction of the educational system, but also those comrades who fought heroically in the jungles of Guinea-Bissau to defeat the colonialists. It would be unlikely that they would fight for twelve years only to sell their interests so easily in the face of some small offer of financial support that we could have made. But let us put this type of criticism aside and try to answer your question.

As I said earlier, the World Council of Churches played an important role in the movements for liberation in Africa. The World Council never ceased to give assistance to those liberation movements, even in difficult times during their struggles. The World Council also saw to it that the contributions it gave during these struggles would continue during the reconstruction of the new societies after independence from colonial powers. It was certainly not inappropriate that the World Council raised about $500,000 to assist the literacy campaign in Nicaragua, for instance. I was part of a team of educators who took part in this campaign in Nicaragua.

But the World Council did not limit its assistance to Nicaragua and Guinea-Bissau. It also offered a tremendous amount of help in Angola, Mozambique, and other countries. So when the department where I worked at the World Council had the opportunity to contribute to Guinea-Bissau, and made a commitment to provide technical assistance, it also accepted the financial commitment that went along with it. That is, even though the department had little money, it paid my salary while I was in Guinea-Bissau, as if I had been in Geneva. The same procedure applied with respect to my trips to Angola, São Tomé, and Cape Verde. But the CCPD, a sector of the World Council that dealt with educational and developmental programs, had the financial means to support certain educational projects and programs in the Third World. The CCPD was interested in the project in Guinea-Bissau, and IDAC presented a proposal seeking financial support from CCPD.

When I first went to Guinea-Bissau, my travel expenses were paid by the World Council. The rest of the team that accompanied me was financed by CCPD. After I received Pereira's letter, I wrote Mario Cabral in Guinea-Bissau saying that I would accept his invitation to put together a team of educators to work there in adult literacy, but that the government did not have to pay the travel expenses, salaries, and other costs that the group would incur. Given the economic conditions of the recently independent Guinea-Bissau, we knew this would have been impossible. By agreeing to provide technical assistance to the literacy campaign, we wanted to try, as much as we could, not to burden financially an already economically depressed country. So it was arranged that the IDAC team going to Guinea-Bissau would continue to be funded by other organizations.

IDAC received a small grant to cover the expenses of an exploratory trip to Guinea-Bissau. When we returned, I talked a great deal about the work we conducted there. The introduction to *Letters to Guinea-Bissau* is a methodological narration of our work during this trip. As you can see, the objectives of the literacy program were developed in Guinea-Bissau, not in Geneva, and they were developed largely by Guineans. Once this program had been developed, we obtained more financial assistance so we could continue to avoid burdening the government of Guinea-Bissau. (Incidentally, I was given the same sort of financial assistance when I went to Nicaragua. The Nicaraguan government did not pay for my trip. The same kind of arrangements were made for my trips to Angola and to São Tomé and Príncipe.)

Macedo: You mentioned that the literacy project in which you, along with other members of IDAC, contributed by providing technical assistance was fully developed in Guinea-Bissau and not in Geneva. However, you have been criticized for trying to implement a plan that was idealistic and populist, that ignored important political, economic, cultural, and linguistic factors that shaped the reality of Guinea-Bissau. Did you and your team from IDAC fully discuss and evaluate the reality of the Guinea-Bissau society before executing your plan?

Freire: I find this criticism scientifically inconsistent. In what way could the IDAC team and I have developed a populist literacy project in Guinea-Bissau? What is the meaning of a political style that is called "populist?" Political analysts say that a populist style necessarily requires the emergence of the popular masses who begin to want, at the very least, to have a different position in the social and political history of their society. It is as if the oppressed suddenly begin to discover the possibility of deviating from the complacent state in which they find themselves; they begin to see the possibility of taking different risks. Symbolically, one could say that before, in their immersion, the risks were preponderantly stagnant. Before, there were risks that only involved survival in the face of exploitation. In certain ways, the subordinate role of the oppressed was perceived as a result of climatic difficulties (for example, there is no rain; therefore we don't have any work or anything to eat) and not as calculated exploitation by the dominant class. During the emergence of oppressed people, they begin to take risks—the risk to say the word; the social, historical, and political risks involved in protesting. There are no clear reasons for this that emerge; maybe it is because of changes in the productive forces of society, because of a situation exacerbated by local members of the dominant class.

These people emerge by taking new and different risks—the risk to be arrested on the street, to go to jail. But there is also the counterrisk: the possibility of being heard. This provokes a response by means of a political style often called populism. Thus, we can say that the populist style of politics is more or an answer than a cause. It is not the populist style that provokes the rising up of oppressed people. It is the rising up of the people that makes politicians change their tactics to remain in power.

What happens then? This new style is given a name: populism. When the oppressed rise and the dominant classes need to defend themselves (to respond defensively to the rising up of the people while maintaining their power), the leadership that was called populist assumes an ambiguity that is manifested in the relationship between the emerging masses and the dominant classes. On the one hand, to continue to be populist, the leadership needs the support of the people on the street. On the other hand, it needs to establish limits in relation to the action of these people so that there is no rupture in the bourgeois style of politics and society in general. These limits are designed to prevent the transformation of society, so that the oppressed do not turn into revolutionaries. Thus, the dominant classes create obstacles to prevent the subordinate classes from transcending their class and gaining class consciousness.

What is the nature of this ambiguity? By limiting the demanding presence of the people, whereby people take to the streets and protest in the parks, the populist leadership cannot stop the people from learning how to use the streets and the parks to voice their demands. The populist leadership can limit its response to the demands of the people. But if it prohibits the people from assembling on the streets, the leadership stops being populist and becomes an overtly repressive regime. To the extent that it only limits its response to certain demands of the people (for example, by allowing demonstrations in designated areas only), it allows the continuance of public demonstrations, which will lead inevitably to an even greater process of discovery whereby the oppressed learn how to make demands. The people end up thriving and assuming their own demands. Thus, the populism that manipulates contradicts itself by stimulating democracy.

There is a point at which political leadership maintains itself by oscillating between manipulation and democratic experience. There is also a point at which the leadership can lean more toward the people. One dimension of its ambiguity has this leadership taking one step to the left and one to the right, with one foot atop the oppressed masses, the other atop the bourgeoisie. When this leadership begins to step with both feet on the masses, there are two possibilities. First, the society can fall into a prerevolution, the so-called populist leadership denouncing populism and entering into its own revolutionary process. Second, the right wing steps in with a coup and installs a rigid, military regime.

From a scientific point of view, which populist characteristics can one find in our involvement in Guinea-Bissau? Which populist aspects are there in our proposals in Guinea-Bissau for the reform of education in general, and adult literacy in particular? We were in contact with a political leadership that had spent years fighting the Portuguese colonialists in the jungles, without traces of populism.

What is the populist dimension of the letters I wrote to the educators of Guinea-Bissau? In the third and fourth letters, for example, where I examine the very serious aspects of dealing with the meaning of a socialist, revolutionary education, or where I discuss the relationship between education and production and the problem of the autonomy of the working class, where is the populist character in these published documents? My impression is that some people probably read the works of a famous Brazilian educator who criticizes me by characterizing me as a populist. Should I be characterized as such for making a contribution to my country under a populist regime?

Today in Brazil, for example, we have begun a historical new phase in political life. Even though I belong to a political party that did not participate in the development of this new government, as a Brazilian I sincerely hope that these democratic moves continue and the system undergoes the necessary transformation to benefit the working class. But no one would claim that Brazil's government is a revolutionary regime. Many of the educators criticizing me as populist are now making their contributions to Brazil's government. It would be interesting to see in ten or twenty years if students working on their theses, for example, would consider these educators populists even though they are contributing to a government that is far from revolutionary.

One is not necessarily populist because one makes certain contributions to a regime that is regarded as populist. Yet what I find even stranger is the claim that the proposals that I made to Guinea-Bissau in conjunction with the team from IDAC were populist. It would be just as ridiculous to characterize as populist my discussion with educators in Angola. There are people who even claim that I did nothing more than transplant my Brazilian experience to Guinea-Bissau. This is absolutely false.

I have also been accused of being indifferent to various ethnic groups in Guinea-Bissau. This is also ridiculous. Why would I reject the idea of learning more? By analyzing and studying the cultural and linguistic diversity in Guinea-Bissau, I was in a better position to comprehend the educational needs of Guinea-Bissau. What I could not do in Guinea-Bissau is overstep the political limitations of the moment. As a foreigner, I could not impose my proposals on the reality of Guinea-Bissau and on the needs as perceived by political leaders. For example, the linguistic question was one of the boundaries that I could not step over, although I fully and emphatically discussed with the educators my concerns about carrying out the literacy campaign in the language of the colonialists. However, the leadership found it politically advantageous to adopt the Portuguese language as the main vehicle in the literacy campaign.

Macedo: As an admirer of Amilcar Cabral, you could not ignore his detailed analysis of the cultural and linguistic character of Guinea-Bissau. Cabral himself showed great concern with respect to the probable difficulties during the postindependence period with the national unification process, given so many diverse ethnic groups.

Freire: Exactly. Amilcar Cabral was a thinker who put his thinking into practice. He was a thinker whom I read over and again and always get new perspectives from.

One of my dreams, which went unfulfilled, was to conduct a thorough analysis of Amilcar Cabral's work. I even have a title for the book that I wanted to write: Amilcar Cabral: The Pedagogue of the Revolution. In this book I would have drawn a clear distinction between "revolutionary pedagogue" and "pedagogue of the revolution." We have some revolutionary pedagogues; but we don't have many pedagogues of the revolution. Amilcar is one of them.

To accomplish this dream, however, I would have had to stay in Guinea-Bissau for at least six to eight months and also go to other African countries. I had neither the finances nor the time to carry out such an ambitious task. I would not ask the government of Guinea-Bissau to pay for my project, in view of the tremendous financial difficulties this new country faced in the reconstruction of its society after independence. I was also reluctant to ask the World Council of Churches to finance my project.

I did some preliminary work, such as conducting interviews with important political leaders who worked closely with Cabral. I interviewed the PAIGC leadership in Guinea-Bissau, for example. I said in one interview with the political director of the time that the project could not be carried out by an intellectual who considers himself objective and free to say whatever he or she wants. My idea was not to go into Guinea-Bissau to carry out research and later write a book in which I say what I might want to say under the rubric of so-called "academic autonomy" or "scientific objectivity." I am a militant intellectual. As such, I wanted to do a serious and rigorous study about Cabral as a pedagogue of the revolution.

But first I would have had to get to know how the party, which was founded by Cabral, and which fought courageously to expel the colonizers, viewed my plan. There were conditions I wanted to establish. If the project had gone forward, before I published the work I would have submitted the manuscript for review by the party. I would not have published the book without the party's approval.

Perhaps the leadership could have responded to my conditions by asking me why I was such an obedient intellectual. I would have said that I am not an "obedient" intellectual. For example, if PAIGC had told me that some of the things I stated were not in the interest of political reform, I would probably have fought with the party to defend my position. But I would also have appreciated the reasons that led the party to conclude that my statements were undermining their goals.

Only after this process would I have submitted the final draft for publication. All the royalties would have gone to political causes that would further advance the humanitarian and social justice that led to both the creation of the party in the first place and the subsequent revolution.

Unfortunately, I was not able to complete this study. I conducted approximately ten interviews, the first one with the minister of education, Mario Cabral. I also interviewed militant youth groups organized during the struggle for liberation. But because of time difficulties and other factors, I decided not to continue with the project. I was thinking of conducting about 300 interviews. Just the work involved in these interviews, the transcriptions of the tapes, the selection and editing of the transcriptions, would have taken years to complete. I could have done the transcription and editing in Europe, but the interviews would have had to be done in Africa, mainly in Guinea-Bissau.

Talking to you about this stalled project highlights how I behaved with respect to the principles of the revolution. I respected the cultural and political autonomy of the people of Guinea-Bissau. I accept it as a fact when people say that I am incompetent in many areas. However, I never tried to succeed by means of criticizing other people's incompetence. That is, by criticizing some people, this criticism could give me visibility and intellectual prestige.

In fact, I do not care about prestige. My major preoccupation is to work honestly and seriously toward the development of a better and just society, as I have done in Guinea-Bissau. If people read *Letters to Guinea-Bissau* they will see my commitment to the educational transformation in that country.

In the book that "talked" with my Chilean friend I made the following observation. In Brazil during the 1950s I defended the position that learners, no matter what level, should allow themselves to experiment with becoming subjects of the act of knowing, which education implies. Now I ask, how could I have done the contrary in Guinea-Bissau? Moreover, in the revolutionary context I must insist that learners become subjects, subjects of the reinvention of their country.

Where is this poor Brazilian educator's populism, an educator who insisted during his meetings with Guinean educators that the people should march and assume their country's history? Have you ever heard a populist talk about the rights of learners to become subjects and assume this history? Ask Fernando Cardenal and Ernesto Cardenal if my work and suggestions for Nicaragua were of a populist nature. These criticisms reveal how superficially my critics have approached my writing. Their brand of ideology prevents them from understanding or wanting to understand the pedagogical proposals I have advanced.

Macedo: How would you confront the process of emancipation through literacy in a society characterized by difficulties rooted in the presence of multiple discourses? This problem becomes infinitely more complex when the society is characterized by many competing languages, such as in Guinea-Bissau.

Freire: We first have to deal with the relationship between literacy and emancipation. The concept of literacy here should be taken as transcending its etymological content. Literacy cannot be reduced to experiences that are only a little creative, that treat the foundations of letters and words as a purely mechanical domain.

In answering your question I will try to go beyond this rigid comprehension of literacy and begin to understand literacy as the relationship of learners to the world, mediated by the transforming practice of this world taking place in the very general social milieu in which learners travel, and also mediated by the oral discourse concerning this transforming practice. This understanding of literacy takes me to a notion of a comprehensive literacy that is necessarily political.

Even in this global sense, literacy by itself should never be understood as the triggering of social emancipation of the subordinated classes. Literacy leads to and participates in a series of triggering mechanisms that need to be activated for the indispensable transformation of a society whose unjust reality destroys the majority of people. Literacy in this global sense takes place in societies where oppressed classes assume their own history. The most recent case of this type of literacy is in Nicaragua.

Interestingly, the nature of this process is different from that of emancipation. Literacy in the case of Nicaragua started to take place as soon as the people took their history into their own hands. Taking history into your own hands precedes taking up the alphabet. Anyone who takes history into his or her own hands can easily take up the alphabet. The process of literacy is much easier than the process of taking history into your own hands, since this entails the "rewriting" of your society. In Nicaragua the people rewrote their society before reading the word.

Further, it is interesting to observe that in cultural history the human being, or, more accurately, the animal that becomes human and the human being who is the result of this previous transformation, first changes the world and much later becomes capable of talking about the world that he or she has transformed. A much longer time elapses before he or she is able to write about the talk generated from this transformation. Literacy must be seen and understood in this global sense. Since the reading of the word is preceded by the rewriting of society in societies that undergo a revolutionary process, it is much easier to conduct successful literacy campaigns in these societies.

But all of this discussion is far more general, more political, and more historical than the literacy process itself. One cannot forget the specific dimension of the linguistic code. In the case of Nicaragua, the only problematic area of the linguistic code (which has its own necessarily ideological, social, and political implications) is the situation of the Mosquito Indians. For the rest, the big problem concerning the Spanish language is the multiple discourses you talked about. These discourses, in my view, are linked to the differences among the various social classes and can be appreciated only in light of class analyses.

The great problem that literacy campaigns face with respect to multiple discourses is dealing with the process of rewriting society. In principle, this rewriting breaks down the rigid hierarchical order of social classes and thereby transforms the material structures of society. Let me reemphasize one point: we should never take literacy as the triggering of social transformation. Literacy as a global concept is only a part of the transformative triggering mechanism. There is a difference of quality between a political crusade and the experience of literacy, even in Brazil today. I recall that in the world conference in Persepolis organized by UNESCO in 1975—participating countries included the Soviet Union, the United States, Cuba, North Korea, Vietnam, Peru, Brazil, and numerous European countries—one of the central themes was the evaluation of literacy campaigns throughout the world. "The Letter of Persepolis," published by UNESCO, states, among other things, that the relative success of literacy campaigns evaluated by UNESCO depended on their relation to the revolutionary transformations of the societies in which the literacy campaigns took place.

This demonstrates the extraordinary role that the reading of the world and reality play in the general reinvention of education and the revolutionary society. It also shows that even in societies with great limitations due to their reactionary stance, for instance, although one would expect less successful results, a literacy campaign can still succeed and help other key factors trigger the transformation of this society. However, it is impossible and inadvisable to forget the linguistic issue.

Now, let's talk about the great problems that we had to confront in Guinea-Bissau.

Macedo: You can begin, I think, by addressing the linguistic challenges you encountered in Guinea-Bissau.

Freire: Guinea-Bissau met the first basic condition that makes the success of literacy campaigns possible: the revolutionary transformation of society. Guinea-Bissau had completed a long and beautiful struggle for liberation, under the uncontested leadership of the extraordinary pedagogue Amilcar Cabral. (In *Letters to Guinea-Bissau* I often refer to the pedagogical aspect of Cabral's leadership, the seminars he conducted during the struggle, not only to evaluate military successes, but also the cultural struggle.)

In brief, Guinea-Bissau had the political, social, and historical contexts, namely the struggle on the part of its people to liberate themselves. But Guinea-Bissau did not meet the second condition, due to its linguistic diversity. Guinea-Bissau has about thirty different languages and dialects spoken by various ethnic groups. In addition, it has Creole, which functions as a lingua franca. Creole gives Guinea-Bissau, Cape Verde, and São Tomé an enormous advantage over Angola and Mozambique, for example.

Creole, a linguistic creation that combines African languages and Portuguese, developed gradually in Guinea-Bissau. Creole is to Portuguese what Portuguese, Spanish, French, and Italian are to Latin: a descendent. Creole is as beautiful and rich and viable as Portuguese. No linguistic expression or language is born ready-made. For example, there is no need for Portuguese, Germans, and Spaniards to be ashamed of using a word like *estress* (stress), which is directly borrowed from English. I do not know any other possible word for stress in Portuguese. The development of the productive forces of technology and science have a great deal to do with linguistic development as well. We have to accept [or *stress*] hundreds of such words, *know-how* for instance.

We see Brazilian products made in Brazil that say, in English, "Made in Brazil." This commonplace wording internationalizes communication. I am not ashamed of using such terms. Thus, should Creole speakers be ashamed if they borrow certain terms from the Portuguese language to address the technological development of their society?

You cannot establish by decree the inviability of such development. And this is, more or less, what I said to the commission on education. At the peril of being misinterpreted by the president's security guard, I put my hands on Luís Cabral's head and said "Mr. President, I understand why you get headaches when you speak Portuguese for a long time. The fact is, your mental structure is not Portuguese, even though you speak Portuguese very well. Your thinking structure, which deals with the way you talk and express yourself, is not Portuguese."

There was a Guinean newspaper, *Nô Pintcha*, that at that time customarily printed one of Amilcar Cabral's texts in every issue. *Nô Pintcha* played an important role in disseminating Cabral's ideas. By an odd coincidence, the day following my speech *Nô Pintcha* printed the only Amilcar Cabral speech with which I disagree. In it he said that the most beautiful gift the Portuguese left Guineans was the Portuguese language. (Cabral's statement should be interpreted in the context of the struggle for liberation. In fact, I learned later that there were political reasons for Cabral's statement. Cabral was trying to use Portuguese as a unifying force to calm the friction between the competing linguistic and ethnic groups in Guinea-Bissau.) I read Cabral's text as a direct message to me: "My comrade Paulo Freire, we like you very much, but don't butt into this business of language in our country. Amilcar Cabral himself said that Portuguese was a beautiful gift from the colonizers."

Notwithstanding this message, I continued to fight, along with the members of IDAC, about the role of Portuguese in the literacy campaign. An IDAC colleague, Marcos Arruda, fought intensely over the language issue. We finally were able to bring to Guinea-Bissau two linguists (one Belgian, the other African, also financed by IDAC) to discuss and evaluate the linguistic dilemma in Guinea-Bissau. Both were from the Language Institute of Dakar. The Belgian was a specialist in Creole languages; the African a specialist in African languages. At the same time I contacted a Brazilian linguist who taught in Leon and was a specialist in Creole languages. (He was working on a dictionary and grammar of Creole in Guinea-Bissau.) He never came to Guinea-Bissau, but we discussed at great length the issues of language in Guinea-Bissau.

We proposed to Mário Cabral a seminar in Guinea-Bissau that would include the five African countries liberated from Portuguese colonialism. The purpose of this seminar would be to discuss the politics of language planning and literacy training in their respective countries. We wanted to see a general discussion about the politics of culture, within which you find the politics of language.

It was at this seminar that I became absolutely convinced that Portuguese could never be a viable language in the literacy campaign. I then wrote a letter to Mário Cabral in which I reiterated the impossibility of continuing to do literacy work in Portuguese. In this letter I also analyzed the consequences of insisting upon using Portuguese as the only vehicle of education. One consequence, for instance, is that while Portuguese would function as the official language, it would have to assume the role of the national languages as well.

Why? To the extent that you expect a language given official status to become the mediating force in the education of youth, you are understandably asking this language to assume the role of national language. It would be inconceivable to expect Brazil, for example, to adopt Spanish as the only language of education if Brazil were to undergo a revolutionary process, Cuban-style, or in another example that might better serve the interest of the Brazilian bourgeoisie, to implement English as the sole language of instruction and business.

In my letter to Mário Cabral, I said that the exclusive use of Portuguese in education would result in a strange experience characterized by Portuguese as a superstructure that would trigger an exacerbation of class divisions, and this in a society that was supposed to be re-creating itself by breaking down social classes.

To continue to use Portuguese in Guinea-Bissau as the mediating force in the education of youth and to continue the practice of selecting students on the basis of their knowledge of spoken and written Portuguese would guarantee that only the children of the elite would be able to advance educationally, thus reproducing an elite, dominant class. The people of Guinea-Bissau would again find themselves locked out of the educational system and higher economic and political echelons. For these reasons I made proposals for an alternative to using Portuguese as the language of instruction.

Macedo: Why didn't you include in *Letters to Guinea-Bissau* the letter you wrote to Mário Cabral in 1977, in which you raised these concerns about the role of Portuguese in the literacy campaign?

Freire: I did not include this letter for political reasons, among other things. I knew that in Guinea-Bissau, as well as in Cape Verde, the question of the Portuguese language in education was not only a problem, but also was not discussed openly. I was familiar with the high level of ideology regarding the issue of language. This was easy to understand, given that the Portuguese colonizers spent centuries convincing the people of Guinea-Bissau that their languages were ugly and that Portuguese was more cultivated.

The colonizers spent centuries trying to impose their language. They did this by decree, giving the impression that the national languages were naturally inferior, that they were only tribal dialects. Creole was also viewed as a mixed and corrupted jargon, and thus could not be considered a natural language. This profile was established by colonizers (only those in power can profile others) and forced upon the people of Guinea-Bissau; and it was never rejected, even during the war for liberation. Many leaders of Guinea-Bissau were still influenced by these myths while being linguistically assimilated and colonized.

One of my great struggles in these ex-Portuguese colonies was to affirm the viability of the national languages. I am reminded of a radio debate I had in São Tomé in which the minister of education stated that the language of education in São Tomé had to be the Portuguese of Camões.[1] I remember

---

1. An illustrious Portuguese poet (1524–80) and the author of the Portuguese masterpiece *Os Lusíadas.*

responding to him by saying that even in Lisbon today one cannot teach the Portuguese of Camões, much less in São Tomé, where the majority of people do not even speak or understand Portuguese.

To a certain extent, I respected the divisions among these ex-colonies regarding language planning because I am not an imperialist. But I never missed an opportunity to let them know my real concerns about the role of Portuguese in education.

I did not publish the letter I had written to Mário Cabral because, as I have said, I felt the timing was not appropriate with respect to greater political concerns. I remember that in the last conversation I had with President Luís Cabral before he was ousted, he said: "Comrade Paulo, I can understand the controversy among ourselves concerning the language issue." I said that I understand the negative reactions of many of the leaders regarding national languages, but that it is necessary to have courage. It is necessary, in fact, to tell the world that you are not going to do to your own people what even the Portuguese colonizers could not do. That is, you should not attempt to eradicate the national languages and impose Portuguese. You need to take a stand and abandon the notion of teaching the Portuguese alphabet, so to speak.

I could not have said these things in public at that time. Today I can say them.

Macedo: Are you sorry for not having taken a public position on the linguistic issue in Guinea-Bissau?

Freire: No, because often there are reasons of a political character that require silence from the intellectual, even if this silence is sometimes misinterpreted. I assumed this silence and today I have broken it because I believe now is the time to talk about these issues. With or without Paulo Freire it was impossible in Guinea-Bissau to conduct a literary campaign in a language that was not part of the social practice of the people. My method did not fail, as has been claimed. Nor did it fail in Cape Verde or São Tomé. In São Tomé and Cape Verde there is a history of bilingualism. And even though bilingualism was less prevalent in Cape Verde than in São Tomé, it was still possible to learn some Portuguese with or without my help.

This issue should be analyzed in terms of whether it is linguistically viable to conduct literacy campaigns in Portuguese in any of these countries. My method is secondary to this analysis. If it is not viable to do so, my method or any other method will certainly fail. The letter to Mário Cabral analyzes the viability of the Portuguese language, as well as the political and cultural consequences if a linguistic colonialization were to continue in this newly liberated nation.

Macedo: One problem some evaluators have in considering your work is that they ask technocratic questions, ignoring the political, cultural, and ideological dimensions of both your theories and practices. It could be that they overemphasize the mechanical acquisition of reading while they fail to assess the development of a critical attitude on the part of learners, that is, the extent to which learners in literacy campaigns become aware of their civic and political responsibilities. For example, to what extent do learners acquire an analytical attitude toward authority in their own daily existence? One should not apply quantitative means and methods to measure results that by their nature are qualitative. Can you comment more specifically on this evaluation problem?

Freire: First, in any evaluation of our involvement and contribution, the question to be asked should not be whether twenty, thirty, a hundred, a thousand, or more people mechanically learned how to spell in the Portuguese language. On the contrary, such an evaluation has to consider the extent to which we are also learned in the process of our involvement. For instance, one learns how difficult it is to remake a society, whether through revolution or otherwise; one cannot remake, reinvent, or reconstruct a society by means of a mechanical act. The reinvention of a society is a political act taking place in history. It is thus important to inquire into the difficulties of the reinvention of the society of Guinea-Bissau. It is also important to ask whether our involvement had any significance for the political educators of Guinea-Bissau.

Again, in this book I wrote with Faundez where I address some of these questions and criticisms about my work in Guinea-Bissau, I said that one day I would like to return to Guinea-Bissau and find the same openness, camaraderie, and political dimensions as before. I would like to return and talk with Mário Cabral, who received me with open arms. I would like to talk with all those comrades with whom I worked. I would ask them if, in our previous meetings and dialogues, some of our concerns had touched them. I would also ask them if these concerns had any impact on the reformulation of the educational process in Guinea-Bissau, as I believe this to be an important part of my evaluation.

Speaking of evaluation, I would again insist that the so-called failure of our work in Guinea-Bissau was not due to the "Freire method." This failure clearly demonstrated the inviability of using Portuguese as the only vehicle of instruction in the literary campaigns. This is a fundamental point.

The importance of our involvement should be measured against examples such as the one I used in my letter to Mário Cabral. A Guinean team was conducting an evaluation of the production work on the collective farm that they had created. One of the participants said in his native language (which was translated into Portuguese for me): "Before we did not know that we knew. Now we know that we knew. Because we today know that we knew, we can know even more."

This is such a discovery, such an affirmation, that it immediately becomes political and requires a political posture on the part of this man in the more general process of the reinvention of his country. This affirmation has to do with a critical theory of knowledge, resulting from the inviability of spelling in the Portuguese language. Among other things, this man discovered that he did not know before that he knew, but that now, for this reason, he discovered that he can know much more. I have asked myself what could have more value in a general evaluation of society that begins to find itself struggling against the colonizers.

A rapid and mechanical codification of the Portuguese language certainly could not have the same weight as the political awareness that was achieved during our debates on the learning of Portuguese. The mastery of the Portuguese alphabet does not compare with the political, epistemological comprehension of this man's presence in the world as a human being who can now know why he transforms himself. Without negating the probable need to master Portuguese or, even better, his own language, I cannot underestimate the significance of the second order of knowledge that this man acquired.

This is true precisely because there is no pedagogical experience that is not political in nature. This man's statements have great importance whether they are evaluated from a pedagogical or political perspective. To forget or, more manipulatively, to omit this critical aspect from the evaluation surpasses the limits of *ba-be-bi-bo-bu;* pure decodification of syllables are meaningless to those who have played a huge role in the reinvention of their society. The challenging task of reappropriating their culture and history could not be achieved through the language that negated their reality and attempted to eradicate their own means of communication.

Macedo: Do you think it is possible to conduct a literacy campaign in Portuguese in Cape Verde, where there is some degree of bilingualism in Portuguese and Creole?

Freire: From the political point of view it is not advisable to do so, for the many reasons we have already discussed. From the linguistic point of view, unlike Guinea-Bissau, where teaching in Portuguese is not possible, in Cape Verde it would be less violent to do so, particularly in urban areas, where the colonialist presence brought about some exposure to the Portuguese language and capitalist development required people to learn some Portuguese. I think, however, that Cape Verde should also opt for Creole as the official national language.

Macedo: We should not lose sight of the danger of reproducing those colonialist values that were, and still are, inculcated through the use of Portuguese. I believe it is impossible to re-Africanize the people through the medium that de-Africanized them. Even if it made sense linguistically (and I feel strongly that it does not), in political terms, any decision to continue to use Portuguese as the official language and the only vehicle of instruction in Cape Verde would seriously undermine the political goals set forth by Amilcar Cabral.

Freire: Then the ideal situation would be to stop literacy in Portuguese, attempt to accelerate the development of Creole, particularly the standardization of its written form, and begin gradually to substitute Creole for Portuguese as the language of instruction. Obviously this could not be done all at once. Just imagine the capital required to change the entire educational system overnight. Cape Verde would have to quickly translate into Creole all of the basic texts required by the curriculum. All of the texts on geography, reading, math, and science would have to be translated. Even teacher training in Creole would be no small accomplishment. But as in Tanzania, one could begin slowly to replace Portuguese through a transitional bilingual model in which Creole would play a greater role in education, while Portuguese would diminish considerably over time. Creole could be used effectively, for example, in the first ten years of schooling.

In this way, at some point you could substitute Creole for Portuguese in the early years of schooling and gradually Creole would be introduced in increasing amounts in all areas of the curriculum. This is what Tanzania did when they replaced English with Swahili. I am not sure whether Swahili is used today at the university level in Tanzania, but my impression is that primary and secondary education is conducted mostly in Swahili.

In any case, I think instruction in Creole is required, even from the perspective of those productive forces that may need Portuguese. And, of course, the people of Guinea-Bissau and Cape Verde can continue to learn Portuguese as a foreign language. But to take it for granted that Portuguese is the national language and the only vehicle for education is totally absurd. In São Tomé, where the degree of bilingualism is much higher than in Cape Verde, it would be somewhat easier. Even in the rural areas of São Tomé people seem to converse more easily in Portuguese. This could be attributed to the small size of the island.

Macedo: The issue of language instruction hides myriad problems that have led to the creation of a neocolonialist literacy campaign in Cape Verde and Guinea-Bissau under the guise of eliminating illiteracy. Even if literacy training in Portuguese were totally viable, we need to raise the crucial question as to what extent, whether successful or not, the continued use of Portuguese would debase the literacy campaign as well as the cultural capital of subordinate Cape Verdians. The debate over the viability of Portuguese as a vehicle for literacy in Cape Verde rests on the technical issue of whether Cape Verdian Creole is a valid and rule-governed system. I think the question to be raised has to be infinitely more political. We need to question the resistance to literacy in Creole supported by claims that Creole lacks a uniform orthography. Excuses like this are used to justify the present policy of using Portuguese as the only medium of instruction. We should ask why Cape Verdian Portuguese speakers rely on the common argument that Portuguese has international status and therefore guarantees upward mobility for Portuguese-speaking educated Cape Verdians. This position, by the way, implies the supposed superiority of the Portuguese language.

The sad reality is that while Portuguese may offer access to certain positions of political and economic power for high echelons of Cape Verdian society, it holds back the majority of the people, those who fail to learn Portuguese well enough to acquire the necessary level of literacy for social, political, and economic advancement. In fact, to continue to use the language of the colonizer as the only medium of instruction is to continue to provide manipulative strategies that support the maintenance of cultural domination. Thus, what is hidden in the technical debate concerning Cape Verdian language instruction is a resistance to re-Africanization, or perhaps a subtle refusal on the part of assimilated Cape Verdians to "commit class suicide." If we are to understand fully the political and ideological factors underlying the language issue, we must reorient our questions from a technical level to a more political level. Can you evaluate the political and ideological consequences of teaching only in Portuguese in Cape Verde?

Freire: This is a political question rooted in ideology. When I was in Cape Verde, President Aristides Pereira gave an excellent speech in which he said, "We threw the Portuguese colonialists out of our land and now we need to decolonialize our mentality." The decolonialization of mentality is much more difficult to achieve than the physical expulsion of the colonialist. Sometimes the colonizers are thrown out but they remain culturally, because they have been assimilated into the minds of the people they leave behind.

This terrible presence haunts the revolutionary process, and, in some cases, it hinders the movement toward liberation. Language does not remain unaffected. The more this colonialist presence haunts the assimilated spirits of the colonized people, the more they will reject their own language. In fact, language is so much a part of culture that by rejecting it, the reappropriation of one's culture becomes a revolutionary illusion.

The ex-colonialized in many ways continue to be mentally and culturally colonized. The colonized people were told either verbally or through message systems inherent in the colonial structure that they did not possess effective cultural instruments with which to express themselves. They possessed an ugly dialect, a bastardization of the colonial language. This language profile imposed by the colonizers eventually convinced the people that their language was in fact a corrupt and inferior system unworthy of true educational status.

People end up believing that the way they speak is savage. They become ashamed of speaking their own language, particularly in the presence of the colonialists who constantly proclaim the beauty and superiority of their own language. The colonizers' behaviors and tastes, including language, are the models that were imposed by the colonial structure over centuries of oppression. At some point the ex-colonized internalize these myths and feel ashamed.

I remember a story you told me concerning a Cape Verdian who vehemently denied that he spoke Creole, but at parties constantly sang in Creole. When confronted with the fact that if he sang Creole so well he must also speak it, he defensively stated that he only knew how to sing but not speak Creole. Maybe he was not aware of it, but he was totally assimilated into the cultural value system of the colonialists. He was convinced that he did not speak his own native language. In fact, he forbade himself to speak his own language. This process is sometimes unconscious. It is the colonializers' ghost whispering in his ears, "Your language is no good . . . it is savage."

You are absolutely right in your analysis of the language issues in ex-colonialized countries. I have always said in my conversations with the people of Guinea-Bissau, Cape Verde, São Tomé, Angola, and Mozambique that the expression "Portuguese Africa" is a misnomer. When intellectuals from these countries use the term, I always tell them that there is no Africa of the Portuguese, nor of the French, nor of the English. There is an Africa upon which the Portuguese language was imposed at the expense of the native languages. If viewed from this perspective, the notion of Portuguese Africa hides the true linguistic issue.

I think we can safely say that in exceptional cases Cape Verdians should study Portuguese, but only as a second language.

Translated by Donaldo Macedo

5

LEARNING TO QUESTION:
A PEDAGOGY OF LIBERATION

Learning to Question

António Faundez: I think that in this conversation of ours we could take as our starting point either particular themes or our actual experience. In the first case, we would discuss particular concepts, how they can be applied to actual situations, how they in fact change as they are applied to different situations, etc. In the second case, we could speak of our experiences in Africa and Latin America, experiences which are common to us both, or even those which are not.

Paulo Freire: Or it could be a combination of the two. Let's accept both possibilities and so give ourselves freedom of scope so that each of us will spontaneously make our particular contribution to the development of the themes. I think it's a good idea.

Why a "Spoken" Book?

Anyway, I think that we ought to give a sort of introduction in dialogue form to this book that we are beginning to "speak," an introduction in the course of which we would not only indicate the themes or experiences we are going to deal with, but already engage in some reflection on them.

I also think, for example, that it would be interesting to tell our readers that the idea of making this book together, even if it didn't actually come to birth, was revived one evening in your home, about six months ago, accompanied by some good Chilean wine, and some equally good *empanadas* as well.

So here we are again today in Geneva, in your office, to begin the task we set ourselves. And I have the impression that at the outset of this shared task we should tell those who tomorrow will pick up this book to read it something about the reason for a book like this, the reason for a "spoken" book, rather than a book written by us both—some chapters by you, and some by me—or two books, one written by you and the other by me. And so we shall both begin our conversation. I shall say my piece and then you will say yours. In that way we shall draw each other out in this first session, and at the same time prepare ourselves for the experience of "speaking" the book so as to bring our project to fruition.

I would venture to tell our readers at this stage something about the reason for a book like this.

First of all, I don't know whether you will agree with me but I believe that this is an interesting intellectual experience, a rich and truly creative experience. An experience which is, in fact, not unknown to me. I have been working in this way for two years and nothing has happened to suggest to me that I should stop doing it.

In fact, "speaking" a book with one or two others instead of writing it alone represents to some extent at least a break with a certain individualistic tradition in the production of books, and—why not admit it?—by taking us out of the pleasant cosiness of our study, it opens us up to each other in the adventure of thinking critically.

In our case now, thinking about the practical work, with its many different aspects in which we were involved, sometimes together and sometimes separately. And this thinking, which is basically a rethinking, has to do on the one hand with what I did together with others directly in Africa and other parts of the world when I was working here with the World Council of Churches, and which I often discussed with you; and, on the other hand, it has to do with what you went on to do when you took over from me in the Education Department of the Council when I returned to Brazil in June 1980.

I can remember, for example, some work we did together, although not in the dialogue form in which we are doing this book. I am thinking of the texts for the literacy campaigns and post-literacy campaigns in São Tomé e Príncipe—which we wrote separately, but submitted to each other for discussion.

I have no intention at all of denying the value of writing a book alone, and both of us, as will countless intellectuals, will continue to write individually. But I am convinced of the value of our producing a book together in dialogue form, and so here we are seated at this table "speaking" our book. And, in so doing, we are consenting, responsibly, to expose ourselves to the meaningful experience of sharing in a common task.

This does not mean, however, in any way that this shared commitment will deny or cancel out what is distinctively mine or yours, as an expression of our deepest selves, in the final joint product. I find this shared work, this dialogue experience, immensely interesting. As I said just now, I am doing it in Brazil, and I have just experienced something similar in Canada, in Vancouver, where I "spoke" a book with an outstanding North American intellectual, Ira Shor. In it we attempted to respond to some of the issues which he and I have picked up in our visits to various university centres in the USA and Canada. I must say that this sort of experience has enriched me, but I must also say, repeating what I've just said, that being involved in it does not mean giving up writing by myself. And this is what is happening to you, too. But I do think that committing ourselves from time to time to the task of creative work together in an attempt to overcome the temptation to be always alone, to write alone, is a meaningful and valuable intellectual exercise. The experiences we talk about, discuss critically, and which are now being recorded on tape will come out in a lively, free, spontaneous and dynamic conversation. It's important, nonetheless, to stress that the liveliness of the conversation, the lightness of the spoken word, the spontaneity of the dialogue are not in themselves a denial of the serious intent of this work or its requisite intellectual rigor. There are people who have the naive idea that rigorous analysis can only take place when you shut yourself up within four walls behind a door securely locked with a large key! Only there, in the silent intimacy of library or laboratory can serious scientific work go on! No, I think that here, in privacy, yes, but at the same time open to the world, including the world of nature outside your office, we can engage in serious and rigorous thought—and are doing so. The style is different, because the language is spoken—with a more colloquial touch, more feeling, more freedom.

Well, those are my first thoughts which I would like to share with the probable readers of this book on the reasons for a "spoken" book. I don't know whether you would like to add anything to what I've said by way of a continuation of this sort of informal joint introduction.

Faundez: I agree with your analysis, particularly with what you say about this break with intellectual cosiness, I mean, the attempt to make intellectual work a joint activity. And the method which best lends itself to this attempt is, without doubt, dialogue. In fact, you and I have been engaged in dialogue ever since we first met in November 1979, and the dialogue which began then has gone on ever since. And what we are doing today is simply a further stage in the history of our dialogue. As you will remember, it was through an interview with our friend Lígia Chiappini that we got to know each other and began our dialogue.

Freire: That's right. That interview with Lígia in which you took part was in a way a short trial run for what we are doing today.

Faundez: In that way our dialogue began at our very first meeting. After our interview with Lígia you invited me to work together with you, and from that time onward in the course of our work we have kept up a constant dialogue, particularly in connection with our experiences in São Tomé e Príncipe. Among these ongoing conversations, I remember one in particular, when the actual idea of a book, a recorded conversation, first came up. We were walking back from lunch at the ILO in Geneva, when in the middle of our conversation on conceptualization and the meaning of the power of intellectuals, you stood still and said to me: "Antonio, we should put all this on tape, because this conversation shouldn't be a conversation just between you and me: we should make it possible for others to share in it and share in conversation with us through our conversation." Do you remember?

Freire: Very well. Actually, that is where the earliest roots of the project for this book are to be found. Then, six months ago, I passed through here on my way back to São Paulo from the United States and we committed ourselves to begin "speaking" our book today. In fact, we have had within us the desire to hold this conversation, the interest in this project, as you rightly said, since 1979, when, through Lígia, our friendship began. Our openness to dialogue—which does not mean that we are always in agreement with each other—has been a constant feature of our friendship. It never ceased during the last part of my time here in Geneva, which coincided with your arrival, and it has been kept alive since then when I have been passing through Geneva. And so I agree with you when you say that our conversation is still going on even when we are a long way from each other. We only need to meet up again and we can take up the conversation more or less where we left off the last time. It's as if we were saying to each other: "As I was just saying . . ." I think, Antonio, as we continue this conversation by way of introduction, we should explore each other's past and present experiences and related issues. As we examine and discuss them, they will give content and breadth to our conversation.

Intellectuals in Exile

So, why don't you tell me, and tomorrow's readers, something about your experiences as a Chilean intellectual in exile? About your experience in Europe as a person who has been uprooted, not because you wanted to be, but because you were forced by history to be uprooted, which, in its turn, involves putting down new roots?

One of the basic problems facing exiles lies precisely in how to resolve the acute tension between being uprooted, of which they are victims, and the need to put down new roots, which can only be within certain limits. If you put down roots too deeply in your new environment, then you run the risk of denying your origins. But, if you put down no roots at all in your new environment, then you run the risk of being annihilated in a nostalgia which it will be difficult to free yourself from.

What has happened to you happened to me as well. I felt, as you are feeling, the ambiguity of being and not being in the situation of exile, but I grew in the course of that tragic experience. It is a mistake to think of exile in purely negative terms. It can also become a deeply enriching, deeply creative experience if, in the fight for survival, we exiles achieve a minimum of physical comfort. Here the question is whether we are capable or not of understanding the situation in which we are placed in exile and then learning from it.

I should like to press you to tell us something about your present experience of being uprooted and having to put down new roots. Tell us a little about being uprooted, about that break with your past, and the subsequent need to put down new roots as an existential affirmation of your new situation.

Faundez: Paulo, what you are asking me to do is to tell my whole life story, and all the experiences of my life, both intellectual and emotional, because exile is, as you say, a break with the past, and that break with the past is a negative, on which we must bring another negative to bear in order to achieve a positive result, as Hegel said. This is the challenge facing us intellectuals: we must overcome what is negative and reach a level where exile becomes in effect something positive, both regarding our work and regarding the help it can give to effect historical change. Therefore, it's impossible to reach an understanding of my exile without speaking of Chile. So I must explain, for example, that my work in Chile was basically at the level of ideas, of philosophy.

I was teaching philosophy at the university, but already at that time philosophy was being interpreted in a practical way. I and my colleagues in the department wanted to understand what was going on in Chile, we wanted to discover how ideas took concrete shape in action, in the myths of the social classes of Chile, in Chilean intellectuals. So we were not simply thinking about the great philosophical systems, about Hegel, Plato and Aristotle, but we were thinking of how ideas take concrete shape in the actions and minds of individuals and groups, in order to interpret the historic situation and change it, or not change it. Thus there was already in that experience a quest in the direction of concrete reality.

Freire: But, if I may, I shall now more or less play the part of a journalist—although I never was one! I know, in fact, a little about your life in Chile, which is after all the place which has left its mark on your personality as an intellectual and as a person. For that reason I think it important, simply for the sake of the continuity of our book itself, for you to say something more about your experience as professor of philosophy at the University of Concepción in Chile—a university which was, when I was there, highly thought of for the quality of its work.

I think it would be interesting for you to tell our readers a little about how, at this time when Gramsci was the great influence, as a young philosopher you taught this concrete philosophy to which you were referring. I think you ought to tell a bit more and not be so modest about it because, as you explain a little how you actually did philosophy at Concepción, you will be preparing our readers to follow your historic step, your going into exile, first in France and then in Switzerland. So as to understand your university work in Europe and even so as to understand your more recent outstanding academic work, which you began to do with the World Council of Churches when you took over from me in the Education Sub-unit. Academic work, but not of the ivory-tower sort, because ivory-tower academics occupy themselves with high-sounding words and descriptions of ideas, rather than with a critical understanding of the real world which, instead of being simply described, has to be changed. That is valid academic work in that it is concerned with the relation between practice and theory.

I would like you to say something more about Chile, and how you brought with you into exile the experience you gained in your native land.

Faundez: I'm afraid I couldn't. It would be impossible for me to speak of *my* experience: I would have to speak of the experience of *my generation*—the experience of a generation which lived and acted and was shaped in a particular context, which was shaped in a context which underwent rapid change as it was affected by the struggles of the people of Chile as they sought actually to change society and create a new society. And that was the process in which our generation was educated, with the stimulus of various international movements, such as liberation in Africa, the struggle of the Algerians against French colonialism, the Cuban revolution, and all those Latin American experiences, which were an invitation to us to change reality. It was impossible then for us students of philosophy or those just beginning their philosophical studies to keep ideas and this attempt at change in separate compartments. Philosophy was for us a means of analyzing the political situation in our land and our life in the real world. So studying Hegel, Marx, Sartre, or even ancient philosophy, was a way of assimilating certain ideas and developing the critical capacity to understand *our* situation, and not merely wrangling about the teaching of the philosophy of systems or of systems of philosophy.

I would say that we were studying philosophy in order to solve problems and not to learn about philosophical systems. And how did that work out in practice? I could say something, for example, about our approach to research: for us research didn't mean constructing a metaphysics of metaphysics. Rather it was understanding how ideas take concrete shape in the minds and actions of a culturally dependent people, like the Chilean people, particularly in the different social strata. One of the research projects we undertook was an attempt to understand the influence of mutualist, socialist, or anarchist thought among the workers of Lota e Schwager, a coal-mining district in Chile, during the period 1890–1925. These workers, who had come in from the countryside or the surrounding areas, had been ideologically educated in a distinctive traditional Roman Catholic world-view, which was totally alienating. What we wanted to see was how these two ideological elements—mutualist thought and Catholic education—functioned in the minds of the workers; what changes they underwent as they left the countryside for an industry which comprised a different social organization; what it meant for them to work together, to organize, and jointly present their demands, and so forth.

It is obvious that research of this type could not be traditional research. It was not possible to go along to a library to understand and solve the problem nor to refer to books written by other philosophers, in order to discover, for example, whether the concept used by such and such a thinker was correctly used or not, or whether the origin of a particular word was this or that, and so on. This type of research required other sources. Where were they to be found? How could we discover the elements which could help us understand this process of ideological change? They were, for example, to be found in conversations with those who had lived through the period in question.

We had to find the original sources. We had to go and talk with those who had lived through that historic period—the oldest miners who had been working at that time. We had to seek out contemporary newspapers, disciplinary acts by the company against union leaders; we had to find out the penalties imposed on them simply because they wanted to organize, how they defended themselves in the courts, and where they got their ideas from, particularly the anarchists.

Strangely enough, Paulo, in our research we discovered that members of the working class felt a sort of moral obligation to record their experiences, and we found diaries which tell the whole story. Family and personal details and desperate defences made by individuals intermingle with what was going on in society, the strikes then taking place, the role of the church, the guards in the mines, who were a veritable private army. All of it, Paulo, expressed in living language, the language of history as it is being made. Unfortunately, all this has now been lost with the *coup d'état*. The diaries have disappeared and are lost for ever. It is amazing how a *coup d'état* can destroy a whole area of a country's intellectual life.

How those diaries were read and discussed! And it was not done exclusively by the philosophy staff. The work was done by an interdisciplinary group made up of professors belonging to our generation, professors of history, literature, geography, political sciences and sociology. Everyone in the team brought their own particular perspective to the reading of these extraordinary notes written by a worker. And each one interpreted the texts from the point of view of their own specialty. The literature specialist interpreted them as literary texts; the sociologist performed the analysis from a sociological standpoint, establishing what social strata were involved and what role they played, etc.; and the philosopher attempted to understand the ideological struggle. All this brought us together in meetings which were quite fantastic, real occasions of collective learning and teaching. The joint seminars with the students were truly impressive, Paulo. I believe that there, in the study of real situations, students and professors alike, we were learning how to do philosophy, we were learning history, literature and sociology. And each one of these disciplines was directly related to the actual situation of the country, and was not imprisoned in transcendental alien realities.

Freire: I think I can understand the direction taken by your research, how you attempted to reach a critical historical understanding of a particular moment in the life of Chile at the end of the last century and the beginning of this, how you understood critically the position of workers in the clash of ideologies. And I can see, for example, how it was possible on that basis to find an entry point into the contemporary experience of Chile and to study with the students the power of ideologies. I lived in your country—which I reckon to be mine as well—before Allende came to power. I left Chile in 1969, but I returned during the Allende regime, at the time when you were working in Concepción. Now, hearing you speak about the very lively research which you were doing, I can imagine the rich contribution which that material could have made to the debate on the contemporary situation of Chile at that time—how it was possible to see the past as shedding light on what was happening then.

I regard the teaching and research that you were doing with your colleagues then as so significant that I would like you to say a little more about it, because, basically, all this is what you were later going to bring with you into exile in Europe. All this very lively past of yours, together with your colleagues, your generation—as a young, aware philosopher, you brought all this with you in your memory, including those diaries which you were not able to bring. So I think it is essential for those who will be our readers for you to tell us something more about all that you brought with you into exile.

Faundez: It was, of course, an experience which left its mark on me and on my intellectual future. You will understand how difficult it is to go into exile when you don't want to.

Freire: Only too well! No one, in fact, ever chooses to go into exile!

Faundez: You were asking me how I was able to continue my work, an experience which, once begun, you cannot escape from, because you have discovered what real intellectual work is: work in which theory and practice and all intellectual activity is done with the aim of understanding reality and, if possible, of changing it. That is work that does not get lost in a mere play of ideas.

So then what plans did I have for myself in Europe? I planned to make a political analysis of positivism in Chile, which was my sociology thesis in Paris. Because the world of Europe was not my Latin American world, or, more exactly, the world which was mine in Chile, in Concepción. It was a different world, in which I did not participate politically. My intellectual work did not have a foundation in concrete history in the sense that it manifested itself in concrete action deeply rooted in a historical situation. But the research which I planned to do was only apparently traditional. In fact it was an attempt at an interpretation of positivism in Chile from a political standpoint: tracing how this ideology determined behavior, justifications, actions, explanations, interpretations of the situation in Chile by certain intellectuals and certain social groups; studying how social groups used ideologies to remain in power or to come to power—the political use of ideology. In that sense it was not traditional research, but a new sort of research, a fresh interpretation, a *political interpretation* of positivism in Chile, which included sociological interpretation, etc. In it, therefore, ideas were considered in action and not as part of an abstract history of ideas.

This program of research inevitably involved me in working basically with documents in the traditional sense of the term. Thanks to that, I was given the opportunity to discover, in Paris, many unpublished texts by Chileans who were the ideologues of this positivism which has marked the cultural, intellectual and political history of Chile, and which played a very important role in the thought and action of Balmaceda, the first anti-imperialist Latin American president. In his fight against British imperialism on the basis of nationalism, Balmaceda's aim was to change a dependent nation into an independent nation. Positivism was of undeniable importance for this, and its most comprehensive statement was the political analysis done by the group of intellectuals and by the social strata connected with Balmaceda, a particular interpretation of positivism which was to result in action to change the situation.

I should add, however, that this was not the only form of positivism to be found in Chile at the time. There was the version of the so-called heterodox positivists, who interpreted the positivist ideology in a different way and were opposed to the orthodox approach of Balmaceda's supporters. This shows the complexity of the ideological struggle of the time, which I have attempted to describe in my thesis. But, anyway, it cannot be denied that this work was more removed from reality than that which I had previously been doing. And here, Paulo, I must recall that our meeting enabled me to rediscover reality. Our meeting each other led to your enabling me to work again with the people, with people who at that time were making their own history.

Freire: You've just mentioned something in which I was personally involved. You referred to when we first met, when I proposed that as soon as possible we should enter into a regular conversation with each other, which finally gave you the opportunity to experience a real life situation once again, even though it was not your own, an experience which was very necessary for you at that time.

While you were recalling that meeting, I was reminded of something which an old friend, the great Brazilian philosopher Alvaro Vieira Pinto, said to me one autumn afternoon in Santiago. Dejected and sad, he said to me: "Paulo, when you are in exile, you are living a borrowed life." As an exile too, no one could appreciate better than I what he was saying. Ever since then I have quoted his words from time to time, but not always mentioning that conversation. Now, as I quote them in this spoken book, I feel I must make a point of giving their source.

That's exactly it: "When you are in exile, you are living a borrowed life." Exiles have to learn—as you have, as I have, and as many of our friends, Chileans, Brazilians, and from other countries, have—to live in a constant state of tension—radically existential, historical tension—between our original world which we have left behind, and our new borrowed world. Precisely as you do that, amid all the longing for the past, you begin to experience, not a numbing asphyxiation of your present, but a flame shedding light on the need to put down roots in your new environment.

Only as exiles learn to live in their new environment, to stand apart from it but still remain in it, experiencing the tension of their two opposing environments—the one which shaped them, which they consciously bear with them in their bodies and with which they are impregnated, and their new one—only so can they maintain a continuing interest in their original environment without it casting an inhibiting shadow on their present.

Your body is impregnated, as is that of any exile, with your original environment, with its history and culture. Impregnated with the dreams you dreamed there, the struggles you were involved in, your commitment to the working classes. Impregnated with your hopes and ideals for that world.

Wherever exiles finally settle, they tend to experience from the moment they arrive the ambiguous feeling of freedom on the one hand, freedom at having escaped from something threatening them, and on the other of having suffered a tragic break in their history.

Learning to live with that ambiguity is difficult but it has to be done. You have to learn to cope with the tension, the break with your past brought about by exile. You must not make the break any greater than it is. Exiles have to learn to live with that tension, without on the one hand denying their original environment, as if it were possible to disown it, as if, in anger at having had to leave it behind, they were trying to punish it by saying "I don't remember you," and on the other without rejecting their borrowed environment. If they do succeed in doing so, then their time of waiting in exile, actively waiting, will become for them a time of hope.

That is why I spoke of the tension of the opposition between your original environment and your new environment. Either we learn to surmount the negativity caused by the break with the past, so as to discover and seize the opportunities presented by the new environment, or else we perish in exile. And you and I both know quite a few cases of friends who could not cope with this tension, who could not stand up to it. One way I have discovered, Antonio, which other exiles have also discovered, is precisely to have a continuing interest in my original environment, without however using that interest as mere psychotherapy. On the other hand, you have to make a certain level of affective, emotional and intellectual investment in your borrowed environment. And if and when possible, on that basis, with sufficient political clarity, to move out into other areas which might open up to us as fields of action. So, when, while I was still in Chile, I received the invitation from Harvard University and three or four days later the invitation from the World Council of Churches (Harvard was inviting me for two or three years beginning in 1969, and so was the World Council of Churches, the only difference being a few months in the starting date), that was why I proposed to Harvard to go there until the beginning of February 1970 and to the World Council of Churches to begin my contract with them in mid-February that same year. I thought that it was very important for me as a Brazilian intellectual in exile to pass through, albeit rapidly, the centre of capitalist power. As I said to my Brazilian and Chilean friends whom I left in Santiago, I needed to see the animal close to on its home territory. But on the other hand, I was by then already absolutely convinced how useful and fundamental it would be for me to travel the world, be exposed to various environments, learn of other people's experiences and to take a fresh look at myself through the cultural differences. And, indisputably, the Council was offering me that more than any university.

One question I asked myself concerned the opportunity of systematic teaching presented by the university but not by the Council. But the essential element in that, however, could be experienced in the work that the Council was offering me, in that I would only give up the work with regular students which a university post involves. But with the Council, I would still have practical political-pedagogical work and research, as well as the opportunity of wide contacts with countless universities. So with the Council I continued, and indeed expanded, my work as an educationalist.

Harvard and the World Council of Churches accepted my proposal. I left with Elza and the children for Cambridge, Mass., where, apart from Harvard, I shared in an interesting programme with a good group of intellectuals, Jim Lamb, Joao Coutinho, Denis Goullet, Denise Loreta Slover, among others, at the Center for the Study of Development and Social Change, now sadly closed.

There in Cambridge we made the final preparations for my coming to Geneva, Finally, in February 1970, I began a new stage in my career, which at the time I could not foresee would later be fundamental in my personal life and also as an educationalist.

I knew that the World Council of Churches, I must repeat, was not a university, but I also knew that, by working in its Education Department, I would be continuing and expanding my work as an educationalist. People like you and me (I hope readers will forgive this lack of modesty, which you are not responsible for!) do not need classrooms in order to be educationalists, however much we may love them and do not dispense with them.

Basically, a university, however good, however famous or however great, gave me the opportunity to work, in term, with groups of students—twenty, say, or thirty. But the World Council of Churches was offering me a worldwide chair, not the sphere of a university, but of the whole world. It was offering me the largest possible environment, its various experiences, a vision of some of its tragedies, its situations of poverty, its disasters, but also some of its beautiful moments—the liberation of the peoples of Africa, the Nicaraguan revolution, the revolution in Grenada.

In the course of covering this vast field of activity given me by the World Council I became a world traveller. It was by travelling all over the world, it was by travelling through Africa, it was by travelling through Asia, through Australia and New Zealand, and through the islands of the South

Pacific, it was by travelling through the whole of Latin America, the Caribbean, North America and Europe—it was by passing through all these different parts of the world as an exile that I came to understand my own country better. It was by seeing it from a distance, it was by standing back from it, that I came to understand myself better. It was by being confronted with another self that I discovered more easily my own identity. And thus I overcame the risk which exiles sometimes run of being too remote in their work as intellectuals from the most real, most concrete experiences, and of being somewhat lost, and even somewhat contented, because they are lost in a game of words, what I usually rather humorously call "specializing in the ballet of concepts."

So when you say to me now that the invitation I gave you in this building on the fourth floor where I had my office all those years ago enabled you to work with people struggling to make their own history and that that helped you as an exile, I feel very happy. However, I must make it clear that that invitation was not gratuitous nor given out of a desire to help! Oh no! At our first meeting I had already sensed the seriousness of your quest, your honest way of searching, your curiosity. On the other hand, I also sensed that your creativity and your critical capacity could help me in the research I was doing. But I was also equally very certain, when I consulted you as to your willingness to discuss concretely with me the experiments in which I was involved, that, by that invitation which at that moment opened up new paths for you, I was helping you to confront the existential tension you were experiencing as an exile in the conflict between your original environment and your new, borrowed environment.

Let me say in conclusion that it was precisely this opportunity to lay hold on the real, the concrete, which saved me as an exile and as a person. In saying all this I must have been rather emotional, but I don't think there's anything wrong in that!

Faundez: I am emotionally very happy with your analysis. I am very happy that we are having this conversation. The interesting thing about it is that it does not only have an intellectual content: it also has an emotional, real-life content.

I completely agree with you, Paulo, particularly with one of your points: how to surmount your lot as an exile. For exiles, there is this tension between their original environment, which has educated and changed and shaped them for the whole of their lives, and their *new environment*, which must be relived and to which they must adapt, or not, and which they must assimilate, or not. I believe that, in order to surmount this negative experience, we need to set a conversation going between these two environments.

For our environment to become yet richer, mentally, physically and emotionally, I think we need to discover a different environment. Basically, as you know, as we all know, in order to discover ourselves, we need to see ourselves in the other, to understand the other in order to understand ourselves, to enter into the other.

According to Fichte, the "I" creates the "not-I" in order to know itself. Now, we do not create the "not-I"—we are not philosophical idealists. Our "not-I" is not of our creating: it is objective. The "not-I" is this borrowed environment, as you put it, which is essential for the enrichment of our lives and of our original environment. "It was the world which helped me to understand and comprehend my own country better." That idea of yours I have developed in a short summary I made in English of your book *Der Lehrer ist Politiker und Künstler.*

I should like to emphasize one important aspect of your intellectual experience: it was precisely your work in Africa and Asia which not only enabled you to discover Africa and Asia, but also to discover, or rediscover, what your own country, Brazil, was really like. That's the positive side of it.

I, too, gained a better understanding of Latin America, and of Chile in particular, through understanding other countries and other experiences. And I would add that I came to a better understanding of the village where I come from and where I was born. Because basically, I think that my great university has been the two small villages of Lebu and Pehuen, where I experienced childhood and adolescence. Lebu is a mining area, the poorest in Chile. Lebu is where I taught my father to read and write—my father who would turn his hand to anything, sometimes working as a peasant, sometimes as a workman. Pehuen was an Indian village where I used to go and work in my school holidays. I would spend three months among the Indians, living as a peasant, sharing their hard life, and working in the fields from five in the morning to midnight, in order to earn a sack of wheat, a sack of oats, a sack of food. Lebu and Pehuen were the two great universities which were to shape my intellectual life.

It is not surprising that both names are of Araucanian origin. Lebu *(leufu)* means "river," and Pehuen is the name of a tree *(Araucaria araucana),* the fruit of which is one of the staple foods of that native people. In Lebu, among other things, I experienced the people's solidarity in the fight for survival and a better life. In Pehuen, I discovered the importance of writing as a means of exploitation, or as a weapon in the fight against exploitation, depending on who is using it. On this last point, I can remember how, when I was working in an Araucanian family as one of them during my student holidays, I and they discovered the importance of being able to read and do sums.

They were a family of sharecroppers. That meant that they would receive from the landowner seeds, some tools and a plot of land to cultivate. The crop they produced was divided as follows: first of all, the owner took out the seed he had lent; then the hire charge for the use of the harvester (10–20%); and, lastly, what was left over was divided into two, one half for the owner and one half for the family.

When the crop was divided, which was done at threshing time, the sacks were weighed by the foreman, who was the only one who could read and write. One day I realized that as he weighed the sacks he was noting down inaccurate figures, lower than those shown on the scales. On discovering this, I went to the head of the family and told him what I had found out. He was afraid of accusing the owner's representative of theft, but he asked me to undertake to note down the figures so that we could do our own sums. I told the foreman that I had been asked to note down the weight of the sacks, so that we too could do the calculation and determine how much was due to us. The foreman had no alternative but to accept this "innocent" request. So we became aware of the importance of writing for the people in their struggle against injustice.

And when you made it possible for me to return to that sort of situation, it was in a way as if I was going back to my childhood, to my two universities of childhood and adolescence, in order to struggle alongside the people against the injustices which I had already experienced at that time and which have continued and evolved up to the present day.

Paulo, I would like to put a question to you about living in exile. People have the impression that going into exile is simply an emotional break with the past at the level of ideas. But exile also involves—and I'm sure you'll agree with me here—all the details of everyday life. So I should like to ask you to tell us, exiles and non-exiles, a little about how you have experienced everyday life in this different environment from your original one.

Everyday Life in Exile

Freire: I believe that this is a basic question which we exiles must ask ourselves every day. I mean, ask ourselves every day how we are understanding this borrowed daily life we are living as exiles, and how it is possible, for example, to operate in it more effectively and less traumatically.

My starting point, the beginning of my experience of a different way of daily living, was precisely in Chile, your country, which I now reckon mine as well. Of course, in a very much less dramatic way than in Europe. After all, Chile, despite its being a somewhat Europeanized country, is in essence Latin American.

One of the first lessons which living in exile taught me, as I took my first steps in the environment that was receiving me, as regards living as opposed to merely surviving in a different daily setting, was that cultures are not better or worse than one another, that the ways in which cultures express themselves are not better or worse than one another: they are simply different. Like ourselves, on the other hand, culture is not static, it is constantly evolving, and we cannot forget its class character. That first lesson, that you just can't simply say that cultures are better or worse than one another, I learned in Chile, when I began to experiment in real-life situations, with different cultural forms—even something as simple as attracting someone else's attention. I don't know whether you have noticed, for example, how difficult it is in a restaurant in a strange culture to attract the attention of the waiter! Each culture has its own particular way, which must not be departed from. There is a certain code of behavior, isn't there? I remember one occasion in Chile, in the Ministry of External Relations—I don't know whether that is what it is called or whether it is Foreign Affairs. Anyway, I had a problem to sort out concerning a document I needed for residence in the country. I stood at the counter in the office and no one attended to me. No one looked in my direction. Suddenly, an official looked up and saw me. I made a gesture to him with my hand to indicate that I was waiting. The man came up to me, and in the voice of one highly offended, told me that that was not a polite way in which to attract someone's attention. In my surprise I for once became totally indecisive. I blurted out: "I had no intention of offending you, sir. I am Brazilian . . . ." "You may be Brazilian, but you are in Chile, and in Chile we don't do that," he said categorically. "Well, then, I apologize again. I apologize for what you took to be offensive in my gesture, not because I intended to offend you, because I didn't. I mean, subjectively, I had no intention of offending you, but, objectively, I did offend you." What a mysterious thing culture is! He attended to me, but I don't know whether he understood me, and I went out into the street deep in thought. How we need to understand the most minor details of everyday life!

We inevitably make comparisons between cultural expressions, those of our own environment and those of our borrowed environment, but if we don't try, Antonio, to understand critically what is different, we run the risk of making rigid value judgments which are always negative towards the culture which is unfamiliar to us.

For me, that is always a false and dangerous attitude. Respecting the different culture, and respecting our own also, does not imply, however, denying our preference for this or that feature of our original environment or for this or that feature of our borrowed environment. Such an approach even reveals a certain degree of maturity—which we sometimes achieve and sometimes don't—which is indispensable as we expose ourselves critically to cultural differences.

We must always be aware of one thing as we learn these lessons from cultural differences, and that is that culture cannot be lightly judged by simply saying "this is better" or "that is worse." But by that I do not mean that cultures do not have negative features which have to be surmounted.

An exercise which I had earlier set myself in Brazil some years previously was to expose myself as an educationalist to cultural differences from the point of view of social class, without ever imagining that in a way I was preparing myself for the necessity to understand cultural differences which I was later to experience in exile. Class differences and also regional differences. Questions of taste, not only as regards the color of the clothes you wear and how you furnish a room, the practice of hanging photographs on the walls (which I don't like), but also taste as regards food, what seasoning you use. People's preference at dances for having the sound of the music turned up high. Distinctive differences in language, in sentence construction and meaning. My long exposure to these differences has taught me that to hold on to my class prejudices against them would be a fatal denial of my political stance. It has also taught me that actually to overcome their negative aspects, which requires change in the material basis of society, means that the working classes must assume their role as subject in their effort to revive the expressions of their culture.

But that's already another conversation . . .

Basically all this has taught me a lot. It has taught me to have an attitude, to practice a virtue which I reckon to be fundamental, not only from the political standpoint, but also existentially: *tolerance.*

Tolerance doesn't in any way imply giving up what seems to you to be right and just and good. No, tolerant people do not give up their dreams:

they are determined to fight for them. But they do respect those who have a different dream from themselves.

For me, at the political level, tolerance is the wisdom or virtue of being able to live with what is different so as to be able to fight the common enemy. In that sense it is a revolutionary virtue and not a liberal-conservative virtue.

You see, Antonio, living in exile, experiencing a different everyday life, has taught me tolerance to an extraordinary degree. This learning to live in a different daily setting began, as I've already said, in Chile, developed in the United States in my year in Cambridge, and continued during my ten years of life in Geneva. And it is amazing how I succeeded—and it wasn't easy—in becoming truly integrated into a different world, a different everyday life, with certain values which are, for example, a feature of day-to-day life in a city like Geneva, and are part of a culture which is multicultural, as Swiss culture is.

It was fantastic how I learned the rules of the game, consciously, without giving up what seemed to me to be essential, without denying what I basically was, and so without conforming to my borrowed environment. In that way I learned to cope with differences which I at times found annoying. One of these differences which I learned to live with, but which never became part of my being, was a certain connection, not always explicit or universal, between the human body and sin. In Europe and the United States, this connection was often evident in the way people behaved. Of course, the younger generation is learning in practice to transcend this virtual denial of the body. I have always found this cold remoteness of the body an embarrassment and quite extraordinary. It is the human body, young or old, fat or thin, of whatever color, the conscious body, that looks at the stars. It is the body that writes. It is the body that speaks. It is the body that fights. It is the body that loves and hates. It is the body that suffers. It is the body that dies. It is the body that lives! It has not been unusual for me to put my hand affectionately on someone's shoulder only to find my hand suddenly in mid-air, while the body I wanted to touch shrunk away refusing contact with mine.

When I am speaking with someone I usually emphasize some of my points by lightly tapping the body of my listener, and it is difficult for me to refrain from doing it.

Another of these differences has to do with the question of feelings, which, it is said, should be expressed in a controlled way out of respect for others. Feelings of happiness, sadness, tenderness, affection and endearment—all of them must be rigorously disciplined.

I can still remember the mingled pleasure and surprise on the face of a European colleague, who worked as a secretary in one of the Council's sub-units, when, on meeting her at the entrance to the building one spring morning, I warmly complimented her on the bright colors and stylishness of her clothes, all of it (I said) matching so well her young, vivacious air. She was somewhat disconcerted, and then pulled herself together and said to me simply: "You're joking."

For me, this much-vaunted respect for others has also in a way to do with a certain fear of becoming committed. I mean, to the extent that I close up, shut myself up, to the extent that I don't express happiness at seeing you, for example, in talking and discussing, I can throw up an emotional barrier between me and you, which warns you not to enter into my territory to request something, to ask for greater commitment from me. That was something else I had to cope with. And that was difficult as well, because as a person from the Northeast of Brazil I have a warm personality and sometimes cannot contain myself. So, without ceasing to be myself, I have had to control myself so as not to hurt others.

Running through all this is the tension of which we have already spoken a lot, the break with the past, the problem of knowing how far you can go, which raises the question of how far we can express our feelings. We must not go too far either way. If we give in too much, we compromise the roots of our being. If we go far beyond the bounds of what is acceptable, we provoke the natural reaction from our environment, which we have, as it were, invaded. And when we invade territory which is not our own, we are punished. You are constantly learning.

Another sensitive area in daily life in Geneva—which is, however, not unique to Geneva—which caused me a lot of trouble, was the question of silence, and of what people considered to be an acceptable level of noise. I shall never forget the occasion when a neighbor of ours rang our doorbell insistently at ten past ten at night. I opened the door. He managed a polite "good evening" and told of his dissatisfaction at not being able to get to sleep because of my son's violin playing.

Joaquim, who now teaches classical violin at the Fribourg conservatoire, was then in his 'teens, and was diligently studying for six hours every day. He was practicing a Bach suite, and our neighbor couldn't get to sleep! So at ten past ten he had come down to complain!

I can remember how, with some humor, I said: "It's interesting how different we are. Bach can send me to sleep!" He left as politely as he had appeared. I told Joaquim, who stopped playing his violin. And our neighbor would have slept in peace.

There are a lot of stories, some of them true, and others no doubt more the product of Latin American imagination, about silence and noise.

As regards this feature of Swiss everyday life, although it is not unique to Switzerland, I have never met a Latin American who did not have some story to tell about it or some complaint. Which brings us back once again to this question of limits. Without remaining too far on this side of the limits or going too far beyond them, we have to face up to them.

I believe, moreover, that the worst aspect of a culture which is so insistent on silence is the often thinly veiled feeling, intolerantly encouraged by society, against those whose bodies are the source of the rhythm, the sound and the voice that can be heard, considering them to be representative of inferior uncivilized cultures. Intolerance is always prejudiced.

As you know, Antonio, when you live alongside other people in their everyday lives, it is a constant learning experience. I always used to say this to the children at home. Because, you see, one of the basic features of our behavior in our everyday life is precisely that we do not examine it critically. One of the basic features of our experiences in everyday life is precisely that we generally pass through it, taking account of the facts, yes, but not necessarily gaining real insight into them. As I say this, I am reminded of that outstanding book by Karel Kosik, *A Dialética do Concreto*, in which he engages in critical discussion of the significance of everyday life.

However, when we leave our original environment and enter another, our experience of everyday life becomes heightened. We find everything in it more stimulating, or potentially so. Challenges multiply. Tension sets in.

I think that one of the serious problems which exiles face is that in their original environment they were immersed in their everyday life, which was familiar to them, while in their borrowed environment they have constantly to stand back from their daily life and ask themselves questions about it. It is as if you were always on your guard. And, if you are not willing to give honest answers to your own questions, if you lapse into nostalgia for your original environment, then your tendency is also to begin to reject everything which your borrowed environment can give you, which you need to overcome the tension created by the break with the past brought about by exile.

Faundez: An analysis of everyday life such as yours is essential for an understanding of exile, because exile is not simply a break at the epistemological, emotional, affective, intellectual, or even political levels: it is also a break in your daily life, which is made up of gestures, words, loving human relationships, relationships with friends and relationships with things. You certainly cannot explain exile apart from this, let us say, personal way of relating to a different world, a new and different environment. We begin, I would want to say, to become literate at the level of being.

And it begins with what you were talking about—discovering other people, discovering a different world, with different things, different gestures, different hands, different bodies. And, since different languages have left their imprint upon us, and we are used to different gestures, different styles of relationships, this new learning process of discovering, of relating to the world in a new way, takes a long time. And yet the differences are the starting point for this learning process. You discover people who are different and, linked, with that discovery of other people, the need to be tolerant of them. This means that through the differences between us we must learn to be tolerant of those who are different, and not to judge them according to our own values, but according to their values, which are different from ours. And here it seems to me to be fundamental to link the concept of culture with the concepts of difference and tolerance.

You were saying that to discover another culture is to accept it, to be tolerant of it. Now, I think that your view of culture, which I fully share, is not an elitist view.

Culture is not only artistic or intellectual phenomena expressed through thought: culture is to be seen above all in the simplest actions of everyday life—culture is eating in a different way, shaking hands in a different way, relating to people in a different way. So that it seems to me that these three concepts—culture, differences and tolerance—are old concepts being used in a new way. Culture for us, I would insist, includes the whole range of human activity, including everyday life; and it is basically in everyday life that we make the discovery of what is different, what is essential. And this understanding of what is essential is different from the traditional one, which views the essential as those features which are held in common. However, for us—and I think you will agree with me—the essential is what is different, what makes us different people.

When we discover and accept that this is the essential, that the ingredient of tolerance is required in this new relationship, then we must initiate dialogue between our differences and thereby enrich one another. So you are right when you say that we cannot judge another's culture according to our own values, but we must accept that there are other values, must accept that differences exist, and accept that fundamentally these differences help us to understand ourselves and our own everyday lives.

Freire: It is, in fact, a difficult process in which you learn something every day. On the basis of my long experience (because, after all, I did live in exile for almost sixteen years, learning this every day), I believe I can say that it really is not easy. Sometimes you almost despair, in this process of learning without forgetting the past. Learning to cope with what is different, which is often hurtful to the distinctive cultural marks we bear with us in our souls and bodies. Sometimes I also got weary. But I always fought back, attempting to reach a balance in my life between what had left a deep mark on me from my own culture and what had begun to leave its positive, or negative, mark on me from the new, different environment.

I also discovered, Antonio, something else obvious. Many people must have already said what I am about to say. I discovered how strong the distinctive marks of our culture are, but how much stronger they become if we don't treat them as absolutes. In fact, as soon as you begin to say, "no, only what is Chilean is good." the distinctive marks of your culture are weakening. But if, instead of treating the marks of your culture as absolutes, you cherish them and seriously cultivate them, without absolutizing them, then you see that were it not for them you would even find it difficult to learn new things which, placed alongside your own personal history, can also be meaningful.

I remember in this connection a letter I wrote to a great Brazilian friend of mine, in which I spoke of my travels around the world. I said: "If it were not for the distinctive marks of our culture, which are present and living within me and which I cherish, my travels, which as it is because of my culture are of deep significance to me, would become nothing more than aimless drifting across the face of the earth." It is interesting to observe what an extraordinary contradiction this is. If you give up the distinctive marks of your culture, you do not genuinely take on the distinctive marks of your new culture, and your life in the new culture is a pretence. But if you cherish your culture, without treating it as absolute, then you can afford to let yourself be influenced by the new culture. In other words, the new culture does not invade you, but nor is it repressed. Basically, it too gives you something. This learning process, which, I repeat, is not easy, is an experience you cannot avoid when you are in exile. That was why Elza and I always made an effort to stop our homesickness for Brazil from ever becoming a sort of sentimental disease. We missed our country very much, we missed our people, we missed our culture—all the things you were talking of: the particular way of greeting people, of walking down the street, of turning a corner, of looking behind you. All that is culture. And we missed it all—but we never allowed the fact that we missed it all to develop into a nostalgia that would drain our lives of color or make us depressed with no purpose to our lives.

But when exiles get involved in some sort of activity and discover some purpose for their lives in it, then they become increasingly better prepared to confront the basic tension between their original environment and their new, borrowed environment. So much so that at a given moment their borrowed environment, although it remains a borrowed environment, does, however, become a channel for their nostalgia. In other words, it enables them to grow as people. Now that is what happened to me when I accepted the post with the World Council of Churches and so had the opportunity through the Council of widening the scope of my activity by working in Europe, Africa, Latin America and the United States, doing something which seemed to me to be worthwhile and which gave justification to my life, even at the distance I was forced to live from my original environment.

The small contribution I was able to make to various countries—and I acknowledge that it was small, but it was also in some way significant—basically gave meaning to my exile. For me, Antonio, one of the key points in the exile experience is to discover, as you were saying at the outset of our conversation, to what extent it is possible or not to take what is negative in the break with your past and turn it into something positive in your daily life in your new environment; to what extent we struggle to create or find ways to escape from the monotony of days with no tomorrows by making some sort of contribution. This is one of the lessons which exile can teach us, provided, however, that we exiles become subjects in the learning process. In fact, exile is not an entity above history, omnipotently issuing orders to people in exile as it wills. Exile is simply people in exile. Exile is people accepting critically their situation as exiles. And if exiles accept their situation, they become subjects in the learning process which their new circumstances impose on them. And if they are good learners, I believe that they are preparing themselves very well for their return home. It is quite clear to me that the more capable exiles become of effectively learning the lessons of exile, the more effectively, when the time comes, they return home to their environment, convinced above all that on returning they cannot arrive home with the intention of lecturing and instructing those who had remained behind. They must arrive home with the same humility they had to have in exile in order to learn how to live their daily life there. Basically, their time away means that when they return they have to be reintegrated into everyday life, which will in many respects have changed while they have been away. The history and culture of their original environment have not stood still waiting for them! And then, returning exiles, as I have often said, must have towards their own environment almost the same humility which they should have had at the beginning of their exile, when they had to learn to live day by day in and with a new environment. Obviously, relearning your original environment is much easier than learning a borrowed environment, but the need to learn still presents itself in one way or another. I sometimes feel, when I think about these things, that there is a fairly dynamic relation between the period before exile, the "pre-exile," and return from exile. During the period before exile, exiles are politically active and have a fairly clear vision of their aims. In exile, too, they can have the clear aim of attempting to live out the tension, which we have already spoken of at length, learning tolerance and humility, learning the meaning of hope, not simply passive waiting, but hope expressed in action. To the extent that that is the case, exiles are preparing themselves to return home without arrogance. They return without believing that their environment owes them something for the mere fact of their having been exiled. They return without claiming to be superior to those who remained.

Some time ago in the course of our conversation, you said something which has to do with what I have just been saying. You said that the opportunity to become involved in an actual experience of making a contribution to other peoples added a different dimension to your exile. At that moment, I am sure, you were definitely preparing yourself for a better return home.

Faundez: That's exactly it, Paulo. I should like to continue our conversation on everyday life, which seems to me quite basic. And come back to what you were saying about reflecting on everyday life, how exile demands of us that we do reflect on it. I would say that my personal experience of reflecting on everyday life began before I was exiled, in a sort of pre-exile, as you put it. Because, basically, this change in the teaching of philosophy which we were making, or were attempting to make, with the rising generations in a particular political context, meant that we had to think about reality in one way or another, that we had to think how ideas take concrete form in daily political and individual acts. And for that Gramsci was essential reading for us. I would also add Lukács, although at a different level, and Kosik, both of them intellectuals who attempted to enter into the history of the society in which they lived and attempted to understand it as a whole, of which daily life is a vital part. They were the thinkers who in one way or another bound us to the reality we were experiencing at that time when changes were taking place in Chile. They were the ones who made us reflect on everyday life. Certainly exile represented a qualitative leap, because in it daily life was a break with the past and the discovery of a different life.

I would say that this analysis of everyday life can take us much further in our thinking, because, when all is said and done, I believe that the question of everyday life raises this other question: how do we relate our ideas and values to our own actions? Everything we affirm and defend, both at the political level and at the philosophical and religious level, must find expression in relevant action. When people do not reflect on their everyday lives, they do not become aware that there is a gap between these ideas and values and the acts we perform in our daily lives. While we affirm certain values at the intellectual level, these values are empty if they are removed from our everyday life, from our relations with our wife, our children, our friends and the people we meet in the street, whom we do not know, but with whom we have a relationship. All these ideas of personal, communal and moral values which should govern our relations with things and persons are no doubt very beautiful ideas; but, to the extent that we do not reflect on them and try to ensure that they and our actions coincide, there continues to be a gap between what we think and the values we affirm and the acts we perform with regard to things and persons. And this is equally applicable to the field of religion, in which there is a gap between what is affirmed and what is practiced day by day, and to the political plane, where there is a gap between what is affirmed and the day-to-day struggle. Because one of the things we learned in Chile in our early reflection on everyday life was that abstract political, religious or moral statements, excellent in themselves, did not produce change, did not take concrete shape in acts by individuals. We were revolutionaries in the abstract, not in our daily lives. I believe that revolution begins precisely with revolution in our daily lives.

It seems to me essential that in our individual lives we should day by day live out what we affirm. Another concept I reckon to be important is that of breaking with the past. I believe that through breaking with the past we learn that life's great lesson is that life is a succession of such breaks: a break which has to be destroyed in order to be transcended, and this fresh break has to be transcended by another. I think that breaks with the past, both great and small, are what really teach us something as we go through life, and teach us to respect others, to be different, and, basically to be modest and humble.

The process of becoming aware is a slow process, but in the final definition, it gains its strength in the course of real life experiences. In my journeys to Africa and Latin America, when people learn that I work, am involved in experiments in popular education in various continents, they always ask me the same question—whether they are Latin Americans or Africans: "Are they better or worse than us?" I reply that you just cannot say that they are better or worse. What I can say is that they are completely different experiences, and that you cannot arrive at a judgment that one is better or worse than the other, because they cannot be estimated or evaluated in comparison with others. They are different experiences, and as such they must be experienced differently. And because they are different, some can teach something to others, and some can learn something with the others. We learn only if we accept that others are different—otherwise, for example, dialogue is impossible. Dialogue can only take place when we accept that others are different and can teach us something we do not already know.

Freire: Of course. There is another aspect of daily life which I should like to bring out, on which you might possibly say something as well. It seems to me, António, that a critical search for an understanding of everyday life shows the need for a basic analysis to reach an understanding of how the fight, the struggle is conducted between the dominant ideology, which attempts to dominate the whole of life, and the dominated ideology, which resists this universal domination.

I believe that an attempt to study and critically examine how things happen in the world of everyday life can be very useful to political analysts in their understanding of how the dominant ideology does not succeed in subjecting all the cultural expressions and creativity of the people to itself, the dominant ideology. Sometimes, in our uncritical understanding of the nature of the struggle, we can be led to believe that all the everyday life of the people is a mere reproduction of the dominant ideology. But it is not. There will always be something of the dominant ideology in the cultural expressions of the people, but there is also in contradiction to it the signs of resistance—in the language, in music, in food preferences, in popular religion, in their understanding of the world. In fact, there was recently published in Brazil a very interesting study with the meaningful title *A Festa do Povo, Pedagogia de Resistencia* (Festival of the people, the pedagogy of resistance). What do you think?

Ideology in Action

Faundez: I consider such an analysis to be essential. And I repeat that this is not an issue for political and social scientists alone, but for all the disciplines in the social sciences. I would say that this is a subject which is also of interest to psychologists and biologists and others. In the final analysis, when people speak of ideology, they wrongly think only of ideas, and they don't realize that these ideas gain strength and are really a form of power only to the extent that they take concrete shape in the actions of our daily lives. And that is where we should begin our analysis. Our starting point should be ideology in action, not ideology in ideas. And not only in the action of groups of intellectuals (although that should also be analyzed), but fundamentally in the action of the people, where the political strength of a movement resides. The power of an ideology to rule lies basically in the fact that it is embodied in the activities of everyday life.

Freire: Ideology is a very concrete thing.

Faundez: Yes, concrete, it is not an idea in action. I believe, then, that it is essential to begin with this analysis and, as we go more deeply into it, we shall discover how, as they confront these dominant ideologies, there are acts of resistance on the part of the masses. I believe that any political, ideological struggle has precisely to begin with an understanding of these acts of resistance. In other words, you should not fight ideology with ideas alone, but beginning with those concrete elements of popular resistance. Therefore, any struggle against a dominant ideology or ideologies should be based on the resistance offered by the people, and on that basis you produce ideologies to oppose the dominant ideology or ideologies. Not the other way round, by creating ideologies in opposition to the dominant ideologies, without realizing that you must have a concrete base as your starting point in the form of acts of resistance by the masses. This is fundamental in any political struggle, in any ideological struggle. And that is where the ideological battle will be won—beginning from that and not from ideas. Because to fight ideologies ideologically is to lapse into an ideology of ideology. It is to consider as important—which is what the dominant ideology wants—that the fight should be conducted on the plane of ideas because, when the struggle is conducted on the plane of ideas, it takes concrete shape and is expressed in mass action, so as to allow the political and ideological power of the dominant groups to continue. While we begin the struggle against that embodiment on the basis of the people's resistance to it, the people themselves can and must contribute to the creation of an ideology and of actions to fight against the dominant ideology or ideologies.

Freire: Of course, I am totally in agreement with you on that point. That was something I struggled for, something I insisted on even before the *Pedagogy of the Oppressed,* where I stressed that the starting point for a political-pedagogical project must be precisely at the level of the people's aspirations and dreams, their understanding of reality and their forms of action and struggle.

You are now introducing into your analysis an element which clarifies for me my theoretical analysis by your insistence that the starting point should precisely be *resistance.* In other words, the forms of resistance of the popular masses. If we refuse to acknowledge these forms of resistance because, antidialectically, we believe everything among them to be a reproduction of the dominant ideology, we end up by lapsing into a voluntarist or intellectualist position, into authoritarian speeches proposing courses of action which are not feasible for the people. The problem is how to get closer to the popular masses so as to understand their forms of resistance, where they are to be found among them and how they find expression, and then work on that.

Faundez: I think, Paulo, that in this regard, literacy campaigns—or popular education, whatever we call it—play a fundamental role, because literacy and post-literacy campaigns begin from certain ideas which serve as models: political models, social models, models of conceiving society, whether industrialized or not, socialized or not.

The starting point, therefore, is ideas which are models, which give structure to the literacy and postliteracy programs. By means of them reactionary or progressive models can be imposed. But we do not perceive that we are working at a metaphysical level, at the level of ideas, and we are in fact presenting the people with a concept worked out in our own minds.

It was not the people who produced this concept. Thus, as you demonstrate in your work, literacy and post-literacy campaigns should begin from an understanding of everyday life, an understanding which should be arrived at by the people themselves. And us together with them. We are not the ones to reflect on their everyday life. Our contribution to the people is that we and they together engage in reflection on their and our everyday life. And then they will discover for themselves their moments of resistance, how they express their resistance, the foundations they have on which to build an ideology; and they will discover that it is they themselves who have to build it, in a process in which we of course participate. As Gramsci said: "The people have feelings, they feel and act: intellectuals understand, but they do not feel." What we must do is bring together feeling and understanding in order to arrive at the truth.

Freire: I believe, António, that militant political intellectuals constantly run the risk either of becoming authoritarian or of becoming more authoritarian, if they are not capable of going beyond a messianic concept of social change, of revolutionary change.

It is interesting, too, to observe the ease with which those who take up an authoritarian stance regard those who defend the need for this communion with the popular masses as mere reformers or populists or social democrats.

Guevara and Amílcar Cabral never gave up this communion. In reality, those who defend communion with the masses are not passive: they are not among those who think that the role of intellectuals is simply that of assistants, of mere helpers or facilitators. Their really important and fundamental role will be all the greater and all the more substantially democratic if, as they place themselves at the service of the interests of the working classes, they never attempt to manipulate them by means of their scientific or technical competence or their language and skill with words. The more seriously they seek to play a complementary role, the more they discover the need to bring together "feeling" and "understanding" of the world. To the critical understanding of reality must be added sensitivity to reality, and to attain this sensitivity or develop it they need communion with the masses. Intellectuals need to discover that their critical capacity is of neither greater nor less worth than the sensitivity of the people. Both are required for an understanding of reality.

When they are remote from the popular masses and interact only with their books, intellectuals run the risk of arriving at a rarified rationality, a disembodied understanding of the world.

This reminds me of the reference you made to a conversation you had with a Bolivian peasant, who jokingly asked you: "Do you know why a military coup doesn't take place in the United States? It's because there's no US embassy there!"

Finally, I should like to make it quite clear that I do not intend to idealize the popular masses in any way: they are neither pure nor undefiled!

Faundez: The difficulty, Paulo, in understanding the importance of the analysis of everyday life lies in the fact that we intellectuals are accustomed to working with ideas as models. Now, of course, people, and particularly intellectuals, need ideas in order to understand the world. But if these ideas become models, in other words, if they are not applied creatively to reality, we run the risk of regarding them as reality. And so concrete reality has to be made to fit in with our ideas, and not the other way round. We would then lapse into what I would call "popular Hegelianism": the belief that the Idea is reality, and that reality is nothing more than the development of the Idea by means of concepts. And so, in order to explain the discrepancy between ideas and reality, to explain why concepts and concrete reality fail to coincide, to explain people's failure to understand and change historical reality, it is firmly maintained that it is reality that is wrong and not our ideas or system of ideas.

If we follow that way, the daily life of the people escapes us, as does also their action and resistance. I think that we intellectuals have to have the opposite approach: we must begin with the actual situation, the actions which we and the people engage in day after day—since we are all involved in daily life in one form or another—reflect on that, and then generate ideas in order to understand it. And such ideas will no longer be ideas that are models, but ideas being generated out of real life situations.

In that way I believe we avoid the absolute fondness for conceptual models, the absolute fondness for concepts, which acquire a value greater than reality itself in that they enable us to "understand" and "change" reality.

I think that this can also even be applied to what is wrongly called your "method," because a lot of people think that your method is basically a model. I don't think you ever considered your method to be a model.

Freire: No, never.

Faundez: A method for you is a series of principles which must be constantly reformulated, in that different, constantly changing situations demand that the principles be interpreted in a different way. And thereby enriched. And thus basically your method is a sort of challenge to intellectuals and to reality to reformulate that method in order to translate its principles as the situation demands and thus be a response to different concrete situations.

What do you think of that?

Freire: I am in complete agreement. That is exactly why I always say that the only way anyone has of applying in their situation any of the propositions I have made is precisely by redoing what I have done, that is, by not following me. In order to follow me it is essential not to follow me! Which is exactly what you were saying.

But, Antonio, without changing the direction of our conversation very much, I should like to ask you something. Although your formal teaching experience in Europe has not been very long, how do you view it as compared with your experience in Chile? What are the most important aspects you would want to emphasize in the teaching you have done in Geneva?

The Fallacy of Neutrality in Education

Faundez: It's a rather complex issue, because our academic life in Chile was a life of total involvement in a political context . . .

Freire: . . . which has not been the case here in Geneva . . .

Faundez: . . . so that for us in Chile teaching was bound up with political positions, with a political struggle, with changing reality. Whereas the European context has been completely different and has not had this political dimension. Or rather, it has had a different political dimension. And for that very reason, my work has been fundamentally "neutral" in that respect *(laughter)*.

In fact, I believe that it has been even more political than what was overtly political in Chile. Here politics consists in denying the political dimension, thereby removing all analysis and all thinking from the concrete political context of social struggle.

Freire: I don't want to interrupt your train of thought, but let me just interject a comment in parentheses. A moment ago you were saying how important it is for us to understand how the dominant ideology finds expression in actions and not only in words. The statement that education is neutral is very often more than mere words.

In the same way, a scientist may say to a student: "You have ceased to be scientific, because you have made a value judgment of reality." For that scientist, reality is there to be spoken about, it is there for us simply to . . .

Faundez: . . . describe it!

Freire: . . . yes, for us to describe it, but not to reach value judgments about it, let alone change it! And it is interesting to note how the dominant ideology, by expressing itself in statements like that, attempts to present itself as possessing the full weight of irrefutable, undeniable truth. You are right: by placing such stress on the political neutrality of education and science, their political partisanship is ultimately shown up. The denial that they are political is finally perceived as a political act.

Faundez: Exactly. In Europe that is fundamental. I have worked in the university institute, which engages in study of third-world countries. You can see there how abstract are the concepts about the third world. The very concept of the "third world" is already a total abstraction! The concepts used to reach an understanding of this non-European world are completely abstract. But, as I travel more and more and share in the struggle of the people in various places, I learn to be modest in my claims. When I am asked if I know Africa or Latin America well, I reply "no." And with each journey I know less!

This is a totally different attitude from that of Europeans. They go and stay for two or three years and then become specialists in Latin America or Africa. With every journey I make, I become less of a specialist, a non-specialist, in Africa and Latin America, precisely because I discover these essential differences. Whereas Europeans try to discover what there is in *common,* and that becomes the essential for them, for me the essential is in the "differences," and, since each time I discover more differences, each time I become more aware of how little I know. That is the way of modesty, and it is the essential way.

Freire: Let's go back to your teaching experience in Geneva. Did you, for example, have difficulty in finding students willing to devote some time to at least thinking critically about their actions, on the basis of which you could make in-depth theoretical analyses with them? Or, conversely, did they require you to be a teacher in the traditional sense?

Faundez: No doubt about that! The teacher is the one who is in possession of the truth and, as such, what he says must be true. But none of us possesses the truth. It is to be found in the "becoming" of dialogue. As Hegel said: "The true reality is becoming." It is not being or not being, but the tension between them—what is true is the historical process. Thus, when you put forward the idea that truth lies in the quest and not in the result, that it is a process, that knowledge is a process, and thus we should engage in it and achieve it through dialogue, through breaking with the past—that is not accepted by the great majority of students, who are used to the teacher, the wise man, having the truth, hierarchically, and thus do not accept dialogue. For them dialogue is a sign of weakness on the part of the teacher; for them modesty in knowledge is an indication of weakness and ignorance.

While it is exactly the opposite. I believe that those who are weak are those who think they possess the truth, and are thus intolerant; those who are strong are those who say: "Perhaps I have part of the truth, but I don't have the whole truth. You have part of the truth. Let's seek it together." These difficulties enable someone from the third world, who begins to speak about the third world, to begin really to discover it, because just because you come from the third world doesn't mean that you know it. To propose that we discover it together is for the majority an admission of ignorance, whereas it should in reality be a sign of wisdom. We must not confuse "feeling" with "understanding."

What experiences of this type have you had?

Freire: I have had and am still having some very valuable, very interesting experiences of this type, in the United States and in Europe. In a more or less systematic way in some universities in the United States, in Canada, in Brazil and in Switzerland; and in a less systematic way in various other American, Latin American, European and African universities. I would say that the results of my experience have been much more positive than negative. Last July, before coming to Geneva, I spent a month coordinating three courses, with daily activities, at the University of British Columbia in Vancouver, and at the University of Alberta in Edmonton. I worked *with* the students, not *for* them, and certainly not *on* them. Only rarely have I found such critically aware involvement, such a clear sense of responsibility, such a real delight in taking risks and engaging in intellectual adventure—without which there is no creativity—as I found among the participants in those courses. But there is no way of forgetting that we are also constantly up against this instilled certainty according to which students are there to learn and teachers are there to teach. This casts such a shadow, weighs upon us so heavily, that it is difficult for teachers to realize that as they teach they are also learning. First, because they are teaching, in other words, the actual process of teaching teaches them to teach. Secondly, they learn with those they teach, not simply because they have to prepare themselves for teaching, but also because they revise their knowledge in the quest for knowledge the students engage in. I have insisted for a long time now in my writings that students' restlessness, doubts, curiosity and comparative ignorance should be seen by their teachers as challenges to them. Basically, thinking about all this is illuminating and enriching for the teacher as much as for the students.

The curiosity of students can sometimes shake the certainty of their teachers. That is why, by placing limits on students' curiosity, on their expressiveness, authoritarian teachers limit their own as well. On the other hand, when students are free to ask questions on a subject, it can often give their teachers a new angle, enabling them later to engage in more critical reflection.

That is what I have tried to do in the course of my life as a teacher. I would not say that my way of working is the only way or the best. It's the way I like. But more than simply that, in it or through it I feel that I am being consistent with my political option.

What I am concerned above all to do is to resist, theoretically and practically, two connections which are generally made, although not always explicitly. The first is the connection made between a democratic style and low academic standards; the second is that made between high academic standards and an authoritarian style.

Basically, those who make these connections do not conceal their strong dislike of democracy and freedom. It's as if for them democracy were something that had nothing to do with the seminar or laboratory context. It's as if it were possible for us first, in an authoritarian way, well mannered, carefully guided and well adjusted, to achieve high academic standards, and then afterward, with the standards thus acquired, go out there and do our democratic thing.

Democracy and freedom are not a denial of high academic standards. On the contrary, to live an authentically free life means engaging in adventure, taking risks, being creative. It is licence, which is a distortion of freedom, that compromises academic standards.

Well, in the final analysis, my experience has always been enriching, and I am comforted by the fact that in the course of it I have never begun from the authoritarian conviction that I have a truth to impose, the indisputable truth. On the other hand, I have never said, or even suggested, that not having a truth to impose implies that you don't have anything to propose, no ideas to put forward. If we have nothing to put forward, or if we simply refuse to do it, we really have nothing to do with the practice of education. The issue raised here concerns our pedagogical-democratic understanding or the act of putting forward ideas, proposing. Educators cannot refrain from putting forward ideas, nor can they refrain either from engaging in discussion with their students on the ideas they have put forward. Basically, this has to do with the near mystery of the praxis of educators who live out their democratic insights: they must affirm themselves without thereby disaffirming their students. This radical, or substantially democratic, position stands in contrast on the one hand to authoritarianism and on the other to what I call spontaneism.

I should like to end these comments by saying that the demands I make of myself of living out my democratic principles in my relations with the students with whom I am working, I also look for in revolutionary leaders in their political-pedagogical relations with the working classes, the popular masses.

I do not believe that education is something done for students or to them. I do not believe either—as I have already often said—that revolutionary change is something done *for* the popular masses but *with* them.

The Pedagogy of Asking Questions

Faundez: I think, Paulo, that this whole issue of teaching or educating is a basic one, and that it is definitely connected with what we were talking about earlier: clearly defined political positions in a hierarchical world, in which those who possess power possess knowledge, and present-day society offers teachers a share in knowledge and a share in power. That is one of the ways in which society reproduces itself. So I think that it is a profoundly democratic thing to begin to learn to ask questions.

In teaching, questions have been forgotten. Teachers and students alike have forgotten them, and, as I understand it, all knowledge begins from asking questions. It begins with what you, Paulo, call *curiosity*. But curiosity is asking questions!

I have the impression—and I don't know whether you will agree with me—that today teaching, knowledge, consists in giving answers and not asking questions.

Freire: Exactly! I entirely agree with you. It's what I call the "castration of curiosity." What we see happening is a movement in one direction, from here to there, and that's it. There is no come-back, and there is not even any searching. The educator, generally, produces answers without having been asked anything!

Faundez: Exactly, and the most serious thing, Paulo, is that the students get used to this way of working, and so what teachers ought to teach—because they themselves ought to know it—should be supremely how to ask questions. Because, I repeat, knowledge begins with asking questions. And only when we begin with questions, should we go out in search of answers, and not the other way round. If you produce answers as if all knowledge consisted of them, were already given, were absolute, you are leaving no room for curiosity or the discovery of fresh elements. Knowledge comes ready-made—that is what teaching then is. Whereas I would want to say, "the only way to teach is by learning"—and that statement is just as valid for students as for teachers. I just cannot conceive that teachers can teach without also learning at the same time. In order to be able to teach they must also be learning.

Freire: I agree, but I would put it more radically than that. Take the process at its very beginning. And I am very struck by what you said earlier about asking questions, which is something I emphasize very much—the authoritarianism running through our educational experiences inhibits, even if it does not repress, our capacity for asking questions. In an authoritarian atmosphere, the challenge implicit in a question tends to be regarded as an attack on authority. And even when that is not openly admitted, the experience finishes up with the suggestion that it is not always convenient to ask questions.

One of the disciplines which Elza and I always placed upon ourselves in our relations with our children was never to refuse to answer their questions. Whoever we were with, we would break off our conversation to pay attention to their curiosity. Only after showing our respect for their right to ask questions did we duly draw their attention to the presence of the person, or people, we were talking with.

I believe we begin this authoritarian denial of curiosity at a very early age by making remarks like: "My, what a lot of questions from a little boy!" or "Be quiet, your father's busy!" or "Go to sleep, and leave that question till tomorrow!"

The impression I have is that, in the final analysis, the authoritarian educator is more afraid of the answer than of the question. He is afraid of the question because of the answer it should give rise to.

I believe too that this repression of questioning is only one dimension of a greater repression—the repression of the whole person, of people's expressiveness in their relations in the world and with the world.

What is attempted in an authoritarian way by imposing silence for the sake of order is precisely stifling people's ability to ask questions. You are right: one of the starting points in the training of educators in a liberating democratic approach would be this apparently very simple thing: asking what it means to ask questions. In this regard, let me tell you about an experience I had which touched me very much. It was in Buenos Aires, where I had gone when I was still working here in the Council, just after the return of Perón. I was invited by the ministry of education, and its staff teams, headed by government minister Tayana, Perón's former doctor, for which he had to pay dearly after the military coup, arranged an excellent full-time program of work for me over a week. It was my first visit to Argentina, and until recently I have not been able to return there by express command of the military.

The program consisted of daily seminars with university teachers, rectors, technical staff from various departments of the Ministry, and artists, but an integral part of the program was also visits to the poor areas of Buenos Aires. One Sunday morning I went to one of those areas. We met with what would have been a sort of residents' association. An immense number of people. I was introduced by the educator accompanying me.

"I have not come here," I said, "to make a speech, but to talk with you. I shall ask questions, and so must you. And our answers will make our time spent together here worthwhile."

I stopped. There was a silence, which was broken by someone who said: "Very good. I think that's the right way. We don't really want you to make a speech. I've got a question."

"Let's have it," I said.

"What does it actually mean to ask questions?"

On that Sunday morning that man in a slum area of Buenos Aires asked *the* basic question. Instead of answering him by myself, I tried to draw out of the group what they thought it meant to ask questions. At each moment I attempted to throw light on the points made, emphasizing the curiosity which is expressed in asking questions. You are right. Perhaps this should be one of the first points to be discussed in a training course for young people preparing to be teachers: what does it mean to ask questions? I must stress, however, that the point of the question is not to turn the question "What does it mean to ask questions?" into an intellectual game, but to experience the force of the question, experience the challenge it offers, experience curiosity, and demonstrate it to the students. The problem which the teacher is really faced with is how in practice progressively to create with the students the habit, the virtue, of asking questions, of being surprised.

For an educator with this attitude there are no stupid questions or final answers. Educators who do not castrate the curiosity of their students, who themselves become part of the inner movement of the act of discovery, never show disrespect for any question whatsoever. Because, even when the question may seem to them to be ingenuous or wrongly formulated, it is not always so for the person asking it. In such cases, the role of educators, far from ridiculing the student, is to help the student to rephrase the question so that he or she can thereby learn to ask better questions.

Faundez: Note, Paulo, how we are returning to the beginning of knowledge, to the origins of teaching, of pedagogy. And we are in agreement that everything begins, as Plato said, with curiosity, and linked with curiosity, with asking questions. I think you are right when you say that the first thing which anyone who teaches should learn is how to ask questions. To know how to ask yourself questions, to know what are the questions which stimulate us and stimulate society. The basic questions, which arise out of everyday life, because that is where the issues are. If we learned to ask ourselves questions about our own daily life, then all the questions demanding an answer and this whole question-and-answer process, which is the way to knowledge, would start with these basic questions about our everyday life, these gestures, these bodily questions, which our bodies ask us, as you put it.

I would want to stress that the source of knowledge lies in inquiry, in questions, or in the very act of asking questions. I would venture to state that the earliest form of language was the question, that the first word was at one and the same time question and answer in a simultaneous act. And when I speak of language here, I do not understand it to be only the language of words.

We know that language by its nature consists of gestures. It is body language, a language of the movement of the eyes, of the heart. The earliest language was body language and, since this language is a language of questions, if we limit these questions, and if we only pay attention to or place value on spoken or written language, then we are ruling out a large area of human language. I believe it to be essential that teachers should accord equal value to all dimensions of language, or languages, which are languages that ask questions before they are languages that give answers.

Freire: I agree. I am sure, however, that we must make it clear once again that our interest in asking questions, about asking questions, cannot remain simply at the level of asking questions for their own sake. What is supremely important is whenever possible to link question and answer to actions which can be performed or repeated in future. I don't know if I am making myself clear. I feel it essential to make clear that your defense and mine of the act of asking questions does not in any way regard asking questions as an intellectual game. On the contrary, what is necessary is that the student, having asked a question about a fact, should have in the answer an explanation of the fact and not a mere description of words related to the fact. The student must discover the living, powerful, dynamic relation between word and action, between word, action and reflection. Thus, by using concrete examples of students' own experience in the course of a morning's classroom work, in the case of a class of school children, we can encourage them to ask questions about their own experience, and the answers will then include the experience which gave rise to the question. Acting, speaking and discovering would all belong together.

Faundez: However, we need to clarify the relation between question and action, question, answer and action. I don't think you are claiming that there should be a direct connection between every question and actual experience. There are questions which are intermediate, questions about questions, and these should receive an answer.

What is important is that a question about a question, or questions about questions, and about answers—that this chain of questions and answers should ultimately be broadly anchored in reality, in other words, that this chain should not be broken. Because we are used to seeing this chain of questions and answers, which is basically what knowledge is all about, being broken, interrupted, and not coming to grips with reality. What I insist on is that, granted that there are intermediate questions, they should always serve as a bridge between the primary question and concrete reality.

I think that the act of questioning, or the question itself, as a principle of knowledge, could be understood in concrete groups. I remember, for example, the occasion when, on the eve of my departure for Zaire, I was sought out by a young man from that country who was preparing his doctoral thesis, which was a study of the educational experience of the missionary churches in Zaire.

At the beginning of our conversation, I said to him: "You talk, and I'll listen. Tell me what you think, what facts you have got together, what are the concerns to be brought out in your thesis." For about an hour, this young man gave me an incredible quantity of information: libraries visited, books read, conversations with people who had experienced the missionary period in Zaire. But all this information had no shape to it at all.

Finally, I observed: "What are the questions you are asking yourself in order to give some structure to your thesis?" Because any thesis, like all research, must begin by identifying the key questions to be answered.

I am not saying that it is unnecessary to gather information, but I am saying that it is essential for this curiosity, which leads us to a particular subject, to find concrete expression in basic questions which will be the guiding thread of our work. If we identify five or six basic questions, those questions and the answers to them will constitute an academic thesis.

Freire: And, during the process of finding out the facts which will help us to find answers to those questions, all the indications are that other basic questions will arise as you build up this rigorous, logical, coherent structure, which is what a thesis should be.

Faundez: Yes, I believe that the value of a thesis lies in discovering and formulating basic questions which will arouse the curiosity of other research workers. The value lies not so much in the answers, because the answers are definitely provisional, as in the questions . . .

But, as we identify the basic questions, which will enable us to find answers and discover fresh questions, a chain is being created which will enable the thesis to be constructed. A thesis in which the basic element is not only answers but also this chain of questions, which are always provisional. It seems to me, therefore, that, in order to begin a thesis, it is essential to learn how to ask questions. The task of philosophy, and of knowledge in general, is not so much to find answers as to ask questions, and to ask the right questions.

Freire: I believe in this regard that students engaged in a continuing process of education should be adept at asking questions about themselves. In other words, it should be impossible to pass through a day without constantly asking yourself questions.

I should like to stress once again the need constantly to stimulate curiosity, the act of asking questions, instead of repressing it. Schools either reject questions or they bureaucratize the act of asking them. It is not simply a matter of introducing a question-and-answer session into the curriculum between nine and ten, for example. That is not what it's about. The issue for us is not the bureaucratized asking of questions, but the acknowledgment of existence itself as an act of questioning.

Human existence, because it came into being through asking questions, is at the root of change in the world. There is a radical element to existence, which is the radical act of asking questions.

And precisely when someone loses the capacity to be surprised, they sink into bureaucratization.

I think it important to note that there is an undeniable relationship between being surprised and asking questions, taking risks and existence. At root human existence involves surprise, questioning and risk. And, because of all this, it involves action and change. Bureaucratization, however, means adaptation with a minimum of risk, with no surprises, without asking questions. And so we have a pedagogy of answers, which is a pedagogy of adaptation, not a pedagogy of creativity. It does not encourage people to take the risk of inventing, or reinventing. For me, to refuse to take risks is the best way there is of denying human existence itself.

Faundez: To find an example of this bureaucratized asking of questions we need look no further than the texts to which students are subjected. The questions are questions which already contain their answers. In that way, they are not even questions! They are answers rather than questions.

Students have to know beforehand the answers to the questions they will be asked. On the other hand, if we taught them to ask questions, they would have to ask themselves questions, and creatively discover the answers for themselves—in other words, participate themselves in the process of discovery and not simply answer a particular question on the basis of what they have already been told.

I would want to stress that education as it is consists generally in finding answers rather than asking questions. An education which consists in asking questions is, however, the only education which is creative and capable of stimulating people's capacity to experience surprise, to respond to their surprise and solve their real fundamental existential problems. It is knowledge itself.

The easiest way is precisely the pedagogy of giving answers, but in that way absolutely nothing is put at risk. Intellectuals are almost afraid to take risks, to make mistakes, whereas it is the making of mistakes which enables advances in knowledge to be made. So in this regard the pedagogy of freedom or creativity should be an eminently risky enterprise. People should dare to take risks, should expose themselves to risk, as the one way of advancing in knowledge, of truly learning and teaching. I consider this pedagogy of taking risks very important, and it is related to the pedagogy of making mistakes. If we negate the negation, i.e. the mistake, this new negation will invest the mistake with positive quality: this transition from error to non-error is knowledge. A fresh mistake will never be a completely fresh mistake: it will be a fresh mistake in that the variable elements in it make it a fresh mistake, and this chain extends to infinity. If that were not the case, we would attain absolute knowledge, and there is no such thing as absolute knowledge. As Hegel said, the force of the negative is essential. The force of the negative in knowledge is an essential part of knowledge, and we call it: making mistakes, taking risks, being curious, asking questions, and so on.

Freire: If you do not engage in that adventure, it is impossible to be creative. Any educational practice based on standardization, on what is laid down in advance, on routine in which everything is predetermined, is bureaucratizing and thus anti-democratic.

Faundez: An example of this is the way workers in factories lose their creativity. Work is a creative process but, since the rationality of work is predetermined and with it the steps to be taken, workers are caught up in a process which is not educative and denies them any possibility of being creative.

Think of the immense gain to human knowledge, the human sciences and society itself, if workers' creativity were given room to manifest itself.

Even as it is, it does manifest itself, because workers sometimes solve problems not foreseen in the way work is planned. But the rationality of work requires workers not to be creative. However, if it did allow workers to be so, it would be much more enriched through this capacity which workers have to be creative, particularly in the practical application of thought to actual situations. The whole rationality of work as propounded is in fact a rationality based on models.

The great problem is the practical application of thought to actual situations. And in this regard the rationality of work requires workers not to respond creatively to the problems with which concrete reality confronts this abstract rationality.

Freire: In this regard, work, as it responds to the demand for higher productivity in a capitalist setting, will be the more efficient the fewer workers ask questions, do not ask questions about themselves, and know little beyond the routine task assigned to them by mass production.

Harry Braverman is right in saying: "The more science is incorporated into the work process, the less workers understand that process. The more sophisticated an intellectual product the machine becomes, the less control and understanding of it workers have." Thus in the name of efficiency and productivity what we are seeing is the bureaucratization of workers' minds, consciousness and creative capacity.

Brutalizing the work force by subjecting them to routine procedures is part of the nature of the capitalist mode of production. And what is taking place in the production of knowledge in the schools is in large part a reproduction of that mechanism—although we could do the opposite.

In fact, the more inventive and creative capacity of students is "brutalized," the more they are simply being conditioned to accept "answers" to questions which have not been asked, as you said earlier. The more students adapt to such a procedure, the more, ironically, it is reckoned that this is "productive" education.

At bottom, this is education reproducing the authoritarianism of the capitalist mode of production. It is deplorable how progressive educators, as they analyze and fight against the reproduction of the dominant ideology in the schools, actually reproduce the authoritarian ideology inherent in the capitalist mode of production.

Faundez: Yes, it is abstract thought that imposes the particular power of a particular ideology. And it is certainly very difficult to escape from it.

What is reproduced in an educational process, both at work and school, is also reproduced at a political level in the political process, which is also a major educational process, in which the creativity of the masses is ignored and trampled underfoot. The more the masses listen to the leaders, the less they think—that is considered the supreme political wisdom, whereas the opposite should be the case. This occurs among authoritarian politicians, both of the left and the right. But it is most serious where it is reproduced among progressive politicians of the left.

Basically, they are reproducing a pattern of thought which propounds an unjust society in which some groups possess knowledge, power, the answers, the ability to think, and so on. I would wish to begin with an analysis of the questions being asked, of the creativity of the answers being given, as an act of discovery, as a question-and-answer process which all sharing in the educational process should be engaged in. If we apply this analysis to the political process in the strict sense, we can see how this dominant pattern of thought exercises a fundamental influence on the progressive politics of those leaders who declare themselves to be on the left or who claim to be close to the masses. Political effectiveness is reckoned to be best gauged by the level of response by the masses to the demands made by political leaders. Also, the effectiveness of students is reckoned to lie in their learning progressively to give answers in the form given by their teachers. All this results in the death of the process as such, and in the reproduction of an elitist, authoritarian society, which is a denial of education itself, of the educational process.

Paulo, now that we have analyzed and examined to some extent what we have propounded as a pedagogy of asking questions and a pedagogy of giving answers, I would suggest that we return to a subject we dealt with earlier in the light of these concepts: the cultural manifestations of the resistance with which the masses oppose dominant ideologies. Ideologies which also find expression in the everyday lives of the masses, as you said, but which are not the only guiding forces in everyday life, since it also consists of actions, gestures, and political and cultural manifestations which represent resistance to those dominant ideologies.

Translated by Tony Coates

6

PEDAGOGY OF THE CITY

The Challenges of Urban Education

Terra Nuova: How do you see the situation of Brazil today—on the one hand, the development which makes Brazil a great economy, on the other, the poverty which so harshly punishes the majority of the population?

Paulo Freire: I don't believe anyone with minimum sensitivity in this country, regardless of political position, can live in peace with such a cruel, unfair reality as this. One thing, though, is to feel bad, and immediately find such whiny arguments as "the people are lazy," the people are uncultured," "Rome wasn't built in a day," to explain the tragic situation and to defend purely self-serving hypotheses of action; another thing is to be taken by "just rage" and engage in political projects for substantive transformation of reality.

My sensitivity makes me have chills of discomfort when I see, especially in the Brazilian northeast, entire families eating detritus in landfills, eating garbage; they are the "garbage" of an economy that boasts about being the seventh or eighth economy in the world. My hurt sensitivity does more, however, than just give me chills or make me feel offended as a person, it sickens me and pushes me into the political fight for a radical transformation of this unjust society.

My hurt sensitivity makes me sad when I know the number of poor boys and girls of school age in Brazil who are "prohibited" from entering school; when I know that, among those who manage to get in, the majority of them are "expelled," and people say they "dropped out." My lashed sensitivity makes me horrified when I know that the illiteracy rate among youths and adults has been increasing in the last years; when I realize the contempt with which the public school system has been treated; when I verify that, in a city like São Paulo, there are one million boys and girls living on the streets. But, together with the horror that such a reality provokes in me, there is the necessary anger and the indispensable indignation that, combined, give me courage to fight democratically for the suppression of this scandalous offense.

Terra Nuova: Tell us about your development as an educator; how did it begin; the time of the dictatorship; the exile. Why did you accept the assignment for the Municipal Department of Education?

Freire: Nobody becomes an educator on a Tuesday at four in the afternoon. Nobody is born an educator or marked to be one. We make ourselves educators, we develop ourselves as educators permanently, in the practice and through reflecting upon the practice.

It is true that we have, since childhood, certain likes and preferences, certain ways of being, or of saying and doing things that, sometimes or almost always, coincide with the nature of certain crafts like education, for example. That is why, sometimes, in light of these likes and preferences, adults will say about boys and girls that they were born doctors, educators, or artists. In reality, however, nobody is born ready.

I was a boy with many pedagogical adumbrations, a certain curiosity, an eagerness for knowing, a taste for listening, a desire to speak, respect for the opinion of others, discipline, perseverance, knowledge of my limits.

My career as an educator started exactly in my experience as a student, when one way or another, those likes and preferences were stimulated, accommodated, or denied. Still very young, shortly after I began middle school, I started to "teach" the Portuguese language. And through teaching my students grammar and syntax, I started to prepare myself to understand my role as a teacher. If, on the one hand, this role was not to propose that my students re-create the whole history of the content I taught them, on the other hand, it was not just to lay out a profile of it either. The fundamental thing was to challenge the students to realize that learning that content implied learning it as the object of knowledge. The issue wasn't to describe those content concepts but to unveil them so the students could relate to them with the radical curiosity of those who search and who want to know. It is true that, back at the beginning of this discovery of teaching, to which corresponds an understanding of the dynamic and critical nature of learning, it wasn't yet possible for me to talk about it as I do now.

This epistemological certainty that learning the object, the content, presupposes the apprehension of the object, the realization of its reason for being, accompanies me in every step of my practice and of my theoretical reflection over practice. It accompanied me in my experience as a young, almost adolescent, Portuguese teacher, in my work along the streams and on the hills of Recife, at the beginning of my youth, as a progressive educator, in the formation of the fundamental principles of the so-called

Paulo Freire Method (a designation I don't like), in my activities as a university professor, in Brazil and abroad, an in the present effort for the permanent professional development of educators in the public school system in which I am involved as Secretary of Education of São Paulo, together with the excellent team I work with.

To be more objective in answering your question about my progress as an educator, maybe I could make reference to moments and people who, directly or indirectly, marked me.

The hardships I lived in my difficult, if not tragic, childhood, and the manner in which my parents behaved in coping with these difficulties, were both important in my development as a person, which preceded my development as an educator, without any dichotomy between them. My father's death—when I was thirteen; the trauma of his absence; my mother's kindness in her struggle to put me through school; the figure of an excellent educator from Recife, Aluizio Araujo, the father of my second wife, Ana Maria (or Nita as I call her), to whom I owe the privilege of studying for free in his school; some teachers whose example I still remember today; the beginning of my studies at the Law School of Recife, when Elza, an extraordinary woman and educator, came into my life; also her loss, which almost took me as well, had it not been for another woman no less extraordinary, Nita; ten years of political and pedagogical experience with urban and rural workers in Pernambuco; my academic work, essential readings; a certain camaraderie with Christ and with Marx, which surprises certain Christians and makes naive Marxists suspicious. All these are the ingredients that necessarily permeate and define my progress as an educator. And they are followed by the equally important impact of the rich and challenging exile experience. This exile resulted from a theoretical understanding of education as a political act, of education as a process of discovery, of the democratic education founded on the respect for the learner, for his or her language, for his or her class and cultural identity, also, an understanding of the theoretical explanation of the defense of an education that reveals, unveils, that challenges; above all, the exile resulted from the putting into practice of such an understanding of education. It was that practice that frightened, in the sixties and still does today, the dominant, authoritarian, and perverse classes. It was the putting into practice of such an education that took me to prison, away from the university, and finally to the almost sixteen years of exile.

The opportunities I had to grow, to learn, to reevaluate myself in the exile were such that sometimes Elza would humorously and wisely tell me,

"You should telegraph the general who responds for the Presidency of Brazil to thank him for the opportunity they afforded you to continue learning." She was right.

In the almost sixteen years of exile, I lived in three different places: Santiago, Chile; Cambridge, Massachusetts; and Geneva, Switzerland. From there, I roamed the world as a tramp of the obvious. I taught courses and seminars, participated in conferences and congresses, assisted revolutionary governments in Africa, in Central America, and the Caribbean; I helped liberation movements, ran risks, made friendships, loved, was loved, learned, grew. And while I did all that and "suffered," in the sense of incorporating what I lived and did, I never stopped considering Brazil as a preoccupation. Brazil never was for me a remote, bitter memory.

The Brazil of my preoccupation was exactly the Brazil subjected to the military coup, picturesquely called "Revolution of 64" by its executers. It was the silenced Brazil, with its progressive intellectuals expelled, with its working class manacled, with men like Helder Camara, the prophetic archbishop of Recife and Olinda, threatened and silenced.

All the well-lived time, however, of exile becomes preparation for the comeback. So in June of 1980, we returned to Brazil permanently, settling in São Paulo.

In a first stage, I dedicated myself to what I called relearning Brazil. I visited the whole country again. From north to south I spoke, above all, to youths curious about what we had done before 1964. I feel that I still have an obligation to write about this. I don't know when or whether I'll do it. I went back to being a teacher. I became a professor at the Pontifical Catholic University of São Paulo and at the State University of Campinas. I also wrote, but mostly, I spoke a lot in those years. Still in Europe, I became a founding member of the Workers' Party (PT), in whose administration of São Paulo I am now the Secretary of Education. That was the first time I became affiliated with a political party, with card, name, and address. Everything right. Everything legal. The reason was that, for the first time in this country, a political party was born from down up. The Workers' Party wasn't born rejecting the so-called intellectuals for being intellectuals, but rejecting elitist and authoritarian intellectuals for claiming ownership over the truth of the working class and of the revolution. And, since I have never accepted this type of arrogant intellectuals, I felt comfortable, from the very beginning, as a modest militant member of PT.

And why did I accept being the Secretary of Education of São Paulo?

First of all, because I am secretary of PT's administration, and in particular, within Luiza Erundina's administration. In other words, because I can say, on TV programs, on the radio, and in the newspapers, that at the Department of Education, political clout and political connections cannot surpass anybody's rights. Secondly, because, if I had not accepted the honorable invitation by Erundina, I would have to, for a matter of coherence, pull all of my books out of press, stop writing, and be silent till death. And this was much too high a price. To accept this invitation was to be coherent with everything I have ever said and done; it was the only way to go.

I did accept the position, and I am pleased because I did.

Terra Nuova: Talk a little bit about the Paulo Freire Method—Conscientization or Literacy? How do you position yourself in relation to the criticism you receive in that respect?

Freire: Maybe the best way to address the question you pose is to insist that every reading of the word is preceded by a reading of the world.

Starting from the reading of the world that the learner brings to literacy programs (a social and class-determined reading), the reading of the word sends the reader back to the previous reading of the world, which is, in fact, a rereading.

Words, sentences, articulated discourse do not take place up in the air. They are historical and social. It is possible, in cultures with primarily or exclusively oral memory, to discuss, in projects of progressive education, the greater or lesser extent to which the subordinate group's reading of the world at any given time is a critical one, without the reading of the word. What does not seem possible to me is to read the word without a connection to the learner's reading of the world. That is why, for me, the literacy process with adults necessarily implies the critical development of the rereading of the world, which is a political, awareness-generating task. What would be wrong, and what I have never suggested should be done, is to deny learners their right to literacy because of the necessary politicization there would not be time for literacy in the strict sense of the term.

Literacy involves not just the reading of the word, but also the reading of the world.

Terra Nuova: What are your guidelines as Secretary of Education, and how do you see them in the context of PT's administrations?

Paulo Freire: I am convinced, and this is quite obvious, that progressive administrations like PT's cannot be distant from and indifferent to the issue of progressive education. They are administrations that need to face the issue of the prestige of the public schools, the struggle for their improvement, which in turn is connected to a profound respect for educators and for their permanent development.

The issue of adult and youth illiteracy is related to the quantitative and qualitative deficits in our education. There aren't enough schools to serve the peoples' demand—eight million children in Brazil are out of school—and the education offered is elitist, removed from the expectations of the subordinate classes.

Every year there tends to be a higher number of illiterate youths and adults, on the one hand, because millions are kept from entering school and, on the other hand, because those who fail end up being expelled from school. Therefore, when addressing the issue of illiteracy, it is pressing:

a. That we do it without the remedial nature literacy campaigns usually have. It is important, then, to think about how to incorporate literacy students into the "regular" educational system.
b. That we fight:
  (i) to overcome the quantitative deficit of our school and
  (ii) to overcome the high rate of failure through adequate and efficient teaching in the basic school.

None of this can be done overnight, but it will be done one day.

Terra Nuova: How do you view the role of nongovernmental organizations of cooperation in Europe in relation to PT's administrations?

Freire: I always view organizations of cooperation in a good light, be they European or not, so long as the relationships established between them and us, PT's administrations, are relationships of mutual respect, dialogical relationships, through which we can grow together, learn together. On the contrary, I will always see negatively any so-called organization "of cooperation," which distortedly, however, intends to impose its options onto us in the name of the help it might give us. In reality, there are no neutral organizations of cooperation. For that reason, they should also be very clear about the administrations with which they seek relationships and for which they study cooperation projects.

We demand very little to live well with any organization: only that it treats us with respect.

Translated by Donaldo Macedo

7

PEDAGOGY OF HOPE: RELIVING PEDAGOGY OF THE OPPRESSED

Chapter 4: A Further "Reading of the World"

If my position at the time had been mechanistic, I would not even have spoken of the raising of consciousness, of *conscientização*. I spoke of *conscientização* because, even with my slips in the direction of idealism, my tendency was to review and revise promptly, and thus, adopting a consistency with the practice I had, to perceive that practice as steeped in the dialectical movement back and forth between consciousness and world.

In an antidialectically mechanistic position, I would have rejected, like all mechanists, the need for *conscientização* and education before a radical change in the material conditions of society can occur.

Neither, as I have asserted above, is an antidialectical perspective compatible with an understanding of critical awareness other than as an epiphenomenon—"as a result of social changes, not as a factor of the same" (Erica Marcuse, 1986).

It is interesting to observe that, for the idealistic, nondialectical comprehension of the relationship between awareness and world, one can still speak of *conscientização* as an instrument for changing the world, provided this change be realized only in the interiority of awareness, with the world itself left untouched. Thus, *conscientização* would produce nothing but verbiage.

From the viewpoint of a mechanistic dogmatism, there is no point in speaking of *conscientização* at all. Hence the dogmatic, authoritarian leaderships have no reason to engage in dialogue with the popular classes. They need only tell them what they should do.

Mechanistically or idealistically, it is impossible to understand what occurs in the relations prevailing between oppressors and oppressed, whether as individuals or as social classes.

Only in a dialectical understanding, let us repeat, of how awareness and the world are given, is it possible to comprehend the phenomenon of the introjection of the oppressor by the oppressed, the latter's "adherence" to the former, the difficulty that the oppressed have in localizing the oppressor outside themselves.[1]

Once again the moment comes to mind when, twenty-five years ago, I heard from Erich Fromm, in his house in Cuernavaca, his blue eyes flashing: "An educational practice like that is a kind of historico-sociocultural and political psychoanalysis."

This is what dogmatic, authoritarian, sectarian mechanists fail to perceive, and nearly always reject as "idealism."

If the great popular masses are without a more critical understanding of how society functions, it is not because they are naturally incapable of it—to my view—but on account of the precarious conditions in which they live and survive, where they are "forbidden to know." Thus, the way out is not ideological propaganda and political "sloganizing," as the mechanists say it is, but the critical effort through which men and women take themselves in hand and become agents of curiosity, become investigators, become subjects in an ongoing process of quest for the revelation of the "why" of things and facts. Hence, in the area of adult literacy, for example, I have long found myself insisting on what I call a "reading of the world and reading of the word." Not a reading of the word alone, nor a reading only of the world, but both together, in dialectical solidarity.

It is precisely a "reading of the world" that enables its subject or agent to decipher, more and more critically, the "limit situation" or situations beyond which they find only "untested feasibility."

I must make it clear, however, that, consistently with the dialectical position in which I place myself, in terms of which I perceive the relations among world-consciousness-practice-theory-reading-of-the-world-reading-of-the-word-context-text, the reading of the world cannot be the reading made by academicians and imposed on the popular classes. Nor can such a reading be reduced to a complacent exercise by educators in which, in token of respect for popular culture, they fall silent before the "knowledge of living experience" and adapt themselves to it.

---

1. See, among others, Sartre, Fanon, Memmi, and Freire.

The dialectical, democratic position implies, on the contrary, the *intervention* of the intellectual as an indispensable condition of his or her task. Nor do I see any betrayal of democracy here. Democracy is betrayed when contradicted by authoritarian attitudes and practices, as well as by spontaneous, irresponsibly permissive attitudes and practices.

It is in this sense that I insist once more on the imperative need of the progressive educator to familiarize herself or himself with the syntax and semantics of the popular groups—to understand how those persons do their reading of the world, to perceive that "craftiness" of theirs so indispensable to the culture of a resistance that is in the process of formation, without which they cannot defend themselves from the violence to which they are subjected.

Educators need an understanding of the meaning their festivals have as an integral part of the culture of resistance, a respectful sense of their piety in a dialectical perspective, and not only as if it were a simple expression of their alienation. Their piety, their religiousness, must be respected as their right, regardless of whether we reject it personally (and if so, whether we reject religion as such, or merely do not approve the particular manner of its practice in a given popular group).

In a recent conversation with Brazilian sociologist Professor Otávio Ianni, of UNICAMP, I received a report from him of some of his encounters with young activists of the Left, one of them in prison, in Recife, in 1963. Ianni not only made no effort to hide his emotion at what he had seen and heard, but approved and endorsed the way these militants respected popular culture, and within that culture, the manifestations of their religious beliefs.

"What do you need," Ianni asked the young prisoner.

"A Bible," he answered.

"I thought you'd want Lenin's *Que fazer?* (What is to be done?)," said Ianni.

"I don't need Lenin just now. I need the Bible. I need a better understanding of the peasant's mystical universe. Without that understanding, how can I communicate with them?"

Besides the democratic, ethical duty to proceed in this way, incumbent on the progressive educator, such a procedure is also demanded by requirements in the field of communication, as the young person in Recife had discerned.

Unless educators expose themselves to the popular culture across the board, their discourse will hardly be heard by anyone but themselves.

Not only will it be lost, and inoperative, it may actually reinforce popular dependency, by underscoring the much-vaunted "linguistic superiority" of the popular classes.

It is once more against the background of a dialectical comprehension of the relationship between world and awareness, between economic production and cultural production, that it seems valid to me to call progressive educators' attention to the contradictory movement between culture's "negativities" and "positivities." There can be no doubt, for example, that our slavorcratic past marks us as a whole still today. It cuts across the social classes, dominant and dominated alike. Both have worldviews and practices significantly indicative of that past, which thereby continues ever to be present. But our slavocratic past is not evinced exclusively in the almighty lord who orders and threatens and the humiliated slave who "obeys" in order to stay alive. It is also revealed in the relationship between the two. It is precisely by obeying in order to stay alive that the slave eventually discovers that "obeying," in this case, is a form of struggle. After all, by adopting such behavior, the slave survives. And it is from learning experience to learning experience that a culture of resistance is gradually founded, full of "wiles," but full of *dreams,* as well. Full of rebellion, amidst apparent accommodation.

The *quilombos*—the hiding places used by runaway slaves—constituted an exemplary moment in that learning process of rebellion—of a reinvention of life on the part of slaves who took their existence and history in hand, and, starting with the necessary "obedience," set out in quest of the invention of freedom.

In a recent public discussion entitled, "Presence of the People in the National Culture," in which I participated, along with the Brazilian sociologist I have already mentioned, Otávio Ianni, the latter, referring to this slavocratic past of ours and the marks it has left on our society, brought out its positive signs as well—the slaves' resistance, their rebellion. He spoke of the corresponding struggles, today, of the "landless," the "homeless," the "schoolless," the "foodless," the "jobless," as current kinds of *quilombos,* or "underground railroads."

It is our task as progressive educators to take advantage of this tradition of struggle, of resistance, and "work it." It is a task that, to be sure, is a perverted one from the purely idealist outlook, as well as from the mechanistic, dogmatic, authoritarian viewpoint that converts education into pure "communication," the sheer transmission of neutral content.

Another consideration that I cannot refrain from entertaining in this book is the question of the programmatic content of education. I seem to be misunderstood on this matter at times.

This calls for a reflection on educational practice itself, which is taking shape before our eyes.

Let us "step back" from educational practice—as I now do in writing, in the silence, not only of my office, but of my neighborhood—in order the better to "close in" on it again, take it by surprise, in its component elements in their reciprocal relationship.

As an object of my curiosity, which curiosity is now operating epistemologically, the educational practice that, by "taking my distance," from it, I "close in" on, begins to reveal itself to me. The first observation I make is that any educational practice always implies the existence of (1) a subject or agent (the person who instructs and teaches); (2) the person who learns, but who by learning also teaches; and (3) the object to be imparted and taught—the object to be re-cognized and cognized—that is, the content; and (4) the methods by which the teaching subject approaches the content he or she is mediating to the educand. Indeed, the content—in its quality as cognoscible object to be re-cognized by the educator while teaching it to the educand, who in turn comprehends it only by apprehending it—cannot simply be transferred from the educator to the educand, simply deposited in the educand by the educator.

Educational practice further involves processes, techniques, expectations, desires, frustrations, and the ongoing tension between practice and theory, between freedom and authority, where any exaggerated emphasis on either is unacceptable from a democratic perspective, which is incompatible with authoritarianism and permissiveness alike.

The critical, exacting, consistent educator, in the exercise of his or her reflection on educational practice, as in the practice itself, always understands it in its totality.

He or she will not center educational practice exclusively on, for example, the educand, or the educator, or the content, or the methods, but will understand educational practice in terms of the relationship obtaining among its various components, and will perform that practice consistently with his or her understanding, in all use of materials, methods, and techniques.

There has never been, nor could there ever be, education without content, unless human beings were to be so transformed that the processes we know today as processes of knowing and formation were to lose their current meaning.

The act of teaching and learning—which are dimensions of the larger process of knowing—are part of the nature of the educational process. There is no education without the teaching, systematic or no, of a certain content. And "teach" is a transitive-relative verb. It has both a direct and an indirect object. One who teaches, teaches something (content) to someone (a pupil).

The question that arises is not whether or not there is such a thing as education without content (which would be at the opposite pole from a "contentistic," purely mechanistic education), since, let us repeat, there has never been an educational practice without content.

The fundamental problem—a problem of a political nature, and colored by ideological hues—is who chooses the content, and in behalf of which persons and things the "chooser's" teaching will be performed—in favor of whom, against whom, in favor of what, against what. What is the role of educands in the programmatic organization of content? What is the role, on various levels, of those at the bases—cooks, maintenance workers, security personnel, who find themselves involved in a school's educational practice? What is the role of families, social organizations, and the local community?

Nor let it be said, in a spirit of smoldering, venomous aristocratic elitism, that students, students' fathers, students' mothers, janitors, security people, cooks, have "no business meddling in this"—that the question of programmatic content is of the sole jurisdiction or competency of trained specialists. This discourse is like peas in a pod with another—the one that proclaims that an illiterate does not know how to vote.

In the first place, to argue in favor of the active presence of pupils, pupils' fathers, pupils' mothers, security people, cooks, and custodians in program planning, content planning, for the schools, as the São Paulo Municipal Secretariat of Education does today in the Workers party administration of Luíza Erundina, does not mean denying the indispensable need for specialists. It only means not leaving them as the exclusive "proprietors" of a basic component of educational practice. It means democratizing the power of choosing content, which is a necessary extension of the debate over the most democratic way of dealing with content, of proposing it to the apprehension of the educands instead of merely transferring it from the educator to the educands. This is what we are doing in the São Paulo

Municipal Secretariat of Education. It is impossible to democratize the choice of content without democratizing the teaching of content.

Nor let it be said that this is a populist, or "democratistic" position. No, it is not democratistic, it is democratic. It is progressive. But it is the position of progressives and democrats who see the urgency of the presence of the popular classes in the debates on the destiny of the city. Their presence in the school is a chapter in that debate, and is a positive sign, and not something evil, something to be deterred. This is not the position of self-styled "democrats" for whom the presence of the people in facts and events, a people organizing, is a sign that democracy is not doing well.

Besides considering the importance of this kind of intervention in the destiny of the school in terms of a democratic learning process, we can also imagine what a school will be able to learn from, and what it will be able to teach, cooks, janitors, security guards, fathers, and mothers, in its indispensable quest for a transcendence of the "knowledge of living experience" in order to arrive at a more critical, more precise knowledge, to which these persons have a right. This is a right of the popular classes that progressives have to recognize and fight for if they are to be consistent—the right to know better than they already know—alongside another right, that of sharing in some way in the production of the as-yet-nonexistent knowledge.

Something that likewise seems to me to be important to bring out, in any discussion or conceptualization of content, in a critical, democratic outlook on curriculum, is the importance of never allowing ourselves to succumb to the naive temptation to look on content as something magical. And it is interesting to observe that, the more we look on content as something magical, the more we tend to regard it as neutral, or to treat it in a neutral manner. For someone understanding it as magical, content in itself has such power, such importance, that one need only "deposit" it in educands in order for its power to effect the desired change. And it is for this reason that, when content is rendered magical, or is thus understood, when it is regarded as having this force in itself, then the teacher seems to have no other task than to transmit it to the educands. Any discussion about social, political, economic, or cultural reality—any critical, in no way dogmatic, discussion—is regarded as not only unnecessary, but simply irrelevant.

This is not the way I see things. As object of cognition, content must be delivered up to the cognitive curiosity of teachers and pupils. The former teach, and in so doing, learn. The latter learn, and in so doing, teach.

244 · PAULO FREIRE

As object of cognition, content cannot be taught, apprehended, learned, known, in such a way as to escape the implications of political ideology—which implications, as well, are to be apprehended by the cognizing subject. Once more a "reading of the world" is imperative that stands in dynamic interrelationship with the cognition of word-and-theme, of content, of cognoscible object.

That every reader, everyone engaged in any teaching or learning practice, explicitly wonder about his or her work as teacher or pupil, in mathematics, history, biology, or grammar classes, is of little importance. That all explicitly interrogate themselves, and see themselves, as participating as teacher or pupil in the experience of critical instruction in content, that all explicitly engage in a "reading of the world" that would be of a political nature, is not of the highest necessity.

What is altogether impermissible, in democratic practice, is for teachers, subreptitiously or otherwise, to impose on their pupils their own "reading of the world," in whose framework, therefore, they will now situate the teaching of content. The battle with the authoritarianism of the Right or the Left does not lead me into that impossible "neutrality" that would be nothing but a cunning way of seeking to conceal my option.

The role of the progressive educator, which neither can nor ought to be omitted, in offering her or his "reading of the world," is to bring out the fact that there are other "readings of the world," different from the one being offered as the educator's own, and at times antagonistic to it.

Let me repeat: there is no education practice without content. The danger, of course, depending on the educator's particular ideological position, is either that of exaggerating the educator's authority to the point of authoritarianism, or that of a voiding of the teacher's authority that will mean plunging the educand into a permissive climate and an equally permissive practice. Each of the two practices implies its own distinct manner of addressing content.

In the former case, that of the exaggeration of authority to the point of authoritarianism, the educator is ascribed the "possession" of *content*. In this fashion, educators who feel that they "possess" content, hold it as their property—regardless of whether they have had a share in its selection—since they possess the methods by which they manipulate the object, they will necessarily manipulate the educands as well. Even when calling themselves progressive and democratic, authoritarian educators of the Left, inconsistent with at least a part of their discourse, feel so uncomfortable with critical educands, educands who are investigators, that they cannot

THE PAULO FREIRE READER · 245

bring themselves to terminate their discourse, any more than can authoritarian educators of the Right.

In the latter case, we have an annihilation of the teacher's authority that plunges the educands into the above-mentioned permissive climate and equally permissive practice, in which, left to their own devices, they do and undo what they please.

Devoid of limits, spontaneous practice, which shreds to pieces something so fundamental in human beings' formation—spontaneity—not having sufficient strength to deny the necessity of content, nevertheless allows it to trickle away in a never-justifiable pedagogical "Let's pretend."

And so, when all is said and done, there is nothing the progressive educator can do in the face of the question of content but join battle for good and all in favor of the democratization of society, which necessarily implies the democratization of the school in terms, on the one hand, of the democratization of the programming of content, and on the other, of the democratization of the teaching of that content. The democratization of the school, especially when we have some say-so over the "network" or "subsystem" of which it is a part, so that we can make a contribution to governmental change in a democracy, is part of the democratization of society. In other words, the democratization of the school is not a sheer epiphenomenon, the mechanical result of the transformation of society across the board, but is itself a factor for change, as well.

Consistent progressive educators need not await the comprehensive democratization of Brazilian society in order to embrace democratic practices with respect to content. They must not be authoritarian today in order to be democratic tomorrow.

What they simply may not do, in critical terms, is look to municipal, state, and federal governments of a conservative mold, or to "progressive" governments nevertheless tinged with the *dogmatism* I have always criticized, to democratize the organization of curriculum or the teaching of content. Concretely, we need neither authoritarianism nor permissiveness, but democratic substance.

In 1960 I wrote, for the symposium, "Education for Brazil," sponsored by the Recife Regional Center for Educational Investigations, a paper entitled, "A Primary School for Brazil" and published by the *Revista Brasileira de Estudos Pedagógicos,* no. 35 (April–June 1961). I shall cite a brief passage from this text here for the sake of its bearing on the question under discussion in this part of this book.

The school we need so urgently [I said in 1960] is a school in which persons really study and work. When we criticize, on the part of other educators, the intellectualism of our schools, we are not attempting to defend a position with regard to the school in which the study disciplines, and the discipline of studying, would be watered down. We may never in all of our history have had more need of teaching, studying, learning, than we have today. Of learning to read, write, count. Of studying history, geography. Of understanding the situation or situations of our country. The intellectualism we fight is precisely that hollow, empty, sonorous chatter, bereft of any relationship with the reality surrounding us, in which we are born and reared and on which, in large part, we yet feed today. We must be on our guard against this sort of intellectualism, just as we must be on our guard against a so-called antitraditionalist position that reduces schoolwork to mere *experiences of this or that*, and which excuses itself from performing the hard, heavy work of serious, honest, study, which produces intellectual discipline.

It is precisely the authoritarian, magical comprehension of content that characterizes the "vanguardist" leaderships, for whom men's and women's awareness is an empty "space" waiting for content—a conceptualization I have severely criticized in *Pedagogy of the Oppressed*. And I criticize it again today as incompatible with a *pedagogy of hope*.

But let me make one thing perfectly clear: it is not every conscious mind, not every awareness, that is this empty "space" waiting for content, for the authoritarian vanguardist leaders. Not their own awareness, for example. They feel they belong to a special group in society, which "owns" critical awareness as a "datum." They feel as if they were already liberated, or invulnerable to domination, so that their sole task is to *teach* and *liberate* others. Hence their almost religious care—their all but mystical devotion—but their intransigence, too, when it comes to dealing with content, their certitude with regard to what ought to be taught, what ought to be transmitted. Their conviction is that the fundamental thing is to teach, to transmit, what *ought* to be taught—not "losing time," in "mindless chatter" with popular groups about their reading of the world.

Any concern with educands' expectations, whether these persons be primary-school children, high-school students, or adults in popular education courses, is pure democratism. Any concern on the part of the democratic educator not to wound the cultural identity of the educands is held for harmful purism. Any manifestation of respect for popular wisdom is considered populism.

This conception is as consistent, on the Left, with a dogmatic thinking, of Marxist origin, in terms of which a critical, historical awareness is given, as I have already mentioned, almost as if it were just "put there"; as it is consistent, on the Right, with the elitism that would have the dominant classes, by nature, knowing, and the dominated ones, by nature, ignorant. Thus, the dominant teach when and if they feel like it; the dominated learn at the price of much effort.

A dogmatic activist working in a school as a teacher is indistinguishable from her or his colleague working on behalf of a union, or in a slum, except for the material differences in their respective activities. For the former, it is imperative to "fill" the "empty" awareness of educands with content whose learning process he or she as educator already knows to be important and indispensable to the educands. For the latter, it is likewise imperative to "fill" the "empty" consciousness of popular groups with the working-class consciousness that, according to this individual, the workers do not have, but which the middle class judges and asserts themselves to have.

I can never forget what four German educators, of the former East Germany, said one evening, in the early 1970s, as we sat in the home of one of them. One spoke, while the others nodded their assent: "I recently read the German edition of your book, *Pedagogy of the Oppressed.* I was very glad you criticized students' absence from discussions of programmatic content. In bourgeois societies," he went on, dogmatically, "you have to talk about this, and fire the students up about it. Not here. We know what the students should know."

From this point forward, after what I said to them in response, it was hard to keep up the conversation. The visit came to an end, and I retired earlier than I had expected to the home of a friend who was putting me up.

It took me a while to get to sleep. I thought not only about what I had just heard that evening in Berlin, but about what I had heard all day long there, in a group of young scientists, university scholars. The contrast was huge. The young people criticized the authoritarianism of the regime: for them it was retrograde, antidemocratic, and arrogant. And their criticism was lodged from within the socialist option, not from the outside.

The educators with whom I had just been speaking were an example of the very thing the young scientists had spoken to me about and had opposed.

It was hard to sleep, thinking of the supercertitude with which those "modern" educators wove their discourse, their declaration of unshakable faith: "Not here. We know what the students should know."

This is the certitude, always, of the authoritarian, the dogmatist, who knows what the popular classes know, and knows what they need even without talking to them. At the same time, what the popular classes already know, in function of their practice in the interwoven events of their everyday lives, is so "irrelevant," so "disarticulate," that it makes no sense to authoritarian persons. What makes sense to them is what comes from their readings, and what they write in their books and articles. It is what they already know about the knowledge that seems basic and indispensable to them, and which, in the form of content, must be "deposited" in the "empty consciousness" of the popular classes.

If anyone, on the other hand, assuming a democratic, progressive position, therefore argues for the democratization of the programmatic organization of content, the democratization of his or her teaching—in other words, the democratization of curriculum—that person is regarded by the authoritarian as too spontaneous and permissive, or else as lacking in seriousness.

If, as I have declared above, the neoliberal discourse has no power to eliminate from history the existence of social classes, on one hand, and the struggle between them, on the other, then the rug is pulled out from under the authoritarian positions that characterize so-called realistic socialism and underly a vertical discourse and practice of curricular organization.

Neoliberals err when they criticize and reject us for being ideological in an era, according to them, in which "ideologies have died." The discourses and dogmatic practices of the Left are mistaken not because they are ideological, but because theirs is an ideology that connives with the prohibition of men's and women's curiosity, and contributes to its alienation.

"I do not authentically think unless others think. I simply cannot think for others, or for others, or without others." This assertion, owing to its implicit dialogical character, unsettles authoritarian mentalities. This is also why they are so refractory to dialogue, to any idea swapping between teachers and students.

Dialogue between teachers and students does not place them on the same footing professionally; but it does mark the democratic position between them. Teachers and students are not identical, and this for countless reasons. After all, it is a *difference* between them that makes them precisely students or teachers. Were they simply identical, each could be the other. Dialogue is meaningful precisely because the dialogical subjects, the agents in the dialogue, not only retain their identity, but actively defend it, and thus grow together. Precisely on this account, dialogue does not *level* them, does not "even them out," reduce them to each other. Dialogue is not a favor done by one for the other, a kind of a grace accorded. On the contrary, it implies a sincere, fundamental respect on the part of the subjects engaged in it, a respect that is violated, or prevented from materializing, by authoritarianism. Permissiveness does the same thing, in a different, but equally deleterious, way.

There is no dialogue in "spontaneism" any more than in the omnipotence of the teacher. But a dialogical relation does not, as is sometimes thought, rule out the possibility of the act of teaching. On the contrary, it founds this act, which is completed and sealed in its correlative, the act of learning,[2] and both become authentically possible only when the educator's thinking, critical and concerned though it be, nevertheless refuses to "apply the brakes" to the educand's ability to think. On the contrary, both "thinkings" become authentically possible only when the educator's critical thinking is delivered over to the educand's curiosity. If the educator's thinking cancels, crushes, or hinders the development of educand's thinking, then the educator's thinking, being authoritarian, tends to generate in the educands upon whom it impinges a timid, inauthentic, sometimes even merely rebellious, thinking.

Indeed, dialogue cannot be blamed for the warped use sometimes made of it—for its pure imitation, or its caricature. Dialogue must not be transformed into a noncommittal "chewing the fat" to the random rhythm of whatever happens to be transpiring between teacher and educands.

Pedagogical dialogue implies not only content, or cognoscible object around which to revolve, but also a presentation concerning it made by the educator for the educands.

Here I should like to return to reflections I have previously made about the "expository lesson."[3]

The real evil is not in the expository lesson—in the explanation given by the teacher. This is not what I have criticized as a kind of "banking." I have criticized, and I continue to criticize, that type of educator-educand relationship in which the educator regards himself or herself as the educands' sole educator—in which the educator violates, or refuses to accept, the fundamental condition of the act of knowing, which is its dialogical relation (Nicol, 1965), and therefore establishes a relation in which the educator transfers knowledge about *a* or *b* or *c* objects or elements of content to an educand considered as pure recipient.

This is the criticism I have made, and still make. The question now is: will every "expository classroom," as they are called, be this? I think not.

2. See, in this regard, Eduardo Nicol, *Los principios de la ciencia* (Mexico City: Fondo de Cultura Económica, 1965).

3. Paulo Freire and Sérgio Guimaraes, *Sobre educação—diálogos* (Rio de Janeira: Paz e Terra, 1984).

I deny it. There are expository classrooms in which this is indeed attempted: pure transferrals of the teacher's accumulated knowledge to the students. These are vertical classrooms, in which the teacher, in a spirit of authoritarianism, attempts the *impossible,* from the viewpoint of theory of knowledge: to transfer knowledge.

There is another kind of classroom, in which, while appearing not to effect the transfer of content, also cancels or hinders the educand's ability to do critical thinking. That is, there are classrooms that sound much more like children's songs than like genuine challenges. They house the expositions that "tame" educands, or "lull them to sleep"—where, on the one side, the students are lulled to sleep by the teacher's pretentious, high-sounding words, and on the other, the teacher likewise doing a parcel of self-babying. But there is a third position, which I regard as profoundly valid: that in which the teacher makes a little presentation of the subject and then the group of students joins with the teacher in an analysis precisely of that presentation. In this fashion, in the little introductory exposition, the teacher challenges the students, who thereupon question themselves and question the teacher, and thereby share in plumbing the depths of, developing, the initial exposition. This kind of work may in no wise be regarded as negative, as traditional schooling in the pejorative sense.

Finally, I find yet another kind of teacher whom I do not regard as a banker. It is that very serious teacher who, in conducting a course, adopts a relationship with the subject, with the content, of which she or he is treating, that is one of profound, affectionate, almost loving respect, whether that content be constituted of a text composed by the teacher or a text composed by someone else. Ultimately, he or she is bearing witness to the educands as to how he or she studies, "approaches," or draws near a given subject, who she or he thinks critically. Now the educands' must have, or create and develop, the critical ability to accompany the teacher's movement in his or her attempt to approach the topic under consideration.

From a certain point of view, this kind of teacher also commits an error. It consists of ignoring the fact that the knowledge relation does not terminate in the object. In other words, the knowledge relationship is not exclusively between a cognizing subject and a cognoscible object. It "bridges over" to another subject, basically becoming a subject-object-subject relation.

As a democratic relationship, dialogue is the opportunity available to me to open up to the thinking of others, and thereby not wither away in isolation.

Pedagogy of the Oppressed first saw the light of day twenty-four years ago, under the impulse of this sentiment with which, more touched by it and enveloped in it than before, I revisit it in this *Pedagogy of Hope.*

I began this book by saying that a poem, a song, a sculpture, a painting, a book, a piece of music, a fact or deed, an occurrence, never have just one reason to explain them. An event, a fact, a deed of love or hatred, a poem, a book, are always found wrapped in thick webs, tapestries, frameworks, and touched by manifold *whys,* of which some are more proximate to the occurrence or creation—more visible as a *why.*

A great proportion of the first part of this book has centered on a grasp of certain of the tapestries or frameworks in which *Pedagogy of the Oppressed* took its origin.

Now, in the latter part of this volume, I shall speak of facts, occurrences, tapestries, or frameworks in which I have shared and am sharing and which have revolved around *Pedagogy of the Oppressed.*

Published in New York in September 1970, *Pedagogy* immediately began to be translated into various languages, sparking curiosity, and favorable criticism in some cases, unfavorable in others. By 1974 the book had been translated into Spanish, Italian, French, German, Dutch, and Swedish, and its publication in London by Penguin Books carried *Pedagogy* to Africa, Asia, and Oceania, as well.

The book appeared at an intensely troubled moment in history. Social movements appeared, in Europe, the United States, and Latin America, each with its own space—time and particular characteristics. There was the struggle with sexual, racial, cultural, and class discrimination. In Europe, there was the struggle waged by the Greens to protect the environment. Coups d'état with a new face, in Latin America, with new military governments replacing those of the previous decade. Now the coups were ideologically based, and all of them were coupled in one way or another to the locomotive of the North going full steam ahead for what seemed to it the capitalist destiny of the continent. There were the guerrilla wars in Latin America, the base communities, the liberation movements in Africa, independence for former Portuguese colonies, the battle in Namibia. There were Amílcar Cabral, Julius Nyerere, their leadership in Africa and its repercussions outside Africa. China. Mao. The cultural Revolution. A lively loyalty to the meaning of the May of 1968. There were the political and pedagogical union movements—all of them obviously political, especially in Italy. There was Guevara, murdered the decade before, present as a symbol not only for Latin-American revolutionary movements, but for progressive leaders and activists the world over. There was the Vietnam War, and the reaction in the United States. There was the fight for civil rights, and the climate of the 1960s in the area of political culture overflowed, in that country, into the 1970s.

These, with their numberless implications and developments, were some of the social, cultural, political, and ideological historical fabrics that explain, in part, both the curiosity the book aroused, and with the tenor of the reading and the acceptance with which it met—whether it was accepted or rejected, and what criticisms were made of it.

As I did not systematically keep and duly comment on the letters that came to me from each respective linguistic region of the world after each new translation of *Pedagogy* is something I regret today with an almost physical pain. They were letters from the United States, Canada, Latin America, and after the publication by Penguin Books, Australia, New Zealand, the islands of the South Pacific, India, and Africa, such was the effectiveness of that publisher's distribution network. After the letters, or sometimes with them, came invitations to discuss and debate theoreticopractical points of the book. Not infrequently, in Geneva, for a day or longer, I would host a group of university students, accompanied by their teacher, who would be running a course or seminar on *Pedagogy*, or a group of workers, especially Italian workers, but also immigrant workers in Switzerland, who—from a more political perspective than the one maintained by the university students—wanted to have points explained and aspects illuminated bearing directly on their practice.

I remember now, for example: there was a series of coinciding positions on political pedagogy, my positions in the book and positions in the general view maintained by the Italian union leaders then heading up the battle for what they called the "fifty hours." The movement was finally victorious in obtaining recognition of workers' right to take courses on work time.

On various occasions, in Geneva, or in Italy, I met with some of these leadership teams to discuss points of practical theory in their struggle in terms of dimensions of the book.

It was in those days that we began to form a group and hold discussions just among ourselves. Elza Freire, Miguel D'Arcy de Oliveira, Rosisca de Oliveira, Claudius Ceccon, myself, and, later, Marcos Arruda and the Institute for Cultural Action. The IDAC team was playing a truly important role just then, in seminars on *Pedagogy of the Oppressed* held throughout Europe, the United States, and Canada. A time or two, as first director of IDAC, I participated in some of those seminars analyzing the book.

It would be difficult to exaggerate how much I was enriched by the discussions I held, for hours on end, with German university youth, whether in Geneva or in their universities in Germany. I could not help being struck with their strong liking for theoretical discussion, and the seriousness with which they challenged me on the basis of their careful, rigorous reading, which they had done either by themselves or along with their professor. Or how much it likewise enriched me to engage in discussions with Italian or Spanish labor leaders—with the former, as I have said in meetings in Geneva or Italy, while with the latter I could only meet in Geneva, since at that time *Pedagogy of the Oppressed* was contraband in Spain and Portugal alike. Franco's Spain, like Salazar's Portugal, had shut us both out. *Pedagogy* and me.

It was at that time, and on account of *Pedagogy*, that I came in contact with the harsh reality of one of the most serious traumas of the "Third World in the First": the reality of the so-called guest workers—Italians, Spaniards, Portuguese, Greeks, Turks, Arabs, in Switzerland, in France, in Germany—and their experience of racial, class, and sexual discrimination.

In one of the seminars in which I took part in Germany, on literacy and postliteracy programs for Portuguese workers, I was told by some of the latter that their German colleagues despised them to the point, and in such a way, that they regarded them as incapable of ever speaking their language, so that when they spoke to them in German they put all the verbs in the infinitive mood. And surely enough, one of the Portuguese workers told me, in German, referring to a fellow worker: "He to like the meeting very much, but not to understand everything."

In Paris, in one of these seminars on *Pedagogy of the Oppressed,* a Spanish worker, enraged and almost in physical pain, protested a lack of class solidarity on the part of his French colleagues. "Lots of 'em come up and kick our butt," he said, with irritation, "if we're not lookin'!"

Behavior like this could reinforce today's neoliberal discourse, according to which the social classes are vanishing. They no longer exist, we hear. They existed, though, at the moment of the above-mentioned unburdening on the part of the Spanish worker, and they exist today as well. But their existence does not necessarily betoken a level of solidarity on the part of their members, especially internationally. At the same time, sectors of the dominated themselves are steeped in the authoritarian, discriminatory, dominant ideology. It becomes installed in them, and causes them to see and feel themselves to be superior to their companions who have left the land of their origin and wear the mark of need.

One of the serious problems that alert, politically engaged guest-worker leaders had to confront in the 1970s, and they discussed it with me in connection with their reading of *Pedagogy*, was a lack of motivation on the part of their companions for any commitment to the political struggles transpiring in the lands of their origin.

I myself took part in meetings in Switzerland, France, and Germany with immigrant workers at which I heard discourses evincing far more concern for an easier life in their experience far from their native lands, than of a desire to return to those lands one day in conditions appreciably better than those in which they had once left them. It was readily perceptible, in those days, whether in the meetings I have mentioned, or in conversations with leaders in which I was told of these difficulties of mobilization and political organization, that a great many of the workers who had emigrated to the new, "loan" context were taken, on the one hand, with a feeling of relief and joy that they had *work* now, and at the same time, with a sense of fear: fear of losing the tiny bit of security that they had found in their "loan" context. Their feelings of insecurity were too great for the minimal courage they would have needed for the adventure and risk of political commitment, however slight a commitment. The time that they had spent living in their countries of origin, the hope of employment, of security, had caused them to stake everything on *employment*, in the loan context, instead of on structural changes in their own context. These persons, a great proportion of the guest workers-to-be, had left their context of origin under the crushing burden of a weariness that I called, in those days, "existential weariness"—not a physical weariness, but a spiritual weariness, which left those caught in it emptied of courage, emptied of hope, and above all, seized with a fear of adventure and risk. And with the weariness came what I dubbed: "historical anesthesia."

On one of my visits to Germany for a discussion with Portuguese guest workers, which was held in a Catholic parish that was sponsoring an excellent program in political pedagogy, I heard from a young priest the following story: "A short while ago I received a complaint from three Portuguese workers that they and many of their companions were being severely exploited by the landlords of their little shacks: super-high rent, flouting of the law governing tenant rights and obligations, and so on.

"So I decided," continued the father, "after talking about it at Mass one Sunday, to call a meeting of anyone willing to discuss the question with me and try to figure out what could be done. Several parishioners came to the meeting. We worked together for two sessions, and we programmed a strategy against the almighty landlords: complaints in the newspapers, fliers, walks through the parish neighborhood, and so on.

"So we began putting the plan in practice—until a committee of tenants, including one of the ones who had made the complaint to me in the first place, came to me personally and requested that I call off the campaign. They had been threatened with eviction unless I stopped the accusations." And I still remember the words with which the priest concluded his story: "I felt a powerful tension, an ethical tension, between continuing to fight the exploiters, who now had gone so far as to take advantage of the emotional dependency of the oppressed and were blackmailing them, and respecting the tenant's pusillanimity and calling off the struggle, thereby restoring to them a sense of relative security—basically a false security, but one they couldn't do without—in which they lived."

In line after line of *Pedagogy of the Oppressed,* I discuss this phenomenon. Fanon and Memmi[4] did the same, or had done it before me. I mean the fear that fills the oppressed, as individuals and as a class, and prevents them from struggling. But fear is no abstraction, and neither is the "why" of fear an abstraction. Fear is altogether concrete, and is caused by concrete considerations—or considerations that seem concrete, so that, in the absence of any demonstration to the contrary, they might as well be.

And so the leadership, which, for any number of reasons, enjoys a different, higher level of "immunization" to the fear that affects the masses, must adopt a special way of leading where that fear is concerned. Once more, then, it becomes incumbent upon them to maintain a serious, rigorous relationship between tactics and strategy, a relationship of which I have already spoken in this book. In the last analysis, the problem facing the leaders is: they must learn, through the critical reading of reality that must always be made, what actions can be tactically implemented, and on what levels they can be so implemented. In other words, what can we do now in order to be able to do tomorrow what we are unable to do today? In the case I have just narrated of the German parish, the solution to the problem from which the workers' *fear* could not be eliminated was found in a tactical freeze on the action initiated. Here was an action that could be resumed further down the line, after a project in political pedagogy from which a victory over the fear, at least in part, would be won. That project would reveal to the workers that their landlords are vulnerable,

---

4. Franz Fanon, *Os condenados da Terra;* Albert Memmi, *The Colonizer and the Colonized* (Boston: Beacon Press).

too. Guevara, as well, spoke about this aspect of the dialectical relationship between oppressors and oppressed—of the need for the latter to be given objectives whereby they can become convinced of the vulnerability of the former, as a decisive moment in the struggle. Indeed, the more the oppressed see the oppressors as "unbeatable," endowed with an invincible power, the less they believe in themselves. Thus has it ever been. One of the tasks of a progressive popular education, yesterday as today, is to seek, by means of a critical understanding of the mechanisms of social conflict, to further the process in which the weakness of the oppressed turns into a strength capable of converting the oppressors' strength into weakness. This is a hope that moves us.

While I lived one-half of the decade of the sixties in the climate of the Brazilian transition that was shattered by the 1964 coup, and the other half in Chile, where I wrote *Pedagogy*—in the seventies, with the book multiplying in various languages, I saw myself exposed, along with it, to challenges that sparked analyses on my part, and these analyses in many cases confirmed and reinforced the book's basic theses.

It is impossible, in my view, to overrate the importance of the innumerable meetings and encounters in which I took part with students and professors of German, Swiss, English, Dutch, Belgian, Swedish, Norwegian, French, Latin-American, African, Asian, United States, and Canadian universities. This is why I speak so much of them here. And sprinkled among these meetings of an academic nature, the no less rich Saturdays to which I was subjected by groups of workers.

The tonic administered by the former—a First World audience—with an occasional exception, came in the form of a theoretical analysis. My interlocutors would assess the degree of rigor with which I had approached this theme or that one, or the precision of my language, or the evident influence on me of this thinker or that one (whose work, at times, I had not read!). Or the inconsistency into which I had slipped between something I had said on, for instance, "page 25," and something else on "page 122." The German students loved this kind of critique.

When the encounters occurred with Third World students, a different tonic was administered. Here, discussion turned preponderantly on political questions, and these led us to philosophical, ethical, ideological, and epistemological questions.

In my meetings with immigrant workers, Italians, Spaniards, Portuguese, of whom a large proportion had also read *Pedagogy,* in Italian, Spanish, or French, interest always centered on a more critical understanding of practice in order to improve future practice.

While the university people, generally speaking, tried to find and "understand a certain practice imbedded in a theory," the workers sought to sneak up on the theory that was imbedded in their practice. Regardless of the world I found myself in with labor leaders who were immersed in personal experience of politics and policy for changing the world, this is how it always was. It did not matter whether those leaders belonged to the Third World of the Third or to the Third world of the First. This is always the way it was.

Once or twice, in Geneva or away, I had the opportunity of working in long seminars with workers and academicians, obviously progressive. I hope they still take that position today, and have not given in to the ideology of those who decree the death of the ideologies and who proclaim that the *dream* is a way of fleeing the world instead of re-creating it.

I had one of the encounters to which I have just referred, a hugely rich one, with academicians and a Spanish laborer, one weekend some time in the 1970s, in Germany, in Frankfurt, to be precise. Two or three groups of progressive intellectuals, respectively Marxists and Christians, who did not relate well with each other, agreed to come together for a study day provided I took part.

I have always found it worthwhile to serve as the pretext for a good cause. So I accepted the invitation and went, along with two German friends—theologians, both of them, clear-sighted, creative, serious intellectuals: Werner Simpfendoerfer, who was to translate *Pedagogy* into German, and Ernst Lang, now deceased, director of the World Council of Churches, who had invited my collaboration in that body and who was to write the preface to the German edition.

The language of the meeting was German, with a simultaneous translation into English for me, and from English into German for the others, except for the theologians.

One of the groups had invited a laborer, a Spanish guest worker, who spoke German without any difficulty.

The presence of the Spanish worker had the effect of keeping the meeting on a level of equilibrium between the necessary abstraction and a quest for the concrete. In other words, the presence of the laborer lessened the risk that abstraction might renounce its authentic nature and meander about in a vagueness ever more distant from the concrete.

When we took our first coffee break, the worker came over to me and we began to converse in Spanish. We alone understood each other now. No one in hearing, other than ourselves, understood Spanish, as was to be expected.

After a few perfunctory remarks, with which we were actually working up to a little conversation, the Spanish worker said: "I have to admit intellectual qualities in these young people that make me admire them. They're devoted to the cause of the working class. They work tirelessly. But they seem to think that revolutionary truth is pretty much their private property. Well, now, we guest workers . . .," he added, with a twinkle in his eye, ". . . we're a sort of new game for them."

There was wisdom, there was grace in his discourse, without grief, and without anger. It was as if the truth infusing his words gave him the peace with which he spoke. He spoke of the problem he had mentioned with the tranquility of someone who knew his "why."

We chatted a while longer, commenting on the elitism, the authoritarianism, the dogmatism of the positions he had criticized. At one point he told me: "I have an interesting experience to tell you about—something I was involved in before I read your *Pedagogy of the Oppressed.*

"I'm an activist in a Leftist political movement working both in Spain and outside. One of our jobs is training immigrants politically so that we can then all go out and try to mobilize and organize other guest workers.

"A year ago, or so, five of us got together to try to work out a course in political problems to offer our fellow immigrants. We met for a discussion, just among ourselves, one Saturday afternoon in the home of one of these activists. We figured out what we thought the course ought to be, content and presentation. Finally, the way you academics like to do, we laid it all out in a nice, orderly package ready to bestow on our future pupils. We were sure we knew not only what our people would like to know, but what they ought to know. So why waste time listening to them? All we had to do was communicate to them what they could expect in the course. All we'd have to do was announce the course and enroll the applicants.

"Once we had the program worked out, with the weekend times, the place, the whole thing—we started looking for students.

"Total failure. No one was interested. We spoke to everybody we could. We laid out the content, we visited a number of people and explained how important the program was, how important the course was, and . . . nothing came of it.

"We got together one Saturday to try to figure out why we'd failed. Suddenly I got an idea.

"Why not take a survey, in the factories? Why not talk with lots of people, one at a time, and find out what each one'd like to do? Why not ask them what they prefer, and what they usually do on weekends? Then, on the basis of that, we ought to be able to figure out how to 'get to them,' instead of just starting out with what *we're* so sure they ought to know.

"We decided to give it a try. We gave ourselves two weeks to conduct the survey, and scheduled another meeting of the five of us after that, for an evaluation. And out we went to conduct the survey.

"After two weeks we got together again as planned, the five of us, each with a report on the job we'd done. Lots of the Spaniards liked to play cards on weekends. Then there was a bunch that liked to go for hikes. Some others went to parks, or to supper in each other's houses, or would sit around drinking beer, and so on.

"We picked the card games. Maybe this would be an 'in' with them, to get the political problems. So we practiced up at cards," the Spanish worker went on, enthusiastically, "and we started going around stopping in on the groups that would play cards on weekends, in each other's homes. Then during the week we'd get together, the five of us, for an evaluation.

"Sometimes during a game, with my cards in my hand, not looking at anybody, I'd just kind of casually ask, 'Know what happened yesterday in Madrid?'

" 'No,' they'd say.

" 'Cops raided some of our guys and locked 'em up. For one little protest march.'

"Nobody said a word.

"I didn't either.

" 'Well, gotta go,' I'd say, then I'd stop in on another game, and then another. Another question, a political question.

"All five of us kept doing this, in different places.

"After four months, we could finally get a bunch of them together to discuss if we'd like to get up some systematic meetings on politics. There were thirty of us at the first meeting, and we made a joint decision to run a real course on political problems. And we've had the best results we've ever had."

He laughed when I told him, "That proves that if we want to work *with* the people and not just *for* them we have to know their 'game.'"

This is precisely what authoritarian educators are always fighting. They claim to be progressive, and yet they regard themselves as proprietors of knowledge, which they need only *extend* to the ignorant educands. These people always see signs of permissiveness or "spontaneism" in the respect that radical democrats show for educands.

These people will never understand what it means to *start* with the reading of the world, the comprehension of the world, had by the educands. All surprised, as if they had made a great discovery, they say their practice proves that *staying* on the lower level of knowledge that the groups have, without trying to teach them anything beyond that knowledge, does not work. Of course it does not work. It is so obvious that it does not work that there is no point in bothering to prove it. One of the main reasons for the lack of spirit and inspiration in team members who get together to evaluate their practice is that the person running the evaluation process has no more sophisticated knowledge than the team has. No research is needed to establish the inviability of an evaluation seminar in which the coordinator lacks that particular knowledge with which he or she might explain the obstacles encountered by the participants in their practice. The normal tendency will be the failure of the seminar. So will a physics course fail unless the teacher knows physics. One does not teach what one does not know. But neither, in a democratic perspective, ought one to teach what one knows without, first, knowing what those one is about to teach know and on what level they know it; and second, without respecting this knowledge. One begins with that which is implicit in the reading of the world of those about to learn what the one about to teach knows.

This is what my practice, consistent with my democratic option, has taught me. This is also what the Spanish workers I have just spoken of were taught by their practice.

I should like to suggest certain further considerations in connection with the Spanish workers' experience. First let me present a consideration along the lines of political ethics. Educators have the right, even the duty, to teach what seems to them to be fundamental to the space–time in which they find themselves. That right and that duty fall to the educator by virtue of the intrinsic "directivity" of education. Of its very nature, education always "outstrips itself." It always pursues objectives and goals, dreams and projects. I have asked before, in this book: what sort of educator would I be if I had no concern for being maximally convincing in my presentation of my dreams? But that does not mean that I may reduce everything to my truth, my "correctness." On the other hand, even though I may be convinced, like the Spanish worker-activists, for example, that reflection on the political life of a town or city is essential, I may not on that account dictate the themes on which that political analysis and reflection must bear. A rather moralistic viewpoint would brand as disloyal the tactic of the Spanish workers in using card games to make a political approach to their companions and thereby render viable their objective of seriously studying the political question in Spain with them. This is not how I see it. They are as ethical as academicians could be in their own research.

The second reflection I should like to offer is far more positive. It regards the validity, in Latin America today, not only of the principle invoked by the Spanish workers, but of their work method. The popular educator must make a democratic option and act consistently with that option. I fail to see how popular education, regardless of where and when it is practiced, could prescind from the critical effort to involve, on the one side, educators, and on the other, educands, in a quest for the "why" of the facts. In other words, in a popular education focusing on cooperative production, union activity, community mobilization and organization so that the community can take the education of its sons and daughters in hand through community schools—without this having to mean an excuse for the state to neglect one of its duties, that of offering the people education, along with care for their health, literacy, and their education after the attainment of literacy—in any hypothesis, there is no discarding the gnoseological process. The process of knowing belongs to the very nature of education, and so-called popular education is no exception. On the other hand, popular education, in a progressive outlook, is not reducible to the purely *technical* training of which groups of workers have a real need. This will of course be the narrow training that the dominant class so eagerly offers workers—a training that merely *reproduces* the working class as such. Naturally, in a progressive perspective as well, a technical formation is also a priority. But alongside it is another priority, which must not be shoved out of the picture. For example, the worker learning the trade of machinist, mechanic, or stonemason has the right and the need to learn it as well as possible—but also has the right to know the "why" of the technical procedure itself. The worker has the right to know the historical origins of the technology in question, and to take it as an object of curiosity and reflect on the marvelous advance it implies—along with the risks it exposes us to, of which Neil Postman warns us of in an extraordinary recent book.[5] This is doubtless not only a

5. Neil Postman, *Technopoly—the Surrender of Culture to Technology* (New York: Knopf, 1992).

profoundly current issue of our time, but a vital one, as well. And the working class should not be part of the employer-employee relationship simply in the way the worker in "Modern Times" saw himself wildly struggling to tighten the screws that came alone the assembly line, in the critique we have from the genius of Charlie Chaplin.

It seems to me to be fundamental for us today, whether we be mechanics or physicists, pedagogues or stonemasons, cabinetmakers or biologists, to adopt a critical, vigilant, scrutinizing attitude toward technology, without either demonizing it or idealizing it.

Never perhaps, has the almost trite concept of exercising control over technology and placing it at the service of human beings been in such urgent need of concrete implementation as today—in defense of freedom itself, without which the dream of a democracy is evacuated.

The progressive postmodern, democratic outlook in which I take my position acknowledges the right of the working class to be trained in such a way that they will know how their society functions, know their rights and duties, know the history of the working class and the role of the popular movements in remaking society in a more democratic mold. The working class has a right to know its geography, and its language—or rather, a critical understanding of language in its dialectical relationship with thought and world: the dialectical interrelations of language, ideology, social classes, and education.

In a recent brief trip through Europe, I heard from a European sociologist, a friend of mine recently returned from Africa, that political activists of a certain African country were saying that the "Freire era" had come and gone. What is needed now, they were saying, is no longer an education faithfully dedicated to a critical understanding of the world, but an education strictly devoted to the technical training of a labor force. As if, in a progressive view, it were possible to dichotomize technology and politics! The ones who attempt this dichotomy, as I have emphasized above, are the dominant class. Hence the wealth of discourse with which we are besieged today in favor of the pragmatic ideal of adjusting ourselves to the world at hand in the name of the values of capitalism. In this new history of ours, without social classes, and thus without any conflicts other than purely personal ones, we have nothing other to do than to let the calloused hands of the many and the smooth ones of the few remake the world at last into a festival.

Really, I do not believe in this. But I hear and regret the mistake in which the above-mentioned African activists are caught: the long, intensely tragic experience that has so long victimized them, their rejection as John, as Mary, as persons, as sex, as race, as culture, as history, the disregard for their lives, which to a perversely murderous white supremacy are of no value, so that those lives can just "be there," stand there practically like an inanimate object that nevertheless moves and speaks and is under white command, and any black life can simply die or disappear and white supremacy will not care one little bit. This long, tragic experience, so worthily humanized by their people's struggle, by that fine, high struggle, has nevertheless bequeathed them, through and through, that same kind of existential weariness that suddenly came upon the guest workers in Europe, as I have described above. The illusion is that today's historical moment calls on the men and women of their country to wage a completely different struggle from the one before—a struggle in which technology would replace people's political formation altogether. At the same time, the blurring of political parameters reinforces the fatalism that marks "existential weariness," inviting us to resign ourselves to a "hope" in which only an adverbial change is possible in the world.

But the truth is: regardless of what society we are in, in what world we find ourselves, it is impermissible to train engineers or stonemasons, physicians or nurses, dentists or machinists, educators or mechanics, farmers or philosophers, cattle farmers or biologists, without an understanding of our own selves as historical, political, social, and cultural beings—without a comprehension of how society works. And this will never be imparted by a supposedly purely technological *training*.

Another concern on which popular education must never turn its back is epistemological research, antecedent to or concomitant with teaching practices, especially in peasant regions. This is a task that has become dear to the ethnoscience being plied among us today in Brazil: to know how rural popular groups, indigenous or not, know—how they organize their *agronomic* knowledge or science, for example, or their medicine, to which end they have developed a broadly systemized taxonomy of plants, herbs, trees, spices, roots. It is interesting to observe how they integrate their meticulous taxonomy with miraculous promises—for example an herbal tea that heals both cancer and the pangs of unrequited love, or battles male impotence; or special leaves for protection in childbirth, for "fallen breast-bone," and so on.

Recent research in Brazilian universities has verified the actual medical usefulness of certain discoveries made by popular wisdom.

For example, to discuss with peasants this ongoing university-level verification of their knowledge is a political task of high pedagogical importance.

Such discussion can help the popular classes win confidence in themselves, or augment the degree of confidence they have already attained. Confidence in themselves is so indispensable to their struggle for a better world! I have already made reference to the need for it in this book.

What seems to me to be unconscionable, however, today as yesterday, would be to conceive—or even worse, to practice—a popular education in which a constant, serious approach were not maintained, antecedently and concomitantly, to problems like: what content to teach, in behalf of what this content is to be taught, in behalf of whom, against what, and against whom. Who selects the content, and how is it taught? What is teaching? What is learning? What manner of relationship obtains between teaching and learning? What is popular knowledge, or knowledge gotten from living experience? Can we discard it as imprecise and confused? How may it be gotten beyond, transcended? What is a teacher? What is the role of a teacher? And what is a student? What is a student's role? If being a teacher means being superior to the student in some way, does this mean that the teacher must be authoritarian? Is it possible to be democratic and dialogical without ceasing to be a teacher, which is different from being a student? Does dialogue mean irrelevant chitchat whose ideal atmosphere would be to "leave it as it is to see if it'll work"? Can there be a serious attempt at the reading and writing of the word without a reading of the world? Does the inescapable criticism of a "banking" education mean the educator has nothing to teach and ought not to teach? Is a teacher who does not teach a self-contradiction? What is *codification,* and what is its role in the framework of a theory of knowledge? How is the "relation between practice and theory" to be understood—and especially, experienced—without the expression becoming trite, empty wordage? How is the "basistic," voluntaristic temptation to be resisted—and how is the intellectualistic, verbalistic temptation to engage in sheer empty chatter to be overcome? How is one to "work on" the relationship between language and citizenship?

It is impossible to make education both a political practice and a gnosiological one, fully, without the constant stimulus of these questions, or without our constantly answering them.

Finally, I believe that the way I pose these questions in this book implies my answers to them—answers that express the positions on political pedagogy that I reaffirm in this book.

Translated by Robert R. Barr

· 8 ·

PEDAGOGY
OF THE HEART

The Limit of the Right

If, however, in a given political context I come to be considered a *lesser evil* by the neoliberal, I cannot keep them from voting for me. They are free to do that. What is up to me in this case is to refuse to accept that their tacit vote would be turned into a favor, an element of bargaining. Their voting for me does not make them into my journey companions, nor should it put me in a position to have to promote them politically.

There is another context, a dramatic one, where an activist of truly progressive tradition happily accepts being the *right's limit*. To settle into such a position is to run an excessively high risk of becoming right.

It is easy to fall into such contradiction, jeopardizing much of the dream in shady alliances; it is hard to secure coherent agreements. What is most common is for there to be fighting between the alike and rupture between the different, as if they were antagonistic. I have no doubt that unity within diversity imposes itself to the lefts (plural) as a means to defeating the right (singular) and, thus, democratizing society.

Latin Americans of the left incur an error that I find to be dangerous—and that tends to intensify—as they move backward, believing to be moving forward, in search of the elusive *center*. It is almost always the case that a less perverse right or one self-proclaimed *center* intends to make its reactionarism more suave. It always remains right, though.

In light of the collapse of the socialist world, perplexed leftist activists have been turning *pragmatic* and *centrist*. That alone is no major concern. We all have the right to change, to think and act today in a different way from yesterday. Besides, no one who goes through such change has any reason to hide it. But I am precluded from understanding by reality; how one could justify the change by saying that social classes have disappeared, thus altering the essence of conflicts by removing their social-class-generated antagonistic character. I cannot understand how one would *adopt* the center as the left's new address, how one could move to the center as if that were the only place progressive forces could aspire to today.

I do not accept this form of fatalism also. It is as if, in order to be left, one necessarily has to go through the center; in order to be progressive one needs to go through a conservative stage.

It is one thing to realize that the popular classes have become uninterested in ideological discourses that drift into rambling babble; it is quite another to say that ideologies have died. The popular majority's lack of interest in ideological analyses is not enough to kill ideologies. This very lack of interests is an ideological expression: ideologies can only be ideologically killed.

While converting to democracy and becoming no longer parties of *ranks,* leftist parties must become truly pedagogical instruments. They must respond to the demands of their time and become capable of inventing communication channels to the expropriated and to those adhering to them.

A democratic style of doing politics, especially in societies with strong authoritarian traditions, requires concretely acquiring a taste for freedom, for commitment to the rights of others, and for tolerance as a life-guiding rule. The leftist parties that authenticate themselves through the effort of unveiling truths must not renounce their fundamental task, which is critical-educational.

Instead of converting myself to the center and occasionally coming to power, as a progressive, I would rather embrace democratic pedagogy and, not knowing when, attain power along with the popular classes in order to reinvent it.

The lefts' sectarianism and dogmatism were always most unbearable and made them almost "religious," as they construed themselves into holders of the truth, with their excessive certainty, their authoritarianism, and their mechanistic understanding of history and of conscience. The results of all that were the deproblematization of the future and the decrease of conscience, reflections of the external reality.

This deproblematization of the future and mechanization of science/world relations seriously weakened, and even negated, the ethical nature of world transformation, since opting for other paths was not a possibility. The future was inexorable rather than problematic. Thus, there ensued a lack of concern for pedagogical work, which was put on hold awaiting infrastructural transformation. The final result was the rejection of dreaming, of utopia, very much like today's *pragmatics*.

"Is there a way out for Brazil?" This question is constantly posed to me, and once in a while I bring it with me under my metaphorical tree. My answer is *yes*. Except that there is a way out only to the extent that we are determined to forge it. There is no way out that will become visible by chance.

Societies do not constitute themselves due to the fact that they are this or that; it is not their destiny to be not serious or to be examples of honor. Societies are *not*; they are in the process of being what we make of them in history, as a possibility. Thus, we have an ethical responsibility.

If history were *a time of determinism*, one where every *present* necessarily were the future expected yesterday, and every tomorrow were something already known, there would be no room for opting, for rupture. Social struggle would be reduced to either delaying the inexorable future or helping it *arrive*. One efficient way to delay it is to reproduce the present with cosmetic changes that pass as requirements of "modernity."

The struggle would be between those who, satisfied with today, would make an effort to delay the future as much as possible, to put up obstacles against any substantive change, and those who, exploited today, aspire to a new reality.

Tactic, the jargon of the satisfied, includes true aspects of society's dynamic present, except that they mold those to their ideology. Basing themselves on a real concern, for example, the discussion around the size of government, they advocate its almost complete absence or a role for it of mere management for the powerful.

Thus, we see the greediness with which they defend the privatization of every public company that turns a profit; we see the aggressiveness with which they attack anyone who, while defending a new understanding of the tasks and limits of government, rebels against its confinement to the role of defending the interests of the rich. Democratic fighters are referred to as "old," charged with not having historic *feeling*, and called *antiquity defenders*, having nothing to do with neoliberal modernity. At the same time, the "modern" files away a rigorous agrarian reform, without which any serious transformation is shot dead. Not one modern capitalist society has failed to conduct its agrarian reform, indispensable to the creation and maintenance of a domestic market. That is why among those democracies, agrarian reform is no longer discussed, and not because this process is "ancient" or a "violation of private property."

Once in Africa, I was told that a convenient way to capture monkeys was to prepare as natural a site as possible where a bag of corn was to be placed, tied to a tree trunk. The top portion of the bag was to contain a round wire frame allowing the monkeys to get into and out of the bag easily with their hands, provided that no corn was being held. The monkeys imprison themselves, for once they grab any corn, they never let go.

Within an understanding of history as possibility, tomorrow is problematic. In order for it to come, it is necessary that we build it through transforming today. Different tomorrows are possible. The struggle is no longer reduced to either delaying what is to come or ensuring its arrival; it is necessary to reinvent the future. Education is indispensable for this reinvention. By accepting ourselves as active subjects and objects of history, we become beings who make division. It makes us ethical beings.

Here lies one of the mistakes of some postmodernists who, while recognizing the requirement for fast decisions, brought about by technological advances, in this new historic time, state the contemporariness of a critical pedagogy, which assigns strategic value to the education of women and men capable of realizing, comparing, opting, and naturally, acting. Indeed, the need to make decisions quickly is an important act in societies where information and communication become accelerated. The fundamental problem for the centers of power lies in how to produce so specialized a variety of criticalness that decisions will be produced in line with the truth of the strong—the oppressors—and will always negate the truth of the weak.

Neoliberals and Progressives

From the point of view of neoliberal power and ideology, critical pedagogy is solely concerned with how promptly problems of a technical nature and bureaucratic difficulties can be overcome. Still in this view, social and political-ideological issues do not integrate the spectrum of concerns akin to educational practice, which is essentially *neutral*. This characteristic must be maintained in the *training* and *education* of young workers, in need of technical knowledge that can qualify them for the world of production.

We both, neoliberals and progressives, agree with the current demands of technology. However, we drastically diverge in our pedagogical-political response to them.

For progressives, there is no thinking about technical education in itself, one that does not inquire in favor of what or whom, or against what it operates. From a pragmatist point of view, since there is no right or left any longer, it is important to make people more competent to deal with the difficulties with which they are faced.

One of the fundamental differences between a pragmatic and a progressive is that what is *strategic* to the pragmatic may, under special circumstances, be considered *tactical* to the progressive, whereas what is strategic to the latter is always rejected by the former.

In spite of the differences between the nineteenth century and the present time—which require a refinement of analytical methods, technical reformulations, production of new knowledge—the domination of the majority by the few has not disappeared. I would like to emphasize the uncomfortable situation of Third World intellectuals. Contemporary of their First World colleagues, they discuss postmodernity with them while living with the uncontrolled exploitation characteristic of a dependent, perverse, and outdated capitalism.

Brazilian intellectuals who state that today's fundamental topic is no longer *work* but *leisure*, are dealing with a reality in which 33 million out of 150 million Brazilians die of starvation.

Today's permanent and increasingly accelerated revolution of technology, the main bastion of capitalism against socialism, alters socioeconomic reality and requires a new comprehension of the facts upon which new political action must be founded. Today it is no longer possible to use, in the more modern areas of the Third World, political tactics that were efficient in the middle of the century.

I feel serious work, meticulous research, and critical reflection about dominant power, which is gaining increasing dimensions, have never been as needed as they are today. The activity of progressive intellectuals must never equate that of people who, recognizing the strength of obstacles, consider them to be insurmountable. That would be a fatalistic position, alien to the task of the progressive. Understanding obstacles as challenges, the progressive must search for appropriate answers.

In light of the existing dominion over information, of the ease with which it is managed by and communicated to the network of power, it is not difficult to imagine the difficulties faced by those operating at the extremities of the circuit. How limited is the power of those, for example, working in the soybean fields of Brazil, who can hardly imagine that the possibilities of their production are known with long notice at the Chicago stock exchange.

> One of the main political implications of the possession and utilization of technology associated with remote monitoring and geographic information systems is the ability to make predictions regarding the environment. Environment here is understood as the physical, historical, and social-economic substratum created from the dialectic confrontation between nature and man.
>
> The above-mentioned technologies make it possible to carry out, with cartographic precision, the tasks of defining location and area of occurrence, classifying, evaluating, and predicting environmental phenomena, generating essential information to support political-economic decisions concerning the use of environmental resources.
>
> Such technological support may be directed toward the early assessment, for example, of expected agricultural crops as good or bad; in this case, fabulous profit may be generated in the commodity markets based on early information.
>
> *(Letter from Professor Jorge Xavier da Silva,*
> *Federal University of Rio de Janeiro, to the author, 1994)*

Also, what to say about the ease with which production can be transferred from one area of the world to another, making workers more vulnerable? Their vulnerability decreases their disposition to fight. It is possible that, with the growing globalization of the economy, strikes may lose efficacy in certain sectors of production.

All that and much more makes the domination power of the few over the many more robust and makes the struggle of the latter extremely difficult. Recognizing, however, the tragic nature of our times does not mean surrender. The struggle of men and women may find obstacles; victory may be delayed, but never suppressed.

In place of immobilist fatalism, I propose critical optimism, one that may engage us in the struggle toward knowing, knowing on a par with our times and at the service of the exploited.

As I speak with such hope about the possibility of changing the world, I do not intend to sound like a lyrical, naive educator. Even though I may speak in this fashion, I do not ignore how much more difficult it is becoming to focus on the needs of the oppressed, of those kept from being. I recognize the obstacles the "new order" represents to the most fragile *pieces* of the

world, such as its intellectuals, obstacles that push them into fatalist positions before the concentration of power.

I recognize reality. I recognize the obstacles, but I refuse to resign in
silence or to be reduced to a soft, ashamed, skeptical echo of the dominant
discourse. The quixotic position of Berenger has always excited me. From
the beginning, he was always in opposition to his fellows, who one by one,
became rhinoceroses in spite of his plea:

> *Ma Carabine, Ma Carabine!*
> *Contre tout le monde, je me*
> *defendrait! Je suis le dernier*
> *homme, je le resterai jusqu'au*
> *bout! Je ne capitule pas!*
>
> (*Eugène Ionesco*, Rhinoceros,
> *Paris; Éditions Gallimard, 1959, p. 246*)

I like being a person precisely because of my ethical and political responsibility before the world and other people. I cannot be if others are not;
above all, I cannot be if I forbid others from being. I am a human being.
I am a man and not a rhinoceros as Berenger shouts.

The "Lefts" and the Right

The political-pedagogical practice of progressive Brazilian educators takes
place in a society challenged by economic globalization, hunger, poverty,
traditionalism, modernity, and even postmodernity, by authoritarianism,
by democracy, by violence, by impunity, by cynicism, by apathy, by hope-
lessness, but also by hope. It is a society where the majority of voters reveal
an undeniable inclination toward change. "The popular majority have been
right in deciding what they want, but they have erred in their choice of
the partisan forces that they have brought to power," as Ana Maria Freire
lucidly analyzes. They were right when they chose change, but they erred
when they chose Collor and his entourage.

They want change; they want to win over inflation; they want a strong
economy; they want justice, education, and health care for themselves and
their families; they want peace in the shanty towns and urban centers; they

want to eat and sleep. They want to be happy in a present lived with dignity and in a future whose realization they play a part in. They vote, however, for partisan coalitions, some of whose predominant forces are, by nature, antagonistic to change in favor of the oppressed.

I am certain that the greatest responsibility for such mismatch belongs to the "lefts" themselves. we speak of *the lefts* in the plural and *the right* in the singular. The singularity of the right has to do with the ease with which its different currents unify before danger. Union among the left is always difficult and cumbersome. While the right is only sectarian against progressive thought and practice, the "lefts" are sectarian among themselves. If there are three or four factions within a leftist party, each believes itself to be the only one truly progressive, and they all fight among themselves. Truly leftist-activist members are treated as "the right of the party" or as "managers of the capitalist crisis."

I have no doubt that the radical experience of tolerance is part of the immediate renovation that leftist parties need to undergo if they are to remain historically valid. And here, I speak of a tolerance that must not be confused with status quo. I speak of tolerance in reconciling differing comprehensions of political action by party members, which does not mean lack of principles or discipline. The tolerance that needs to be lived in the intimacy of a leftist political party should transcend its borders. It must not be practiced only among progressive positions within the party, but also between the party and society at large. It should also be effective between the party's leadership and the popular classes, a tolerance made explicit in that leadership's discourse and their practice.

A leftist political party intent on preserving their discourse within an intensely contradictory society such as ours, intent on climbing to power, without which it is not possible *to change* the country, must learn to reread our reality. Learning to reread implies learning a new language. One cannot reread the world if one does not improve the old tools, if one does not reinvent them, if one does not learn to deal with the related parts within the whole one seeks to discover. Likewise, a new reading of my world requires a new language—that of possibility, open to hope. Nowadays we are so vulnerable before unreachable forces—the collisions of an asteroid with the earth, the tragedy of AIDS, the possibility of having my little backyard spied on from halfway across the world—hope has become indispensable to our existence. It is difficult to maintain it, hard to reinforce it, but it is impossible to exist without it.

A leftist party cannot engage in a dialogue with the popular classes using outdated language. As it reveals optimism, it must be critical; its hope must not be that of an irresponsible adventurer. Its criticism of the injustice within the capitalist system must be strong. That, though, does not mean this criticism should be pronounced with anger rather than with the goodness and peace characteristic of those engaged in the good combat. This must not be the discourse of bitterness, without even the faintest trace of hope. On the contrary, it must be hopeful, critically optimistic, and "drenched" in ethics.

I can see no reason why progressive activists, men and women, should be careless about their bodies, enemies of beautifulness, as if looking good were an exclusive right of the bourgeois. Today's youth has nothing to do with that: they paint their faces and take to the streets wearing that beautiful joy that also fills their protest.

In search of its renewal, a leftist party must lose any old trace of *avant-gardism*. It must lose any trace of any leadership that decrees itself as the edge, as the final word, one who defines and enlightens. This word necessarily comes from outside the body of the popular classes. Changing from an avant-gardist party to one of the masses alters not only the party's understanding of its role in the history of political struggle, but also its methods and organization, going from a centralism only strategically called *democratic* to decentralization, truly democratic.

The role of activists in an authoritarian, hierarchical party is a very different thing from their duty within a democratic one. In the first instance, the discourse of activists, while members of the party's hierarchy, comes molded by the party's leadership, which is equally molded by its orthodoxy, myths, and absolute truths. In the second instance, the activists' political-pedagogical practice is far from any savior's dream about the "uncultured masses." Their hopeful discourse is not that of someone intending to liberate others, but that of someone inviting others to liberate themselves together. In an authoritarian practice, different activities seek to blindfold the masses and lead them to a *domesticated* future; in a democratic practice, as they expose their reading of the world to popular groups, activists learn with them how the people know.

By learning *how* and *what* the people know, activists can and should teach better what the people already know. They learn with the oppressed the indispensable *ropes* of their resistance, which are, in an elitist view, classified as "flaws of character."

One of the urgent duties of a leftist party in touch with its time is making all its statements, denunciations, and announcements rigorously ethical. It should never accept that lying pays off, nor should it surrender the people's truth to the oppressor. In my prison experience, I never told the colonel who questioned me that I knew communists. I never lost sleep over that either.

Another duty of a progressive party is to struggle, with the most clarity possible, to make popular classes more aware of the problematic nature of the *future*. It is not true that socialism will come because it is announced; it is not true either that socialism collapsed with the Berlin Wall, or that victorious capitalism is an eternal future that has begun. The truth is that the future is created by us, through transformation of the *present*.

Could it be that the present we are living is a good one? Could it be that this is a more or less just present? Could it be that our society has been at least minimally decent? Could it be that we find it possible to sleep while we know tens of millions starve to death? Could it be that we can accept our educational system as reasonable with its current quantitative and qualitative deficiencies? Should we continue to make deals with the World Bank where we spend more than we actually receive? While Secretary of Education in the Erundina administration, I had the fortunate opportunity to decline, politely but categorically, an offer for one of these deals harmful to our country (see "O Banco do Império," an interview with Marília Fonseca by Paulo Moreira Leite, in *Veja* magazine, 11/23/94).

Could it be that lack of respect for public property is a Brazilian way of being that we cannot escape? Could it be that violence, skepticism, and irresponsibility are unchangeable marks of Brazilian nature? No! To change what we presently are it is necessary to change the structures of power radically.

However, no one can do this alone. No political party, no matter how competent and serious, can do this alone. It is not just any old political coalition that will accomplish it either. Only forces that feel equally at home with certain fundamental principles, even though they may have surface differences, can unite for the needed change. How can we expect agrarian reform, even of mediocre grade, from great land owners? How can we expect unstoppable greed to accept limits to its profits? How can we expect the elitist to propose progressive cultural programs and educational projects?

I can imagine how difficult conversation must be, sometimes, between progressives who accept being the right's limit and their new partners. And here I mean not necessarily conversation about government plans, where the difficulties must be even greater. I mean general conversation that brings back memories of past struggles, around the radicalness of their former colleagues in their dream of world transformation.

When the time comes for those progressives to govern, they must either break up with their allies in the right, requiring support from the left, or try some new partisan configuration, or lie to the people once again. That is why I attribute greater responsibility for such discontinuities to the left itself. The difficulty those in the left find in reaching agreement and sorting their differences, which are much less serious than those they have with the right, winds up helping their opposition.

In an interview in the *Folha de São Paulo* newspaper, the famous Mexican anthropologist, Carlos Castanheda, stated, while discussing the left in Latin America, that, in the case of Brazil, it would have been ideal if the configuration of the presidential race in the second round of 1989 had been that of the first round in 1994.

That would have been, in my view, if the left had already learned to be tolerant, to have historical sensibility, not to claim ownership over the truth. It would have been, if the left had learned the importance of history, the impatiently patient wait. Here I mean a wait where those who wait never settle down, where those who wait more along impatiently patient in carrying out their dreams or projects.

It would have been, if the majority of progressives had already understood that social transformation only really takes place when most of society takes ownership of it and takes the initiative to expand its social radius of acceptance. When transformation is more or less imposed and its implementation is not followed by any effort or explanation about its reason for being, what results is blind obedience, immobilization, passivity, and fear. It may also lead, someday, to uprising.

No one in his right mind would think of a left whose activist force was made up of celestial beings. Politics is a job for concrete men and women, those with flaws and virtues. But one would expect the left to become more coherent, refusing coalitions with its antagonists. One would also demand that the "lefts" overcome their superficial differences, having their common identity as a base.

The democratic, open, critical testimony of progressive leadership before one another has a pedagogical dimension. Undoubtedly, the positions taken by the left, especially those taken by the Workers' Party (PT), have moved the Brazilian political process forward.

For this reason, the right was unable to find any visibility in the presidential race of 1994 other than by decreeing as its limit a man from outside its ranks, one with a political past the right had condemned. If, while having him as its possible limit, the right made him concede more than he should have, it was also forced to take a few steps beyond its natural limits. If the right had chosen a candidate from within its ranks, while the left had remained united, it would not have advanced and would possibly have lost the election.

In this sense, Fernando Henrique Cardoso's victory is as much a result of the Real Plan as of the Brazilian left's struggle, PT included. Logically, added to all that is the president's personality, political skill, and competence.

It is unfortunate that, presently, the advancement experienced by the right is entering undeniable reversal, which, I hope, will not be enough to immobilize popular demands. In order to fight effectively against a possible paralysis, it is necessary that progressive forces be alert and ready to denounce even the smallest attempt to mislead the popular classes.

It is necessary, above all, that the left face some most destructive social infirmities: raging sectarianism, authoritarian messianism, and overflowing arrogance.

In order to stay faithful to my utopia of a less perverse society, I do not need to repeat a discourse that is no longer in line with our times, nor do I need to subscribe to the neoliberal one. As a progressive, I must say *no* to a certain professionalization of the political-partisan practice. It is also indispensable that this practice overcome the voluntary amateurishness of some well-meaning activists. Progressive practice must, however, be kept from sprawling into a mental bureaucracy, one that ties us down to *our* truth, and that we may become enslaved to.

No leftist party can remain faithful to its democratic dream if it falls into the temptation of rallying cries, slogans, prescriptions, indoctrination, and the untouchable power of leaderships. Such temptations inhibit the development of tolerance, in the absence of which democracy is not viable.

No leftist party can remain faithful to its democratic dream if it falls into the temptation of seeing itself as possessing a truth outside which there is no salvation, or if its leadership proclaims itself as the avant-garde edge of the working class.

Any progressive party intent on preserving itself as such, must not lack the ethics of humility, of tolerance, of persevance in the peaceful struggle, of vigor, of an every-ready curiosity. It must not lack hope with which to restart the struggle whenever necessary. It must not defend the interests of the popular classes, their right to a dignifying life, their right to pronouncing the world, and at the same time look the other way while the taxpayer's money is being stolen. Such a party's coherence must be absolute. A political party is not a monastery of sanctified monks, but it should aspire to become an association of truly serious and coherent people, those who work to shorten more and more the distance between what they say and what they do.

A leftist party intent on bringing itself to meet the demands of its time needs to overcome the old prejudice against anything that resembles a bourgeois concession. It must be able to realize that, at a time as needy for humanization as ours, fighting for *solidarity*, before the negation of even minimal rights suffered by most, is endlessly more valuable than any bureaucratic discourse of ultraleftist flavor.

An authentic progressive party must not become sectarian, for that would represent a move away from its normal radical position. Radicalness is tolerant; sectarianism is blind and antidemocratic. Unlike the sectarian, always tied to their truth, the radical are always open to revising themselves; they are always ready to discuss their positions. The radical are not *intransigent*, even though they can never condone unethical behavior.

Radicalness is serene, so long as it does not fear change when it is needed. That is why the progressive are always open to overcoming. Continuing a discussion and defending a certain argument make no more sense to them if someone can convince them of the opposite. That is not the case with the sectarian, who will continue to defend their position even if convinced of their error. Radicals are at the service of truth; the sectarian at the service of their truth, which they hope to impose.

Sectarization is sterile, is *necrophilic*. Radicalness is creative, *biophilic*. Radicals fight for *purity*; the sectarian will settle for *puritanism*, which is make-believe purity. Never has Brazil had a deeper need for progressive men and women—serious, radical, engaged in the struggle for transforming society and in giving testimony of their respect for the people.

There is no denying a certain degree of optimism toward the real changes Brazilian society may experience from now on. Overall, there seems to be an atmosphere of hope. It feels like *fatigue at the highest degree*. And that gets added to outrageous pillage of public money, impunity, and you-scratch-my-back-I'll-scratch-your-back politics, one of the most resilient vices in this country.

Even right-wing forces seem a bit intimidated by the indignation felt within Brazilian society. Any chance of the present government's proving to be effective, while a serious project, will depend on that intimidation. But the fundamental changes to the country will not count on the endorsement of the right. And the right did not vote for Fernendo Henrique because he was a lesser evil. Not at all. The right chose him as its *limit,* and he accepted that condition. My hope—which is based on my personal knowledge of him and on his political life history—is that he will go beyond the limits that they hope to force down on him.

As I see it, the true left, one not afraid or ashamed of defining itself as such, should not play the role of betting on the right's success. Instead, the left should focus on undermining the right's importance and its power of influence over governmental decisions. The critical left's role is to realize that, having completed the stage of democratic transition, we now enter another state, that of democratic *intimacy.* Thus far we had been crossing the road between authoritarianism and democracy. Now, already in democracy, we must, on the one hand, reinforce it and, on the other, move forward in the social domain. Whether it had been under Lula, or be it under Fernando Henrique Cardoso, the government embodies this movement.

Not at any time will Brazil have ever needed so much to count on its radicals' engaging in the struggle for deep social transformation, for *unity within diversity.* This expression is made up of two nouns connected by the preposition *within.* It is interesting how, in addition to its characteristic connective function, prepositions presuppose another: to impregnate a phrase with the very meaning of the relationship it embodies. There is a certain kinship between the relationship-meaning of the preposition and the syntactic status of the word that requires it. When I say, "I live on Valença Street," the preposition *on* means *placement,* coinciding with the syntactic status of the verb *to live,* or *to reside.* For this reason, I cannot say, "living to Valença Street." The proposition *to* indicates movement while the status of the word *street,* regarding the verb, requires the preposition of place *on.* It is just as incorrect to say, "I live to Valença Street," as it is to say, "I went on Pedro's house." *To go* is a verb of movement, thus requiring the preposition *to,* not *on.*

If I say *unity within diversity,* it is because, even while I recognize that the differences between people, groups, and ethnicities may make it more difficult to work in unity, unity is still possible. What is more: it is needed, considering that the objectives the different groups fight for coincide. Equality *of* and *in* objectives may make unity possible within the difference.

The lack of unity among the reconcilable "different" helps the hegemony of the antagonistic "different." The most important is the fight against the main enemy.

Therefore, the "different" who accept unity cannot forego unity in their fight; they must have objectives beyond those specific ones of each group. There has to be a greater dream, a utopia the different aspire to and for which they are able to make concessions. Unity within diversity is possible, for example, between antiracist groups, regardless of the group members' skin color. In order for that to happen, it is necessary for the antiracist groups to overcome the limits of their core racial group and fight for radical transformation of the socioeconomic system that intensifies racism.

The perversity of racism is not inherent to the nature of human beings. We *are* not racist; we *become* racist just as we may stop being that way.

The problem I have with racist people is not the color of their skin, but rather the color of their ideology. Likewise, my difficulty with the *macho* does not rest in their sex, but in their discriminatory ideology. Being racist or macho, progressive or reactionary, is not an integral part of human nature; rather it is an *orientation toward being more*. And that orientation is incompatible with any sort of discrimination.

If I am certain that the only kind of prejudice that can be fully explained by class analysis is the prejudice of class, I also know that the class factor is hidden within both sexual and racial discrimination. We cannot reduce all prejudice to a classist explanation, but we may not overlook in understanding the different kinds of discrimination.

When a so-called minority refuses to join forces with another minority, it reveals a prejudiced certainty: that of the other's natural inability to be fair and decent. I do not understand how, in Brazil, we can maintain feminist, black, Indian, working-class groups separately struggling for a less perverse society. Each group is fighting its own battles.

Unity within diversity is an imposition of the very fight. The dominant know that very well. Thus, one of their golden rules is, "divide to govern." We, who are classified by them as minorities, take on this profile. Therefore, we tend to divide forces fighting among and against ourselves, instead of fighting the common enemy.

Tolerance reveals excessive self-valuation on the part of the intolerant in relation to others, who are considered by the intolerant to be inferior, to their class, their race, their group, their sex, their nation. For this reason, there is no tolerance within a lack of humility. How can one be tolerant if one considers others to be inferior? But one cannot be humble by bureaucratically doing favors to others. In order to be humble, one must be so in practice as one enters relationships with others. One is not humble by underestimating others or overestimating oneself.

The oppressor is not humble, but arrogant. The oppressed is not humble either, but humiliated. In order for oppressor and oppressed to become humble, it is necessary for the oppressor to convert to the cause of the oppressed, and for the oppressed to commit to his own fight for liberation. It is only from that point on that both will have met the requirements to learning humility.

Theories considering liberation as a given fact of history, or basing it exclusively on scientific knowledge, never excited me very much. The same goes for those that did not accept giving any serious consideration, for example, to human nature, even if human nature was understood to be socially and historically constituted. I mean human nature while taking place in history, rather than prior to history. I cannot think the issue of liberation, and all that it implies, without thinking about human nature.

The possibility of discerning comparing, choosing, programming, performing, evaluating, commiting, taking risks, makes us beings of decision and, thus, ethical beings. For this reason, fighting against discrimination is an ethical imperative. Whether discriminated against for being black, female, homosexual, working class, Brazilian, Arabic, Jewish—regardless of the reason—we have the obligation to fight against discrimination. Discrimination offends us all, for it hurts the substantiveness of our being.

Our fight against the different discriminations, against any negation of our being, will only lead to victory if we can realize the obvious: *unity within diversity.* And by unity I mean that of the reconcilable different, not of the antagonically different. Among the latter, in the process of the struggle, there may be a pact as a function of circumstantial objectives serving both extremes. Among the former, unity is based on strategic and not only tactic objectives.

The appropriateness of my discourse might be questioned, for I speak as an activist when I should speak as theoretician and vice versa. I reject such dichotomy: I am not a theoretician, say on Wednesdays, and an activist on Saturdays.

The criticism of capitalism I put forth, from an ethical point of view, derives as much from the educator as it does from the activist, which I seek to continue to be in my own way. My activism can never become dissociated from my theoretical work; on the contrary, the former has its tactics and strategies formulated on the latter. The moment we recognize that food production around the world could be sufficient to feed twice its population, it is desolating to realize the numbers of those who come into the world but do not stay, or those who do but are forced into early departure by hunger.

My struggle against capitalism is founded on that—its intrinsic perversity, its antisolidarity nature.

The argument has been destroyed of scarcity as a production problem that capitalism would not be able to respond to and that would represent an obstacle to the preservation of this system. Capitalism is effective in this and other aspects, but it has shown its other face—absolute insensitivity to the ethical dimension of existence.

It has produced scarcity within abundance and need within plenty. Thus, the neoliberal feel the need to impregnate their discourse with a fatalism, to them irrefutable, according to which "things are the way they are because there is no other way."

This cynical discourse tends to convince that the problem lies in destiny or fate, rather than severely criticize a system that, in spite of lack of scarcity, condemns a large part of humanity to hunger and death. Successive technological revolutions have rendered capitalism bare. They have forced it to expose its own evil—millions of people dying from starvation, head-to-head with wealth.

I refuse, for all these reasons, to think that we are eternally destined to live the negation of our own selves. In order to be in the world, my conscious body, my unfinished and historical being, needs food as much as it needs ethics. The fight would make no sense to me without this ethics backdrop, upon which experiences of comparison, criticism, choice, decision, and rupture take place.

I would be a melancholy and unmotivated being if it could be scientifically proved that the laws of history or nature would take care of surpassing human misencounters without any mark of freedom: as if everything were predetermined, preestablished, as if this were a world without errors or mistakes, without alternatives. Error and mistakes imply the adventure of the spirit. Such adventure does not take place where there is no space for freedom. There is only error when the individual in error is conscious of the world and of himself or herself in the world, with himself or herself and with others; there is only error when whoever errs can know he or she has erred because he or she knows that he or she does *not* know. At last, in this process, error is a temporary form of knowing.

At the very moment I write these lines, I am reminded of Berenger, Ionesco's character. His cries of refusal to become a rhinoceros are a powerful testimony to our rebelliousness, our affirmation as men and women in the exercise of our citizenship, in the struggle for the millions deprived of it.

Translated by Donaldo Macedo and Alexandre Oliveira

INDEX

Also by Paulo Freire from Continuum

Paulo Freire
Pedagogy of Hope
Reliving *Pedagogy of the Oppressed*

This is the eagerly awaited sequel to *Pedagogy of the Oppressed*, in which Freire reflects on the impact his writings have made over the past twenty-five years. *Pedagogy of Hope* represents a chronicle and synthesis of the ongoing social struggles of Latin America and the Third World since the landmark publication of *Pedagogy of the Oppressed*.

With *Pedagogy of Hope*, Freire once again explores his best-known analytical themes—with even deeper understanding and a greater wisdom. Certainly, all of these themes have to be analyzed as elements of a body of critical, liberationist pedagogy. In this book, the reader comes to understand Freire's thinking even better, through the ciritcal seriousness, humanistic objectivity, and engaged subjectivity which, as in all of Freire's books, are wedded to a unique creative innovativeness.

"A powerful, scholarly defense of the radical liberal position."
—*Choice*

Paulo Freire
Pedagogy of the City

This unique book describes the everyday struggles, political as well as administrative, fought in the urban schools of São Paulo. Its forthright examination of urban education has many applications for schools in the U.S.

"Just as unrelenting and visionary [as *Pedagogy of the Oppressed*]. It is all the more powerful precisely because Freire is not speaking theoretically." —*The Other Side*

Paulo Freire & Antonio Faundez
Learning to Question
A Pedagogy of Liberation

Paulo Freire and Antonio Faundez engage in a stimulating dialogue on a variety of topics, from the relation of education and the liberation of oppressed people in the Third World to the part played by popular culture as a means of resisting domination.

Paulo Freire
Education for Critical Consciousness

Two important studies are brought together for the first time. The book comes out of Freire's innovative work in the field of adult literacy in Brazil and his studies of the practice of "agricultural extension" in Chile.

Paulo Freire
Pedagogy of the Heart

Some of Paulo Freire's last writings are in this book, which is filled with reminiscences of his early life and meditations "under my mango tree." These meditations include discussions of Solitude and Community, The Limit of the Right, Neoliberals and Progressives, Lessons from Exile, The "Lefts" and the Right, _Dialogism_, and Faith and Hope. Many of these themes will be familiar to those who have walked with Freire before. For those coming to his work for the first time, _Pedagogy of the Heart_ will open new doors to the interrelations of education and political struggle. Further enhancing the text are substantive notes by Ana Maria Araújo Freire.

Paulo Freire
Pedagogy of the Oppressed

This newly revised twentieth-anniversary edition is modified to reflect the interrelationship of liberation and inclusive language. It represents a fresh expression of a work that has stimulated the thought of educators and citizens for the last quarter of the 20th century.

"Brilliant methodology of a highly charged and politically provocative character."—Jonathan Kozol

"This is truly revolutionary pedagogy."—Ivan Illich

**These titles are available at your bookstore, or may be ordered by calling toll free: 1-800-561-7704.
They may also be ordered through the Continuum website: www.continuum-books.com**

**The Continuum Publishing Company
370 Lexington Avenue
New York, NY 10017**